C
C
C
P

1

2 3

Men
of the
Bombers

Men
of the
Bombers

Crews Who Fought and Won the Campaign

Ralph Barker

Pen &
Sword
AVIATION

First published in
Great Britain in 2005
By Pen and Sword Aviation
An imprint of
Pen and Sword Books Ltd
47 Church Street
Barnsley
South Yorkshire
S70 2AS

ISBN 1 84415 157 3

Typeset by Mac Style Ltd, Scarborough, N. Yorkshire
Printed and bound by CPI UK

Pen and Sword Books Ltd incorporates the imprints of Pen and
Sword Aviation, Pen and Sword Maritime, Pen and Sword Military,
Wharncliffe Local History, Pen and Sword Select, Pen and Sword
Military Classics and Leo Cooper.

For a complete list of Pen and Sword titles please contact
Pen and Sword Books Limited
47 Church Street, Barnsley, South Yorkshire, S70 2AS, England
E-mail: enquiries@pen-and-sword.co.uk
Website: www.pen-and-sword.co.uk

CONTENTS

Acknowledgements vi

1 The Litter-Buggers – The Phoney War, October 1939 1

2 Sir Arnold Wilson, MP – Arch-Appeaser and
Air-Gunner, Dunkirk May 1940 20

3 Pilot Officer W.J.Edrich – The Daylight Boys,
Summer of '41 46

4 Jimmy Ward – Kiwi 'Sprog' Pilot – How and Why He
Got the VC, July 1941 78

5 Reg Howard – Aussie Rear-Gunner – the Man Who
Wouldn't Die, Middle East, September 1942 94

6 How Bill Stannard Swapped a Seat on a London
Bus for a Chariot of Fire – May 1943 109

7 Canadian Gunners – Andy Mynarski and
Pat Brophy – A Reversal of Fates, June 1944 121

8 BAZ – a Father's Letter Earns his Son a VC 1944/45 136

9 'What the Stars Foretold for Jack Cannon' –
October 1944 155

10 Jim Hall – Washed-out Jamaican Pilot Saves Bomber and
Crew, Rhine Crossing, March 1945 178

Appendix One The Edrich Citation....................................192

Appendix Two Evadne Price – A Brief Biogrpahy 193

Index...196

Acknowledgements

The Litter-Buggers. Interviews and correspondence with Alfred Griffin, former RAF Sergeant; also with his son, Robert; personal account from J.H.P. (John) Wynton, later Flight Lieutenant, and correspondence; Harry Budden, later Wing Commander, DSO, DFC, correspondence; Roy Jackson, later Wing Commander, MBE, DFM, correspondence; 51 Squadron Operations Record Book, Public Record Office; *Royal Air Force 1939–45, Volume I, The Fight at Odds*, by Denis Richards (HMSO).

Sir Arnold Wilson, MP, Arch Appeaser and Air Gunner. The Wilson Family – Hugh, son, now deceased, and his wife Helen. Sarah Pennington (née Wilson). Ann Pennant (step-daughter, née Carver). Ian and Eileen Gray, for much correspondence and archival material on their father the late Pilot Officer William 'Dolly' Gray. Cyril Orland, brother of Rex Orland, crew member. Air Chief Marshal Sir Walter Merton (squadron commander). Flight Lieutenant E.J. 'Ted' Butcher, squadron colleague. *Walks and Talks*, the Diary of a Member of Parliament, by Arnold Wilson, KCIE, CSI, CMG, DSO, MP – OUP, 1934, and *Walks and Talks Abroad*, the Diary of an MP in 1934–1936. *Biography of Sir Arnold Wilson*, by John Marlowe (Cresset Press, 1967). 37 Squadron Operations Record Book, Public Record Office. Wing Commander F.F. Lambert, DSO, DFC, Public Record Office. A.W. Cooper, writer and researcher. Newspaper Reports, especially the *Hertfordshire and Bedfordshire Express*.

Pilot Officer W.J. Edrich – The Daylight Boys. Largely based on Bill Edrich's own war memoirs as told to the author, for the *Sunday Express*. Acknowledging permission and help from the Edrich family: Jasper Edrich, Justin Edrich, Mrs Jessy Edrich, Mrs Valerie Edrich. Professor M.M.R. Williams; Julian Horn; Colin Waugh; *A Day to Remember*, by W.F. Corfield, and much other research help; Wing Commander D.G. 'Don' Cameron, MBE; Ron Bramley, editor of *The Turret* (Air Gunners' magazine); David J.M. Armstrong; Lady Broom (widow of Air Marshal Sir Ivor Broom, KCG, CBE, DSO and Bar, DFC); Jim Langston; Barbara

McClear, daughter of Ernie Hope, (Bill's air gunner); Alan Hill and Gavin Mortimer, for recorded details of the DFC award, in *Bill Edrich, a Biography* and *Flights of Glory* respectively; *The Bristol Blenheim – a Complete History*, by Graham Warner, (Crecy Publishing, 2002); and *Blenheim Striker* by Drs Theo Boiten (Air Research Publications).

Jimmy Ward VC, the Wing-Walking Kiwi. Correspondence with Wing Commander Reuben Widdowson, pilot; Flight Lieutenant Joe Lawton, navigator (complete personal account); Sergeant A.R.J. Box, DFM, air gunner. Sergeant Ward's interview with artist C.A.Spencer (*Illustrated London News*); Hector Bolitho, author and journalist; Air Ministry Bulletin No 4459, July 13 1941; *For Valour, the Air VCs*, Chaz Bowyer; *RNZAF – A Short History*, Geoffrey Bentley (A.H. and A. W. Reed); *Return at Dawn*, Hilary St. George Saunders (AMSO); 75 Squadron ORB, and Awards Files (Public Record Office); Correspondence with New Zealand Defence Force, Secretary of Defence, Air Department; Notes taken from numerous newspaper reports.

The Indisciplined Aussie: Reg Howard. Interviews and correspondence with Warrant Officer Reginald Patrick Howard, RAAF; Wing Commander Lloyd Wiggins, DSO, DFC, RAAF; Flight Lieutenant Ralph Wagstaff, DFC; Wagstaffs Chartered Accountants, Stevenage; Squadron Leader A.J.W. Stanscomb; Alan Burgess, Producer BBC; numerous authorities in Queensland and Canberra, Australia.

Andy Mynarski: The Last Salute of a Canuck. Interview and correspondence with Roy Vigars, RAF, crew member; Correspondence with J.W.Friday, (Jack Friday), also crew member, RCAF; Record of Service, Andrew Charles Mynarski; Articles by Jim Kelly, RCAF, also crew member, in *Winnipeg Tribune*, November 1955; *Winnipeg Free Press*; National Museums of Canada; *The Dangerous Sky* by Tom Coughlin; The magazine *The Legionary*, November 1946; Cuttings from Canadian newspapers, mostly 1955; *Canadian Aviation Historical Journal* (CAHS); *The 14th Mission*, by George Patrick Brophy and David Macdonald (Readers' Digest, 1965, and CAHS).

Bill Stannard's Chariot of Fire. Interview and correspondence with William Stannard. Correspondence with Rupert North. Letters from A.H. Vermeulen, an eye-witness, to W. Stannard, in 1958, from an Ontario address. Article by F. VanderMeer in the Dutch magazine *De Spiegel*, including a photo of Bill Stannard and his crew. G.J. Zwanenberg, Dutch historian and researcher.

'Baz': Recommended for a VC - by his Dad

Interviews and/or Correspondence with Ian Willoughby Bazalgette's surviving crew: Douglas 'Jock' Cameron, Charles 'Chuck' Godfrey, Geoff Goddard, Ivan Hibbert and Bob Hurtnall. Group Captain T.G. 'Hamish' Mahaddie, the Pathfinder 'poacher'. The Bazalgette family: Marion (mother), Deryck (brother), Ruth, Charles (Alberta), Ethel Brodrick (sister), letter from C.I.Bazalgette (father) written to the Secretary of State for Air, Public Record Office. Karen White, researcher, BBC Archive. C.P.V. Beaumont, correspondent; Air Vice-Marshal D.C.T. Bennett and his book *Pathfinder* (Frederick Muller); Wing Commander F.F.Lambert, PRO, researcher; Royal Australian Air Force Records; Ministry of Defence Records.

'What the Stars Foretold' for Jack Cannon.

Interview and correspondence with Jack Cannon over a period of years. Tommy Cushing, owner of Little Snoring Airfield; Bert Lee, of Fakenham, aviation archaeologist and his son Arthur; Norfolk and Suffolk Aviation Museum, Flixton; Theatre Museum, London, for obituary of Evadne Price and pictures; National Library of Australia, Self-Portrait by Evadne Price, and Interview with Kenneth Attiwill; Raymond Mander and Guy Michinson, for research assistance; Phyllis Handley, first cousin of Denis and Stuart Richins, for memoirs and photographs; Gwyn Gillard, of Belmont, Victoria, Australia; Gloria Brown, of Narrabeen, NSW, Australia; Frances Cantwell (daughter of Wren Stobo), of Ryde, NSW, Australia; *Herald and Weekly Times*, Melbourne, Victoria, Australia; National Archives of Australia; Australian War Memorial, Canberra; Brian Aherm, Getty Images; East Sussex Federation of Women's Institutes; The Estate Office, Houghton (Houghton Hall); Sarah Fisher, of A.M.Heath, agents; Jeff Watson and Robin d'Arcy of Jeff Watson Productions, Sydney, Australia.

Jim Hall: Washed-out Jamaican Pilot saves Bomber and Crew

Interview and correspondence with James M. 'Jim' Hall. Interview and correspondence with Richard 'Dick' Perkins, pilot, both since deceased. Letters from Donald Freeman; meetings and correspondence with Angela Perkins (widow); research help from Alan W. Cooper, author and researcher.

CHAPTER ONE

The Litter-Buggers – The Phoney War, October 1939

The man in the tail turret of the old Mark III Whitley bomber had endured one of the most traumatic experiences of any wartime flyer.

It had been bad enough for the rest of the crew. Sitting it out at 15,000 feet in a temperature of –30 degrees Celsius for hour after freezing hour, without heating and with inadequate oxygen, had reduced the men in the cabin to a state of mental coagulation and physical collapse. But for the tail gunner, cut off from his comrades by the long pencil-box Whitley fuselage, the pains and discomforts were greatly magnified by the isolation. For the men up front there was always a vestige of warmth – the warmth of companionship. For the man in the tail there was nothing but loneliness.

27-year-old Sergeant Alfred Griffin, a Liverpudlian, had sat alone in the tail of the Whitley for over six hours. That, on one of the earliest and certainly the strangest of all wartime air raids, 27 October 1939, was his job. At first he had joined in the breezy jocularity that each man had attempted on the inter-com. They had even sung to keep up their spirits. 'Roll out the Barrel', 'South of the Border' (rendered as 'East of the Border', to mark the crossing of the German frontier), and even 'We'll hang out the washing on the Siegfried Line' (this was the period of the 'Phoney War', and they still believed it then). But as time passed, voices became as petrified as limbs and extremities.

Now, returning from their target near the end of the flight, the Whitley was circling in darkness over the low, undulating downlands of northern France. Guessing that the men in the cabin were searching for a pinpoint, Griffin called them up on the inter-com.

'Hello Skipper. Tail-gunner speaking. Aren't we getting a bit low?'

There was no feed-back from his earphones. Deafened by the clatter of the two Armstrong-Siddeley 14-cylinder Tiger radials, he nevertheless knew that his inter-com had gone dead. They must know what they were doing up front. Yet, as the creases of the hills loomed closer out of the darkness, he stirred uneasily in his seat. He had no means of knowing that his entire crew had baled out. The awful loneliness he had felt for the last six hours had become reality.

Alfred Griffin's crew, with one exception, were all experienced men in their middle or late twenties who had come up in the Service the hard way, as indeed he had himself. Sergeant T.W. 'Johnnie' Bowles, the pilot, had begun as an engine fitter. Bill Emery, the second dicky and navigator, had once been an orderly room clerk. 'Ali' Barber, the front gunner, the only one married (Griffin had been at his wedding), was an ex-ground tradesman. Even the wireless operator, the 19-year-old Aircraftman 1st Class Roy Jackson (this was before the days of automatic NCO rank for aircrew), was Cranwell-trained.

Griffin's natural amiability hid unsuspected qualities of stubbornness and tenacity, which had enabled him over the years to rise from aircraft-hand general duties – ACH GD, the lowest form of animal life in the Royal Air Force – through air gunner and photographer to air observer/navigator, with a status equal to that of pilot. But for tonight the regular rear gunner was absent, the duties of navigator had been taken over by the second pilot, and Griffin, to make up the crew, was standing-in as Tail-end Charlie.

Griffin's squadron, No. 51, was normally stationed at Linton-on-Ouse, Yorkshire. From there, the target he and his crew were briefed to visit tonight – Munich, in southern Germany – would have meant a round trip of 1,400 miles. But by flying first to an airfield in France – the French were still our Allies – they could avoid the sea crossing and substantially reduce the distance.

The airfield chosen was Villeneuve, forty miles east-south-east of Paris. It was really no more than a week-end flying-club field, owned by the Coty family, with no airport buildings, no fuelling facilities (refuelling was done manually from four-gallon cans), tented accommodation, no kitchens or ablutions, latrine pits instead of lavatories, and, for a bonus, continuous rain that turned areas of the low-lying field into a quagmire. From here, five crews were briefed for the raid, all peacetime regulars, the targets being honoured for 'persuasive' treatment being Nuremburg, Frankfurt, Stuttgart, and, furthest of all, Munich. Bowles and his crew had clicked for Munich, a round trip of some 720 miles. A much reduced mileage, yes, but even this in the slow-moving Whitley meant a flight of five or six hours.

Basing the squadron at Villeneuve had been no more than a temporary measure. They were not expected to be there for more than one night: it was to be a quick turn round. But day after day the operation had been postponed for bad weather, and during all that time the pressure to go, from the highest level, had increased.

For the squadron air and ground crews, in spite of the hardships, there were compensations. Each day, when flying was cancelled, they were made more than welcome at the local *bistro*, where *d*uty-free cigarettes were plentiful and champagne was only half-a-crown a bottle. The crews had nowhere to store their purchases, but there was plenty of room in the aircraft, and there would be no Customs and Excise back at base. They stocked up with a generous supply of goodies to take back to Yorkshire.

Besides Barber, most of them had girl friends, and the 19-year-old Roy Jackson had a sweetheart, with marriage in mind. To the special cargo that was to be carried into the heart of Germany and back, bottles of *eau de Cologne* for mums and sweethearts proliferated.

The official load the crews were carrying was even more bizarre. The persuasive element they would be dropping on Germany from a great height was not some newly-invented deadly war weapon. The Whitleys were loaded not with bombs but with leaflets, propaganda

An alfresco meal at Villeneuve, France, 1939. (IWMC487)

leaflets, persuasive pep talks addressed to the German people, a personal message from the Prime Minister himself.

The RAF were back to their normal peacetime role overseas: issuing stern warnings 'or else' to recalcitrant tribes. The tribe Neville Chamberlain was addressing was the Hun. Having reluctantly accepted that a state of war now existed between Britain and Germany, Chamberlain was making this last-minute appeal – as he imagined – to their good sense and better nature.

In a curious encore to the waving of that scrap of paper at Heston Airport after Munich '38, he was asking the RAF to deliver more scraps of paper to Munich '39 – over a million of them. Pamphlets.

Hitler, anxious to consolidate his gains in Czechoslovakia and Poland, had launched a new peace offensive. Chamberlain, in reply, was asking the German people in these leaflets how Hitler intended to right the wrongs he had done. He sincerely believed that if he could get his message across, the German people would respond. He set great store by the wording of these leaflets, and was impatient to hear, first of their delivery, and then of their impact.

The crews, who had heard all this before, were equally impatient to get the job done and get back to Yorkshire.

Whitleys of Bomber Command had been dropping leaflets on Germany since the first night of the war. The policy had attracted fierce

The leaflets with an English translation. (RAF Museum)

"Germany has agreed with Poland.....a non-aggression pact as a further and more than valuable contribution to European peace, which she will not only blindly observe, but concerning which we have only one wish... that out of it will grow an ever increasing friendliness in our relations."

(Reichstag Speech. 21st May,1935).

THUS SPAKE ADOLF HITLER.

290

NOT TO BE SHOWN TO THE PRESS.

Hat man in Deutschland

die englische Antwort

auf die Rede Hitlers veröffentlicht?

Verlangt von Hitler die Veröffentlichung des vollen englischen Textes!

Hier folgt ein kurzer Auszug.

Herr Hitler wies alle Friedensvorschläge zurück, bis er Polen überwältigt hatte, so wie er vorher die Tschechoslovakei zu Grunde richtete. Friedensbedingungen, die davon ausgehen, Angriffshandlungen gutzuheißen, können unmöglich annehmbar sein.

Die in der Rede des deutschen Reichskanzlers enthaltenen Vorschläge sind in hohem Maße unklar und unbestimmt; sie sagen nichts über eine Wiedergutmachung des an der Tschecho-slovakei und an Polen verübten Unrechts.

Selbst wenn die Vorschläge des Herrn Hitler deutlicher gewesen wären und Hinweise auf die Wiedergutmachung

The issue is therefore plain. Either the
German Government must give convincing proof
of the sincerity of their desire for peace by
definite acts and by the provision of effective
guarantees of their intentions to fulfil their
undertakings, or we must persevere in our duty
to the end.

It is for Germany to make her choice.

293

NOT TO BE SHOWN TO THE PRESS.

Englands Antwort an Hitler!

Premierminister Chamberlain hielt am 12. Okt. eine Rede, in der er unter anderem ausführte:

Nach einem mutwilligen Angriffsakt, der so vielen Deutschen
und Polen das Leben kostete, habe der deutsche Reichskanzler
nunmehr seine Friedensvorschläge vorgebracht. Sie sollten
auf der Anerkennung seiner Eroberungen und auf seinem
Recht, mit dem besiegten Volke nach Belieben zu verfahren
begründet werden. Es sei für Großbritannien unmöglich,
irgend eine Grundlage dieser Art anzuerkennen; internationale
Streitigkeiten sollten durch Diskussion, nicht durch Gewalt
beigelegt werden.

Die Hauptschwierigkeit bei der Behandlung der Hitlerschen
Vorschläge liege in Herrn Hitlers wiederholtem Wortbruch
und in den plötzlichen Kehrtwendungen seiner Außenpolitik.

„Die einfache Wahrheit ist eben," sagte Mr. Chamberlain,
„daß es nach unseren bisherigen Erfahrungen nicht mehr
möglich ist, sich auf das bloße Wort der gegenwärtigen
deutschen Regierung zu verlassen."

„Es gehört nicht zu unserer Politik, ein Deutschland, das
in Freundschaft und Vertrauen mit anderen Völkern leben
will, von seiner rechtmäßigen Stellung in Europa auszu-
schließen."

Im Gegenteil, die Welt lasse sich nicht von ihren Krankheiten
heilen, wenn nicht die berechtigten Ansprüche und Bedürfnisse
aller Länder berücksichtigt werden. Wann immer auch die
Richtlinien eines neuen Friedens festzulegen seien, es würde
in der Zukunft wenig Hoffnung geben, wenn dieser solcher
Friede nicht auf dem Wege der Verhandlung und Vereinbarung
erreicht werden könne.

Nicht aus Rachsucht haben Großbritannien und Frankreich
daher die Waffen ergriffen, sondern einfach um die Freiheit zu
verteidigen. Nicht nur die Freiheit der kleinen Nationen stehe
auf dem Spiele, sondern auch der friedliche Bestand des britischen
Weltreiches, Frankreichs und aller freiheitliebenden Länder.

---

dieses Unrechts enthalten hätten, so wäre es immer noch
notwendig, zu fragen, mit welchen praktischen Mitteln die
deutsche Regierung beabsichtigt, die Welt davon zu überzeugen,
daß Angriffshandlungen ein Ende gesetzt wird und daß
Versprechen gehalten werden.

Die Erfahrung hat gelehrt, daß auf die Versprechungen der
gegenwärtigen deutschen Regierung kein Verlaß ist. Deshalb
sind Taten — nicht nur Worte — vonnöten, ehe wir, die englische
Nation, und unser tapferer und bewährter Verbündeter
Frankreich uns berechtigt fühlen könnten, mit der Fortführung
des Krieges bis zum Äußersten unserer Kraft, aufzuhören.
Erst dann, wenn in der Welt das Vertrauen wiederhergestellt
worden ist, wird es möglich sein, — wie wir, mit Hilfe aller, die
guten Willens sind, es wünschen, — die Fragen zu lösen, die die
Welt beunruhigen, die der Abrüstung im Wege stehen, die das
Wiederaufblühen des Welthandels verzögern und die Besserung
im Wohlergehen der Völker verhindern.

Es ergibt sich daher eine Grundbedingung, die erfüllt werden
muß. Und nur die deutsche Regierung kann sie erfüllen. Wenn
sie das nicht will, dann läßt sich eine neue und bessere Weltord-
nung, nach der sich alle Völker sehnen, jetzt noch nicht verwirk-
lichen.

Die Frage ist also klar. Entweder: Die deutsche Regierung muß den überzeugenden Beweis ihres aufrichtigen
Friedenswillens liefern, einmal durch unzweideutige Taten,
und dadurch, daß sie stichhaltige Garantien gibt, die die
Absicht verbürgen, gegebene Versprechen zu halten. Oder:
Wir müssen bis zum Ende in der Erfüllung unserer Pflicht
beharren.

Deutschland hat die Wahl!

Weitergeben!

LEAFLET NO. 13.
H.290

No. 37a/

SECRET

298

Have you been given the British
reply to Herr Hitler's speech ?

Here is the summary of it.

Demand from Herr Hitler that he
should publish the whole of the reply !

Herr Hitler rejected all the suggestions for peace
until he had overwhelmed Poland, as he had previously
overthrown Czechoslovakia. Peace conditions cannot be
acceptable which begin by condoning aggression.

The proposals in the German Chancellor's speech
are vague and uncertain and contain no suggestions for
righting the wrongs done to Czechoslovakia and to
Poland.

Even if Herr Hitler's proposals were more clearly
defined and contained suggestions to right these wrongs,
it would still be necessary to ask by what practical
means the German Government intend to convince the
world that aggression will cease and that pledges will
be kept. Past experience has shown that no reliance can
be placed upon the promises of the present German
Government. Accordingly, acts — not words alone —
must be forthcoming before we, the British people, and
France, our gallant and trusted ally, would be justified
in ceasing to wage war to the utmost of our strength.
Only when world confidence is restored will it be possible
to find — as we would wish to do with the aid of all who
show good-will — solutions of those question which
disturb the world, which stand in the way of disarmament,
retard the restoration of trade and prevent the improvement of the well-being of the peoples.

There is thus a primary condition to be satisfied.
Only the German Government can fulfil it. If they will
not, there can as yet be no new or better world order
of the kind for which all Nations yearn.

Loading leaflets into a Whitley before flight. (IWMC919)

criticism: while Poland was bleeding to death, Britain was bombarding Nazi Germany with nothing more lethal than Chamberlain's speeches. The public were so outraged that for a time the policy was dropped.

Yet Chamberlain still hoped against hope to avoid war, anyway total war. And it was soon realised that the dropping of leaflets had its uses. What was the alternative? Who was going to start the shooting war? The shame of our inactivity still rankled, but some riposte had to be attempted. The dropping of leaflets might attract scorn, but from experience of German raids on Britain in World War I, British bombers ranging over enemy territory at night would have more than a mere nuisance value, besides being useful for reconnaissance, the gathering of intelligence, and, above all, for training. Before the end of September the Cabinet withdrew its ban, and on paper at least the RAF's new task became marginally more warlike: 'to reconnoitre southern Germany, and to drop leaflets over some of the principal towns'.

Thus it was that at two o'clock on the afternoon of 27 October 1939, Wing Commander James Silvester, aged 42, officer commanding the Whitley squadron and also the detachment at Villeneuve, having suffered three days of restless discomfort, asked again – as he had done daily – for specialist meteorological advice from home. He learned that the forecast included the promise of 'rain, hail and sleet showers, risk of thunder: cloud 7 to 9/10ths, low base 1,000 feet, but 500 feet in showers: freezing level 1,500 feet: heavy icing anticipated in shower clouds up to 12,000 feet.' This was the forecast available, and although better conditions were expected at Villeneuve later, Silvester decided it unquestionably ruled out any flying for that day.

RAF aircraft at this time were just not equipped to operate in these conditions, and indeed no other squadrons were operating. The Whitley had no de-icing gear, no hot-air intakes for the engines, and although hot-air ducts were installed, there were none of the essential heat exchangers. All the crews got was cold air from outside. Yet at five o'clock that afternoon, in contradiction to all that had gone before, orders were received that the Whitleys bound for southern Germany were to take off before dark.

'It can only be concluded' says the Official History 'that those responsible for these orders were impatient for the delay which had already occurred.' It brought panic stations at Villeneuve.

It would be dark in less than an hour. The Whitleys, firmly picketed down, were dispersed round the airfield perimeter. Engine, cabin and turret covers were secured. There was no time for the crews to prepare. Worst of all, they had had no food since midday, and even then, nothing but the inevitable tinned beef stew, heated on paraffin stoves. And there was no time now to feed them again before take-off. There was not even time for them to pick up sandwiches and Thermos flasks of coffee, to sustain them during the flight.

Silvester protested, as well he might. He argued, as forcibly as he dared, that his crews were totally unprepared for a long and arduous flight and that the weather in any case was quite impossible. But he soon found himself heavily outranked. The Prime Minister, he was told, was taking a personal interest in the raid. The optimistic forecast that better conditions were expected for the return flight may be said to have 'cut no ice' at Villeneuve.

Silvester could argue no further. A veteran of RFC days, and for three years an instructor at the RAF's own Central Flying School, he was a man of vast experience, and he had been more frustrated than anyone by the delay. Now they were quoting the PM at him. As detachment commander, he had brought no crew of his own, so he could not lead the raid himself, but he reacted as one would expect. 'If *they've* got to go, *I'm* going with them.' He chose his senior crew, and went as reserve pilot and observer.

By 17.55, when Bowles and his crew boarded their aircraft, the light was failing. A quick check with each crew member in turn on the intercom, and Bowles taxied across the field towards the goose-neck flares that flickered unevenly on either side of the grass runway. At 18.05, Whitley K 8984 (N for Nuts), followed by four others, took off into the gathering gloom.

From the tail turret, Griffin could hear the two Tiger engines struggling to lift the under-powered Whitley into the sky. By the time they entered cloud, at 5,000 feet, they were conscious that the outside temperature was already falling. At 7,000 feet they emerged thankfully into bright moonlight, but the air speed indicator was already iced up.

Wing Commander James Sylvester, shown later when a bomber base commander. 'If they've got to go, I'm going with them.' (IWMCH11243)

Interference from enemy fighters had not been a hazard on these trips, but under a full moon they might be challenged. As they approached enemy territory, Bowles eyed the cloud immediately below them and was ready to dive into it if need be.

Griffin, in what was to him an unaccustomed section of the fuselage, was finding it hard to settle. Despite his Irving jacket, helmet, scarf, silk gloves and gauntlets he was thoroughly chilled. But the songs on the inter-com helped to revive him. When someone volunteered a solo, no one applauded more vigorously than Griffin. It was one way of trying to keep warm.

After about twenty minutes at 7,000 feet, the cloud suddenly enveloped them, and Bowles eased the plane into a gentle climb. Eight, nine, ten, eleven, twelve thousand feet – and they were still in cloud. Finally they reached what seemed to be their optimum ceiling at 15,000 feet, and at this height they could glimpse the moon fleetingly through the cabin roof. Soon afterwards Emery reported that they were crossing the frontier. They were half-way to Munich.

The intensity of the cold in the cabin had become palpable. It was worse in the turrets. Snow was pouring through into the front turret and sweeping aft, and the fuselage, acting as a funnel, was channelling the powdery snow to the rear, where it piled up around Griffin. Ice

Alfred Griffin's 'office' – a stern view of the Whitley. (Simon Parry)

was building up to a depth of six inches on the engine cowlings and the leading edges of the wings and twin tailplane, and the whole exterior was becoming encrusted, like icing on a cake. Even the windows were coated, isolating the crew from the cotton-wool world that surrounded them.

The weight of ice that the Whitley was carrying was making the controls sluggish. Only by frequent movement of the control column could Bowles keep the surfaces free. This somewhat eccentric progress unnerved the crew. So did the alarming thuds against the fuselage as great chunks of ice broke off the airscrews. The further they were from the cockpit, the greater the apprehension. But Griffin, like the others, kept his fears to himself. That was the rule.

The other Whitley crews who had taken off from Villeneuve were suffering similar privations. One crew, beset by misfortune, stuck it for $2^1/_2$ hours and turned back. Blinkered and ice-clad, the roar of their engines strangely muted, the rest lumbered on.

After nearly three hours' flying, Emery judged from his dead-reckoning plot that they were approaching Munich. It was time to prepare for off-loading the leaflets, or, to use the crews' dismissive phrase, to 'paper the town with bumpf'.

The pamphlets, in bundles, but to be unpacked before release, 'in case they hit someone on the head', were reckoned to fall at a rate of 17 feet per second, roughly 1,000 feet per minute. The dropping zone had to be chosen to take account of height, wind speed and direction, all carefully calculated beforehand by the Met boys, and given to the crews at pre-flight briefing. On this particular night, the forecast 'dropping wind' for Frankfurt, remembers sergeant-pilot John Wynton, 'meant that at a height of 16,000 feet we had to fly 75 miles to the north-east of the city to place our bumpf on target.' This was not so much dropping as scattering. Proportional off-setting was to be applied by Bowles and his crew at Munich.

With much the longest journey, Bowles hoped to get a pinpoint before dropping. From half-an-hour or so after take-off they had seen nothing. They were dropping blind, and they had to believe that the Met boys were right. They had no other means of checking their position. Wireless reception had been obliterated by static interference, and radar aids were yet to come.

Emery went back into the radio cabin to collect Jackson, and the two men unplugged themselves from the oxygen supply and crawled aft to the central or 'dustbin' turret. They lowered the dustbin under hydraulic power until it was flush with the floor, then began passing the leaflets through the flare-chute by hand.

There were fifteen parcels of leaflets, each parcel containing twelve bundles, making 180 bundles in all. Each bundle, on release, had to be thrust individually down the chute.

The cold was so excruciating in this part of the fuselage that Jackson felt he could smell it and feel it pressing in on him as a solid, molecular thing, unyielding and tactile. He had taken his gloves off to handle the bundles more readily, and when his fingers touched the steel of the knife he was using to cut the bundles open, they stuck to it. The same thing happened when he put the knife between his teeth to leave both hands free; it pulled away the skin from the corners of his mouth as he removed it.

Slowed down by the lack of oxygen, the work of dropping the leaflets seemed interminable. They couldn't have been scattered more widely. It was not until 21.15 that the last bundle was dropped and Bowles could turn for home. 'Right!' he called, 'Get the turret up, Jacko!' But Jackson and Emery had sunk exhausted to the floor.

When they regained sufficient strength to raise the turret, they found it had frozen in the down position. They expended their last ounce of energy on the emergency pump but still couldn't shift it. That meant additional drag for the rest of the flight.

As they left the cloud over Munich behind – they had still seen nothing of the city – Griffin noticed a change in engine noise, something that, after eight years' flying, his ears were attuned to. Twisting his head round to look forward, he realised that a periodic blue flame about an inch long was escaping from the exhaust stub of the starboard engine. He recognised the symptoms. The rocker gear had broken on one cylinder. It was a familiar fault with the Tiger engine. As the noise and vibration swelled, Bowles fought to maintain height, and they actually crossed the frontier at 13,000 feet. Another ninety minutes and they ought to be overhead Villeneuve. But the danger was that the cylinder would crack where the base fitted into the crankcase.

Then came the explosion they all feared. The cylinder head blew off and came straight through the cowling, like a chicken emerging from its shell. No power was available now from the starboard engine, and with the Whitley's two-speed propeller there was no ability to 'feather'. The engine, like the basin turret, would remain a drag on their progress.

Icing-up of the carburettor was already causing loss of power on the port side, and they were losing height. As they descended, the temperature fell and the accretion of ice thickened.

Bowles was faced with two choices. Either he could let down quickly through the freezing layer or he could try, despite the reduced power, to climb out of it. Below him, as he well knew, the ground rose in places to 1,500 feet. That was assuming their navigation had been accurate. It was a lot to ask. The margin might be narrower. He was making up his mind to hold his present height and increase it if he could, looking for a break in the cloud, when the port engine began dropping revs.

The alternative of holding his height was thus denied him. His rate of descent, suddenly increasing, could not be reversed. The plane was heavily iced up and he was still in cloud. He fell back on a third and final choice. Switching on his inter-com, he called the crew.

'Hallo everyone. This is the pilot speaking. We can't maintain height. Get ready to jump!'

As the height loss continued, down to 1,500 feet and below, and the cloud remained impenetrable, he called the crew again, urgently this time.

'Bale out! Bale out!'

The main exit in a Whitley was through a square hatch in the floor of the nose. The tail gunner had an emergency exit from the turret itself. The first man to go was Ali Barber, the front gunner, but as he slid through the hatch the leads to his helmet twisted round his neck and he hung there helplessly, kicking his legs in space. The deep-frozen effect on his mind and body of the long hours of sub-zero temperatures, exposed as he was, had almost petrified him and he bungled his exit; he was being strangled. Bill Emery managed to release him and push him out, but as his parachute opened it knocked him unconscious. Emery went next, and as he somersaulted through the cloud he was relieved to see Barber pirouetting down.

Seeing that something was delaying them up front, Roy Jackson, already trying to transmit an SOS, clamped the Morse key down so someone could get a bearing on them, then crawled through the centre section towards the door. As he went he heard a final shout from Bowles.

'Out! We're baling out!'

Jackson grabbed his bottle of *eau de Cologne,* slid across the dustbin turret, and grasped the door handle. He had a last look behind him, and seeing no movement from the rear turret he assumed that Griffin had used his emergency door. Staring into the blackness, he curled himself up into a ball and leaned forward until he overbalanced. This was his way of trying to ensure he missed the tail.

There was no automatic pilot, but Bowles throttled back and trimmed the Whitley to fly in a gentle glide. Then, with the plane now well below the height of the highest ground and still in cloud, he made one final call. He was thinking of Griffin.

'Hallo Griff. Have you gone?' There was no reply.

The confusion up front had delayed Barber and Emery. Jackson had stayed on a moment longer to send the SOS. Griffin, decided Bowles, would have been the first to go. A final touch on the trimmers and he too must go. His parachute had barely opened when he came out through the cloud.

Griffin had felt the changed air pressures in his ear-drums and he knew from his watch that they must be nearing the end of the flight. Best of all, it wasn't quite so cold. He was feeling almost relaxed. As with Barber, however, mind and body were taking some time to de-freeze. He could see the occasional gout of flames from the engines, illuminating the cloud, but he had got used to that. It seemed to him that they were circling but it was hard to get any sort of orientation.

Suddenly he was conscious of wisps of cloud rushing past him, ghostly and insubstantial in the darkness, like ectoplasm. One moment he was sitting in a golden-red world, then the flames were no more than a pale reflection on the cloud-base as the Whitley came out in the clear. 500 feet below him he could just see the ground. Patches of indigo blackness, interspersed with battleship grey, told him the land was a mixture of woodland and pasture.

The Whitley was circling, and there was just enough light to make out the contours of the hills. Johnnie and Bill must be looking for a pinpoint. But he could see no feature to fix their position.

He began to wonder why they were still circling. Could they be contemplating a forced landing? They were getting a bit low. Almost alarmingly low. He began calling them up. Nothing. Nothing. The circuit was dead.

At about that moment, Roy Jackson's parachute opened, and as he steadied himself his harness slipped under him to form a seat. He could hear the Whitley, engines complaining, still above him somewhere, and he looked round to see where it was. He was amazed to find that it was describing a perfect clockwise circle, as though still under control. Was someone still flying it?

Johnnie, he thought, must have changed his mind. Or Emery. One of them must be still in there. But as the Whitley steadily lost height, he guessed what had happened. Bowles had trimmed the aircraft like the master he was.

It occurred to him that had it not been for the undulations of the hills the plane might have flown on and on, finally perhaps flying itself majestically into a robot belly-landing without damage. But if it continued on its present circuit, it would fly itself into the side of a hill.

Griffin, sitting alone in the tail, retained perfect faith in the men up front. He could see little or nothing ahead of him and he did not realise there was rising ground lying in wait right on track.

What a night it had been! Cruel, too cruel altogether. Some deskbound warrior had blundered, that was for sure. No one could do their job in conditions of such severity. All to strew bumpf over Germany.

The arc of the circle remained unchanged. Griffin, puzzled though he was, remained blissfully unaware of his plight.

Jackson watched the Whitley, its familiar nose-down attitude slightly exaggerated, pursuing its graceful curve. Even though he thought there was no one in it, he winced at its imminent fate. He had barely touched ground when he saw it plunge into the hillside and burst into flames. The gradient of the hillside was shallow, and the Whitley pancaked so that its first contact with the ground was made by the forward section, somewhere beneath the main spar. This was the section, near the obtrusion of the still lowered basin turret, that suffered the most damaging impact. The rear half broke off amidships, turned over on its back, and continued forward under its own impetus, vaulting over the front half and landing upside down beyond it. It was the front half that burst into flames.

Griffin, upside down in the turret, was facing the way he had been heading, away from the flames. He was slightly singed during the leap-frogging, but apart from minor injuries to the head that knocked him out temporarily he was not seriously hurt.

When he came to he realised two things. First, miraculously, the fire was behind him. Second, it was close enough to engulf him if he didn't move quickly. And third, he thought of the crew. They must be somewhere in that holocaust behind him.

He managed to twist the turret round to give himself room to get out. Working upside down, he had got about two-thirds of the way when his harness snagged. To release himself he had to struggle back into the turret, free the harness, and drop to the ground head first, saving himself with his hands.

As soon as he got his bearings he staggered round to the front to help the others. Already the wreckage was settling as only a fiercely burning metal structure can do.

Somehow he had to get nearer the cockpit, and he stumbled towards it. He was immediately beaten back by the heat. Confronting him was an inferno, a funeral pyre for his crew. No one had got out – unless they were thrown out. And that couldn't be. There was nothing he could do for his comrades. He was the sole survivor.

Still half-concussed, racked by horror and shock, he wandered about aimlessly on the hillside, scarcely able to think. The entire flight had been a nightmare, ending with this ghastly purgatory of waking up. He couldn't think at all. When the ammunition started exploding he thought for a moment it was the champagne corks popping.

He dragged himself to the top of the hill to get his bearings. As soon as he got there, three local French conscripts who had seen the plane crash accosted him at the point of a bayonet and started marching him to the nearest village. They thought he was German, and he could not convince them he was not. But soon, in the village of Passavant-en-Argonne, in an unbelievable moment of joy and hysterical laughter, he was reunited with his crew. All had baled out safely and made their way to the village.

What had happened to the other Whitley crews? Had their experience been similar, or had Bowles and his crew just been unlucky – or even unprofessional? Did the fault lie with those responsible for sending them off on such a desperate errand on such a night?

Of the five crews, one, as we have said, turned back. He could hardly be criticised for doing so. Another, Flight Sergeant J.W.P. Wynton – John Wynton – has sent me his own story, which he calls 'The Ice Flight'. He too had very nearly turned back with an erratic port-engine, but it returned to full power, and he decided that a landing in the weather still prevailing at base would have been even more hazardous than continuing.

Wynton reached their Dropping Zone 75 miles north-east of Frankfurt after three hours flying at 16,000 feet and began to circle. There was a danger of drifting too far downwind, and a clear sky made them a target for the defences, though they weren't hit. 'We conserved our oxygen for the men handling the pamphlets,' writes John Wynton, 'but even so they passed out every few minutes, lay down for a bit, then awoke, then got back to the job. They, nor I, expected less. Fortunately anoxia had not been 'invented' then: the general remedy was to breathe more deeply.'

They dropped their leaflets, but on the return flight it was Wynton himself who collapsed for lack of oxygen, and his second pilot, Sergeant E. Hide, took over. 'The next thing I remember, Hide was punching me awake and the world was a mass of flames.' The starboard engine was on fire. 'Hide was in an impossible position, iced-up aircraft, crew disoriented, pilot and second pilot both suffering from oxygen lack. Then we stalled. I think we were at about 9,000 feet in a cu-nim and we came straight down through the core.

'Hide was absolutely magnificent and his piloting was really superhuman, we both heaved on the control column and we eventually broke cloud at about 500 feet. There was a faint horizon and we lined up on that. God alone knows what our airspeed was.

'Below all was black, and then we realised what we were over was a forest. It was pouring with rain and soon we were down to 200 feet. In the distance on the side of a hill was a light grey patch, just something different, so we aimed the aircraft at that. The plane sank into the tips of the trees, these mercifully broke our speed and we made the grey patch. It was a forest clearing. The crew were safe, but the aircraft was a write-off.'

When Wynton says 'We both heaved on the control column', the man sitting at the radio, 'Tick' Heller, can be more specific. 'They were both' he says, 'standing on the instrument panel.'

John Wynton, who contacted me when I first wrote about Griffin, added: 'I spent 45 years in RAF service, enlisted in 1929, sergeant pilot 1933, a lifetime of adventure and interest.'

The third pilot, Sergeant E. Cotton, had fared no better. The turret and trimming tabs had all frozen up long before they dropped their leaflets, they had a depleted oxygen supply through the panic take-off, and on the way back the front gunner collapsed in a semi-frozen heap. Cotton was forced to let down to an altitude where they wouldn't need oxygen, but there they were peppered by anti-aircraft fire. Despite the conditions the wireless operator managed to get a succession of bearings and they got back to Villeneuve safely after five hours twenty minutes 'iceborne' – to use their own phrase.

Wing Commander Silvester, the detachment commander, had chosen the short straw by going all the way to Munich – not with Bowles, but with his senior pilot, Flying Officer Budden. Yet right from the start – through no one's fault except the leadership back in England – he could hardly have chosen worse.

First, the elevator trimming tabs froze in the climbing position, so that Budden had to apply considerable forward pressure on the control column for most of the flight. Worst of all, in the panic before take-off, they too had had no time for the routine check of their oxygen bottles and only one bottle was charged.

Trying to escape the build-up of ice, Budden climbed to what proved his absolute ceiling of 16,500 feet, but at that height the front gunner slumped in his turret and the navigator lay gasping on the floor, his cheeks pulsating and his lungs pumping like bellows. The cockpit heating, such as it was, proved useless, and they could find no way of relieving their physical agony.

At one point, Silvester and the navigator butted their heads on the navigation table and even on the floor, in a desperate effort to experience some other form of pain as a relief from the tortures of frostbite and lack of oxygen. Budden himself was prostrated with sickness, and, even over Germany, the crew prayed to be overtaken by some disaster that would force them to bale out. They found themselves incapable of cohesive thought and unable to resist the most unfathomable depths of depression.

It was this same incapacity for cohesive thought, due to a combination of hunger, air-sickness (which all the crews suffered from), and the other privations endured, that excused Bowles's crew for forgetting Griffin. In those last moments, under the mounting threat of a fatal crash into high ground, it was easy to believe that Griffin had gone, or even to forget about him altogether. Certainly Griffin always exonerated his crew.

In his subsequent report, Silvester, unable to be frank to the point of disrespect, went as far as saying that the weather had been 'far from satisfactory for the operation to be carried out with success'. This was tact to the point of subservience.

Despite the loss of two Whitleys on what must have seemed in retrospect a truly misguided and even suicidal mission, there seems to have been no subsequent court of enquiry. Presumably it was recognised that the buck, if it was to be passed to anyone, could only stop at the top. The truth was that the operation was based on a number of fallacies. First was the notion that the German people had the freedom and the will, if given the facts, to change their government. Second was the assumption that the air crews of the peacetime Royal Air Force could go anywhere in daylight or darkness in any weather, find their targets, drop their loads accurately by dead reckoning, and fight their way home. They were assumptions which, in that first winter of the war, were to prove tragically misconceived.

At the Air Ministry and at the operational commands and groups, there was an enormous reservoir of talent, but what was lacking was war experience. That experience could only be bought by the men at the sharp end, men like Bowles, Wynton, Cotton, and Budden, and their crews.

Expressing his amazement that the Whitleys in such conditions of icing-up had been controllable at all, Silvester offered the opinion – which no one challenged – that the gallantry, courage, determination and devotion to duty of his crews had been worthy of the highest

King George VI meeting members of Sergeant Bowles's crew at Linton-on-Ouse, November 1939. Right to left: Alfred Griffin (nearest camera), showing scar), Roy Jackson, 'Ali' Barber, Bill Emery, 'Johnnie' Bowles. (Alfred Griffin)

traditions of the Royal Air Force. However, there were few decorations for litter-bugging, and none were awarded on this occasion. Only one pilot had turned back, and he, perhaps, also merited an award – for good sense.

In the climate of the peacetime air force, Griffin's injuries did not even warrant a visit to sick quarters, nor were post-traumatic stress disorders mentioned. But Griffin's fantastic lone experience did appeal to the press, arousing the interest of a certain V.V.I.P.

The cuts on Griffin's face and head were still visible five days later when he and his crew were lined up back at Linton-on-Ouse to tell their story to King George VI.

Notes

Alfred Griffin's help with this account of course was crucial: he later flew with 'ace' bomber pilot 'Willie' Tait. Roy Jackson helped usefully too: he was later awarded a DFM and an MBE and retired as a wing commander. (And in 1942 he married his sweetheart). He and Griffin were together later on Stirlings and Halifaxes, but 'a mighty prang stopped us both'. John Wynton's story has been interwoven: as mentioned, he stayed on in the RAF after the war. Harry Budden retired as a wing commander, DSO, DFC. 'Johnnie' Bowles was later shot down and taken prisoner. He died while attempting to escape.

CHAPTER TWO

Sir Arnold Wilson, M.P. – Arch-Appeaser and Air-Gunner, Dunkirk, May 1940

As the twin-engined Wellington bomber neared the coastal area where the beleaguered British Expeditionary Force was trying to escape from France, the man in the rear turret peered into the darkness, desperately seeking a target for his guns. With his five-man crew, he was there to do all he could to harass and delay the victorious Nazi *blitzkrieg*. It was 31 May, 1940.

The occupant of the turret was in many ways a seasoned veteran – but not as an airman. A distinguished soldier, yes, civil and political administrator, author and politician, knighted for his services to the British Empire, all those things, even for the last seven years a Member of Parliament, for Hitchin, Hertfordshire: but as a wartime air gunner, a novice.

It was back in 1904, 35 years earlier, as a young subaltern, that he had won the King's Award and the Sword of Honour at Sandhurst. What was he doing here, at this crisis moment in World War II, a middle-aged man and a devoted husband and father, volunteering for this most vulnerable of aircrew duties at the age of 55?

Marrying late, he had fathered two young children, both now at school: Hugh, 14, at Eton, and Sarah, 12, privately, at Westmere, near Thetford. Yet he had seen it as his duty, for hugely personal as well as patriotic reasons, to get into the front line immediately in the fight against Nazi Germany.

Throughout the 1930s he had been an arch-appeaser, a vilified apologist for the Fascist dictators, for whom he professed understanding and admiration, and with one of whom, at least, he had been on visiting terms: Adolf Hitler.

In 1934 he had been granted a special interview at the German Chancellery with the Fuehrer. But that was six years ago. Tonight he was planning to leave a less formal visiting card for his erstwhile friend. Two tons of bombs.

As a Member of Parliament since 1933, the year Hitler came to power, Arnold Wilson had been a controversial figure. It was not only for his defence of the Fascist dictators, Hitler and Mussolini: that alone had earned him widespread opprobrium. He had also earned a reputation for the espousal of social reforms which branded him as a firebrand eccentric, even by the most radical Tory standards. The measures he introduced, or tried to introduce, were aimed not so much at factions abroad as at frictions at home. They were measures designed to alleviate the genuine grievances of the masses, the have-nots of the 1920s and 30s, the sick, the disadvantaged, and the unemployed.

He was working on Bills to improve the lot of the working man – Workmen's Compensation, Industrial Assurance, Burial Reform, Funeral Costs, and Old Age Pensions. These Bills, years before the Beveridge Plan, were among the campaigns which he pursued, relentlessly and provocatively, through speeches in the House, through lecturing, and above all through writing books, or collaborating in the writing of them. In all this he was years ahead of his time. Yet in one outstanding area he had been proved spectacularly wrong.

For a long time he had refused to accept it. Some of his speeches in the House had ended in uproar. He had been a fanatical defender of Neville Chamberlain, and of Munich. He had entertained high-ranking Germans in his home. Even after war was declared and the policy of appeasement was in ruins he had gone the last mile, pleading that Hitler's peace overtures should not be dismissed out of hand.

Finally had come a dramatic recantation, of staggering proportions, even for a politician. No man could have confessed his faults and eaten his words more abjectly. His eleventh-hour volte-face, meant as atonement and expiation, left him open to contempt and ridicule: it had come too late. He was one of the guilty men who had brought Britain to the brink of disaster. What could he do about it? The answer, it seemed, was nothing. Yet he was absolutely determined not to leave the terrible reckoning of the wasted inter-war years, with all that it now threatened in carnage and destruction, exclusively to the young.

Tall and thick-set, with a moustache that like his hair had turned from jet-black to iron grey, and with prominent eyes, heavy eyebrows and an unflinching gaze, he had, as soon as war was declared, started exercising daily to improve his physical fitness, hoping that a call might come. With all his contacts, he was quite sure it would. But not even the Secretary of State for Air, to whom he addressed a final, heartfelt plea, imagined that he was capable of slimming down sufficiently to squeeze into a Wellington bomber's turret.

How was it that, in something approaching advanced middle-age, this former lieutenant-colonel and civil administrator had transformed himself into Pilot Officer Sir Arnold Wilson, tail gunner extraordinary, talked his way into the first major crisis of World War II, and was even now about to pound away at advancing German *panzers* as they closed in around Dunkirk?

Wilson was elected Conservative and Unionist MP for Hitchin in 1933. Soon he was professing an understanding of the racial theories propounded by Hitler and looking forward to the unification of Germany and the re-creation of the old German Federation, which he saw as a strong and stabilising force in Europe. These views were counterbalanced by continual urgings, equally unpopular at the time, that Britain must re-arm. Soon his sympathies came to the notice of the German ambassador in London, Herr von Ribbentrop, and this led, in May 1934, to an invitation to visit Germany to lecture widely on industrial subjects at major cities, including Munich, Dusseldorf, Hamburg and Bonn, and also to students at various Public Works Service camps. His visit was to culminate in a meeting with Herr Hitler.

'The day before meeting Hitler,' he wrote, 'I was received at his office by Herr Rudolf Hess, one of his right-hand men.' It was a softening-up exercise. Hess was the man who had built up the voluntary Storm Troop organisation. 'He is a fine looking man of forty-five years or so … We exchanged a few reminiscences about the war.' For Germany, said Hess, there were now only two courses open, the servitude that the Russians now endured, or the stony, upward path of regeneration. The Allies at Versailles had inflicted almost incurable wounds on Germany, but Germany had successfully applied the remedy.

'Hitler's aim,' Hess told him, 'is to change the whole outlook of the German people. Peace within will bring strength without. Hitler has already succeeded, but it will be years before the full results will be apparent. The real reserve of the revolution is the Hitler Jugend. The SA (subsequently absorbed by the SS) is not a military force but it inculcates the soldierly attitude towards life, a spirit of unity and selflessness born in the trenches in August 1914.'

Next he met General Blomberg, Minister of Defence, who spoke English well and freely. 'We spoke not of war but of peace.' He told

Wilson that the racial basis of Nazi doctrine forbade them any desire to rule other races. But self-determination must recognise the right of all Germans to unite politically.

'The list of your demands,' said Wilson, 'is long.'

'That is one of the foreseen consequences of the Treaty of Versailles.' Finally he met the Chancellor himself.

'I was received by Herr Hitler at his office, a fine but unpretentious modern building. There was no military display: a couple of SS sentries at the door and two more on the first floor. This was the only external indication that the building housed the ruler of the new Germany.

'The interview had been fixed for one o'clock, and, accompanied by my host, Herr von Ribbentrop, I was ushered punctually at that hour into the great room.

'Herr Hitler left on my mind an indelible impression of single-mindedness, with great reserves of strength. He spoke with vigour and vivacity in German so clear that the services of an interpreter were scarcely needed.' He asked what impression I had formed during my week in Germany. I spoke with admiration of the Public Service Works Camps and mentioned our own Ministry of Labour Training Centres, to the advantage of the latter. He listened intently and forecast great expansion of their own Centres. He cross-examined me on everything I had seen, and said I'd seen more in a week than some Germans saw in a year.

'He was critical of the slant often given in our newspapers. Did we realise how essential unity was for Germany, even at the expense, temporarily, of ancient liberties? Did we realise the significance of his racial policy? Every man should be proud of his own race and nation. Did I understand how profoundly the German nation was devoted to peace? The German people deserved above all things the understanding of the English, their blood relations, but they would work for peace with all: Peace on terms of honourable equality at home and abroad.'

For Wilson, the manner of this harangue was of greater interest than the content, 'which', as he wrote, 'was but an echo of his many speeches, broadcast, printed and distributed through a thousand channels.' He was more impressed with one of the Public Works students, who, after six months in London, had compared his impressions of London with conditions in Dusseldorf or Cologne.

'In London were beggars at every corner, ex-servicemen, blind men, helpless old men and women, unemployed miners: such were not seen in German towns. In London, for weekly flag days, there was a vast, ill-organised stream of charity, undertaking what should be the functions of the State. Had we no respect thus to parade the inadequacy of our social system? Where were there such slums as in England? Such degrading conditions? There was poverty in Germany, but no degradation and no real slums. What appalled him in England was the amount of misdirected energy and misused money. We had yet to learn the meaning of the German motto – 'Public welfare before self-interest'.

Judging by his subsequent attempts in the House of Commons to introduce legislation to correct some of these social black spots, Wilson returned from Germany far more obsessed with the need to clean up Britain than with nourishing or defending the Nazis. His conscience had been pricked by this German student, with striking results to his social awareness.

Unlike most of his contemporaries, Wilson made no distinction between the Nazi leaders and the German people. The Nazis, he had reason to believe, had the passionate support of many and the assent of the majority. In a ten-minute BBC talk on his return, he concluded:

'It is not for us to criticise or to condemn, but to understand.

'I have seen German youth displaying in work and play an energy and enthusiasm which, because it is wholly unselfish, is wholly good. Great dynamic forces have been developed, even greater forces are in reserve. Whatever be the aims of their leaders I believe that the temper of the people is peaceful.'

The same was true, he thought, of Mussolini and Italy. 'I cannot withhold my admiration for the achievements of the Fascist Government in Libya and in Italy itself.'

Mussolini's case in Abyssinia was strong: he had simply handled it badly. Our attempt to apply sanctions had been a disastrous mistake. And he accepted the Italian propaganda line. 'I have no reason to doubt what I have been told, that people in those areas which Italian troops have occupied regarded these troops as liberators.'

His postbag, after this broadcast, brought a shoal of letters – of thanks and abuse in about equal measure. Almost all the abusive letters were anonymous. Two months later he visited Germany again.

When Hitler marched into Austria in 1936 Wilson argued that he had only taken forcibly what he might have had by consent. Hitler's action was no more than the expression of popular feeling. So far as England was concerned, popular feeling, he felt, was in favour of accepting the German proposals. 'The people of this country are determined not to be carried away by any sentiment that could lead to acute opposition to Germany.' He warned that the treatment by Czechoslovakia of German minorities in the Sudetenland would cause trouble, 'and when it occurs we shall do well not to assume too readily that Germany is the aggressor.'

Several times he journeyed to Germany to lecture, and he was not afraid to stress his dismay at Nazi excesses, especially against the Jews. But he still found much to admire. After a visit in September 1937 he wrote: 'Herr Hitler appeared to have mellowed.'

He had no more trenchant adversary in the House of Commons than Winston Churchill, with whom he had clashed many years earlier when he was political commissioner in Iraq, defending Britain's mandate, and Churchill, as Colonial Secretary, spoke against it. But he understood that the Nazis only respected strength. 'Moderation,' to use his own phrase, 'is not a German virtue'. Meanwhile he was pilloried as a warmonger because like Churchill, he campaigned for rearmament and conscription. 'We cannot hope as in 1914 to have eighteen months, or even eighteen weeks, in which to improvise an army.'

After the absorption of the Sudetenland into Germany in 1938 and Chamberlain's 'Peace in our time' meeting with Hitler at Munich, Wilson welcomed the redrawing of frontiers and told Conservative Central Office he would gladly speak as often as they wished in support of Chamberlain. He addressed fifteen meetings in October and another fifteen in November. 'What we are seeing today is the growth of German federation. There is no intention on the part of the German people or those in control of their destinies to dominate this country or France. What they are asking is that they control every German hearth in Europe and nothing we can do will stop that process. With good sense and wise statesmanship Britain can look forward to a longer period of peace and prosperity than ever before.'

Summarising these meetings, he wrote, pointedly: 'Those who clamour for "no surrender to dictators" are mostly beyond military age.'

But his allegiance underwent a dramatic revulsion when, in March 1939, Hitler double-crossed his sympathisers by swallowing up the rest of Czechoslovakia. No one was more outraged than Wilson. Like

Chamberlain, he had been duped. In his anger he railed above all against Hitler himself, accusing him of treachery and perfidy. 'Hitler killed all confidence when he entered Prague.' But he was still ready to pay another visit to Germany. More in sorrow than in anger he told his audiences: 'We have tried to negotiate again and again in the last two years, but we have not found Herr Hitler willing to do likewise. Our patience is almost unlimited, but if war is forced upon us we shall display a staying power which will eventually decide the issue.' He was now injecting a note of defiance. 'We shall win the last battle.'

This challenging declaration of faith, coupled with his demands for rearmament and conscription, should have distanced him from the ranks of the so-called 'guilty men' of the Thirties. But he still believed that appeasement was the only rational policy. 'Britain's young men must not be thrown again into the furnace of war unless and until all possibility of compromise is not only past, but past beyond recall.' If and when that stage was reached, however, 'War must be prosecuted to the limit.'

On 3 September 1939, when the Chamberlain government declared war on Germany, Wilson began an attempt at metamorphosis. He stopped smoking, shunned alcohol, walked long distances – an exercise, even a pastime, he had always enjoyed – and went on a diet. 'What war work I shall have to do I do not yet know,' he told his son Hugh at Eton; but he was determined to become fit enough for a combatant role.

The Army must be his first call and he wrote to General Ironside, Chief of the Imperial General Staff. He could hardly go higher than that. And Ironside was a personal friend from way back. But Ironside could offer him nothing and nor could the Admiralty, who would not even consider him for the crew of a minesweeper. They simply said he was too old. The Colonial Office 'had him on their list', and he knew what that meant. In any case he wanted something at the sharp end. What about the Royal Air Force?

He had spent many happy times with the RAF in Iraq when he was a civil commissioner there, twenty years earlier. Would they remember? For two and a half years, from April 1918 to October 1920, as Acting Civil Commissioner in Baghdad, he had been continually on the move to and from the districts, almost always travelling by plane with the RAF. He had used their services regularly, visiting remote areas under his control for which any other form of transport was impracticable. At the time it was regarded as an unconventional mode of travel for a high government official, but not only did it save a great deal of time and discomfort, it introduced him to the camaraderie of a group of pilots and Air Force personnel, of whom he soon became inordinately fond.

'I have seen a lot of Air Force officers,' he wrote in his diary, 'they are the best company in Baghdad; their training brings out the strongest point in their race… They are more devoted to their jobs than anyone I know and they never tire or expect others to tire of their shop; very open too to other people's shop, but not platitudes… Flying does me good and lightens my burden. I wish I could chuck my job and go in for it, but I fear I have not the mechanical proficiency required for it. But I believe I could make a good observer …'

What the local RAF men thought of him – and most of them were non-commissioned, pilots, observers, and ground crews – was summed up after several incidents with rebel tribes, who in 1918 supported Germany and were pledged to oppose the British. Wilson, being air-lifted as a passenger, had actually manned the guns. Once they were actually shot down, the crippled British plane fortunately falling within friendly territory. After this the RAF in Iraq granted him the honorary title of 'observer', with a brevet to go with it.

The memory encouraged him to have one more go, this time with the RAF. But was it a pipe dream? He was beginning to lose hope. First he decided that a final attempt at finding a peace formula ought to be made, before the real shooting started. He told a reporter: 'It may be argued that no peace is possible with Hitler. This is not true.' Now that Britain had declared war, Hitler, it seemed, was hesitating. 'I believe he has seen the red light. It may be said that a peace negotiated now will not endure. I do not agree.

'I am regarded by the authorities as too old to fight, but I do not wish to live behind the rampart of the corpses and maimed bodies of the youth of Britain and France.'

In his constituency, he noted, his remarks aroused 'extreme indignation and widespread disapproval'. Nevertheless he penned a final appeal to Neville Chamberlain, expressing grave anxiety at the long road ahead and the heavy casualties that must be sustained before victory could be won. He agreed that Hitler's terms were unacceptable, but suggested that an armistice now might give Britain the opportunity to put forward her own terms.

Chamberlain conceded that it would be wrong, if peace proposals were made, to refuse point-blank even to hear what they were. 'But we must not forget that the main purpose for which we entered the war was to put an end to the constant threat of German aggression. I must confess that I find it difficult to imagine that any peace could be concluded now which would secure for us this fundamental object.'

With this rebuff from no less an appeaser than Chamberlain, Wilson made his final approach, this time to the Air Minister himself, Sir Archibald Sinclair. He had a feeling that the RAF might take a less orthodox view, and he was right. 'You can join the RAF as an air gunner,' said Sinclair at length, 'if you can pass the medical.'

That was the next hurdle, but if Sinclair thought this would be the end of the matter, he underestimated his man. 'I wish you could have seen me doing my medical examination,' he told Hugh. 'Eyesight exceptionally good, hearing very acute, heart full strength. Held my breath for 65 seconds and could have gone on. *They tried to find some defect but could find none.'*

He shocked his constituents a second time by telling them that, having been finally convinced that the war must be fought to a finish, he had no desire as their MP to shelter himself and live in safety behind the bodies of millions of young men. 'I have obtained leave and have been passed medically fit to take my place in the armed forces of the Crown.' This proud boast was heard in sullen silence by his constituents.

He was told by Chamberlain, in a personal letter: 'You have taken on the most dangerous job in the Air Force.' And to Hugh he wrote: 'Your mother has agreed that I am doing the right thing. Your job is clear – to take more pains than ever to look after her, for she will be much alone.'

He told the editor of *The Times*, in an unpublished letter, that he hoped no one would suggest that his action was either impulsive or ill-judged. Once decorated for bravery – as he had been – a man was no longer a free agent. 'I am going with my wife's full consent, and she lost her first husband in the RAF in the last war – killed in action, so the credit is hers.'

Now that he had passed the medical – which no one had expected him to do – there was no stopping him. Early in November 1939 he began his training at No 1 Air Armaments School at Manby in Lincolnshire. 'This is a great show I am in!' he exulted to Hugh. 'I have to learn every detail of three guns – Lewis, Vickers and Browning – how to take them to bits and put them together – what to do when there is a stoppage.' (Stoppages were frequent and clearing them in the air a tiresome process: the price of failure, as he noted in his diary, was death.)

He was equally enthusiastic about the Central Gunnery School at Warmwell in Dorset, where he was posted in December. 'This is a great place. We fly every day – often at great heights – cold enough to make a man cry – but as I have had cold baths all my life I stand it better than most younger men.' Nearly all the gunners were 20-25, some younger, but 'I think I am up to average in class and hope to do better.' The young trainees went all out to beat him – their pride saw to that – but he tired less easily than they did. 'I walk long distances and hope soon to be the same size I was in 1917 when I was "a fighting man".'

For Wilson junior at Eton, unique in having a father training to be an air gunner, this was heady stuff. His father's letters were sometimes accompanied by diagrams and photographs, including a panoramic shot of a Wellington in flight. 'I have marked my favourite turret, also the front turret, which I like second best. There is also a mid-turret or "dustbin", which is let down and hangs underneath the belly of the machine. I can use it but it is rather small.' In fact because of his size he had difficulty in getting in and out of all the Wellington turrets, although in case this was held against him he wouldn't admit it.

A contemporary recalls that during that bitterly cold winter of 1939/40 Wilson rose before six o'clock, made tea for his fellows, then lit the coal-burning stoves in the classrooms.

Soon he was training with a regular crew. And the choice of pilot was surely more than coincidence. They had met years before, so it emerged, back in Iraqi days, though no record of their actually synchronising can be found. The airman in question had graduated over the years to pilot training, for which he had been recommended. Wilson, with his admiration for the airman professionals of pre-war days overseas, could not have arrived at a better choice.

There were of course a great many airmen who had served in Iraq, and it may well be that Wilson, on qualifying as an air gunner, indicated a preference. Or perhaps an imaginative personnel department may have directed him similarly.

Who were his new companions? His pilot, Flight Sergeant William Alfred Gray, from Cumberland (born in Dalston, near Carlisle), had joined the RAF on an apprenticeship at the age of 18 in 1926. He completed courses as Fitter Airframe and Fitter Engine (FAE) at Halton before joining No. 602 Squadron, and in 1931 he was posted with his squadron to India. Assessments were always 'Very good' or 'Superior', and transfer to pilot was recommended many times, but it was five years coming through, and meanwhile he passed the requisite Service courses in Higher Education. Finally he began training at No. 4 Elementary Flying Training School in Iraq in 1932. Passing out as a sergeant pilot in 1934, he returned to Home Establishment in 1936. Meanwhile he had distinguished himself by flying VIPs (important passengers) on notable long-distance inter-Command flights in the Middle East (the sort of work with which Wilson was himself familiar), and had become a fully qualified flying instructor. He was teaching young pilots to fly heavy bombers and training them in cross-country flying, night flying, and bomb-aiming. Artistic, his off-duty interests included music – playing the piano and singing – and in Service life he was much in demand on Mess occasions, with a beer lined up on the piano-top to keep him going.

The accolade for non-operational flying for non-commissioned officers in peacetime came his way when the London Gazette, on 8 June 1939, recorded his award of the Air Force Medal (AFM), a rare distinction indeed.

During his time in Iraq, as we have seen, Wilson had made many friends in the RAF, and at what point Gray had been among them is uncertain. The earliest Gray could have reached Iraq seems to have been 1931, and long before that Wilson had retired from the Indian Political Service. But in 1923 he had accepted a prestigious appointment as representative of the Anglo-Persian Oil Company in the Persian Gulf, placing him in commercial charge of the area over which he had recently exercised political control. 'I go wherever I can be most use,' he said, and he still travelled widely, presumably by air, in pursuit of the company's business.

Wilson was an enthusiastic believer in Pax Britannica, helping the development of Iraq under the British Mandate. In 1922 he had married a war widow in Rose Carver, then aged 30, formerly married to Lieutenant Robin Carver, killed in 1918 in the Royal Flying Corps – another link with the junior Service. She brought with her a daughter, Ann. From all accounts it was a 'happy ever after' union. They set up home at Khorramshahr, between Basra and Abadan, and they too started a family, Hugh in 1924 and Sarah in 1926, both actually born in England. Finally he was promoted and posted to the oil company headquarters in London, though he still made frequent visits to Iraq. This did not end until 1932, when at some financial sacrifice he retired from the oil business, bought a house (Wynches at Much Hadham, in Hertfordshire), and resolved to pursue a political career. He was then 48. But he still visited Iraq, and somewhere in this period he met Leading Aircraftman Gray, or Sergeant Gray, or Flight-Sergeant Gray – which by 1937 he had become.

They met up again when they got to No. 37 Squadron, a front-line Wellington squadron based at Feltwell, in Norfolk, in late March 1940. Writing to his Mum and Dad on 29 March, Gray told them: 'We have an interesting addition to our Squadron, in the person of Sir Arnold Wilson, MP, ex-Governor of Iraq and Malaya and goodness knows what else. He is a rear gunner in one of our machines.' Very soon he was assigned to Gray's crew.

Soon Wilson was writing to Hugh. 'My crew are A1, cheerful, courageous and determined. We have never failed to reach our objective.'

Wilson and Gray had much in common. Wilson was descended on his father's side from a line of small farmers in Cumberland. Gray was Cumberland born and bred. Gray, like Wilson, was a great walker, loving the Kurdistan Hills, and it may well be that their wanderlust brought them together in Iraq. Certain it is that they had become friends, and in August 1937, when Gray married – 'to the finest woman I know' – Annie Margaret Lewis, aged twenty-one (he was twenty-nine), at Dalston Parish Church – they were especially proud of the wedding present Sir Arnold gave them: a handsome bookcase. And very soon they had further points of reference when he and 'Nan', as he called her, started a family, a girl, Eileen Margaret, 2.11.38, and a boy, Ian William, 27.2.40.

The inscription written in Martineau's Guide to the English Lake District, and given to Pilot Officer Gray four days before the last flight over Dunkirk. (Ian Gray)

In that same letter, Gray told his parents: 'I shan't be happy until I have Nan down here with me.' Meanwhile an appointment to a commission was in the pipeline.

What sort of chap was 'Dolly' Gray, as he was inevitably known? Short and stocky, with crinkly fair hair, he had a countenance which always reflected friendliness and good-humour and a Service record of thirteen years of almost unbroken keenness and reliability, marred only by a reprimand in 1935 for minor damage to Service equipment, bringing a fine of £2.10 shillings, just to prove he was human. A former colleague, Ted Butcher ('Butch'), then a sergeant observer on the squadron, writes: 'Dolly Gray AFM and 'Bomber' Brown (second pilot and bomb-aimer) were great friends of mine in those days and were regarded as the most experienced pilot and navigator/bomber respectively on the squadron.' Since there were commissioned officers in charge of both Flights, this was high praise.

Butcher also recalled Arnold Wilson. 'I well remember him giving extremely entertaining talks in the flight (office) when we were grounded.' This was in the 'Wait and See' period of the 'Phoney war', the 'blue-birds over the white cliffs of Dover' time, when any serious bombing effort was circumscribed, for fear of what it might incite. 'In particular,' writes Butcher, 'he developed and demonstrated a method of extracting the rear gunner from his turret if he were wounded. This involved swinging on an overhead bar and pinning the gunner by the legs before pulling him out. We were amazed that an 'old man' was so fit!'

Another man who remembered Wilson was the new commanding officer of the squadron, 'Willie' Merton (later Air Chief Marshal Sir Walter). He found Wilson already installed as gunnery leader. 'Though at the time he was only a very junior member of the squadron I always referred to him as "Sir Gunner"', says Merton. 'This pleased everyone.

I found him indefatigable, a leader who spent hours training and encouraging the young gunners. He was so keen to fly on missions that I had to instruct that he only flew with his own crew as he was always volunteering to fill gaps as they occurred in other crews.'

After succeeding in getting exactly where he wanted, Wilson was even more frustrated than most by the policy of temporary non-aggression. North Sea sweeps and leaflet raids over the German periphery were play-acting. He actually visited Charles Portal, then C-in-C Bomber Command, and complained that they weren't doing

Sir Arnold Wilson. Told by Neville Chamberlain, then P.M., 'you have taken on the most dangerous job in the air force. (Hugh Wilson)

'Sir Gunner', standing at the left of the back row, with the rest of the crew. Left to right - back row – Sir Arnold, Sgt. Jim Brown and Sgt Jack Axford. Front row – LAC Rex Orland, Pilot Officer Bill Gray – and an unknown member who was not on the final flight. (Cyril Orland)

enough. He even asked for a transfer to a day fighter squadron, either Blenheims or Defiants, and Portal promised to forward an application if he made one. But he was only needling Portal, and no such application was made. He was in fact, as he told Hugh, perfectly happy with his crew.

Although Wilson, according to Merten, kept very much to himself in the Officers' Mess and off-duty seemed always to be busy writing (he was in fact expanding an old diary of his Persian past into a book), his real friends were amongst his crew. They were all long-serving peacetime airmen. In addition to Gray, about to join him in the Officers' Mess, there were also 'Bomber' Brown, Sergeant James Francis Brown, twenty-six, revered in the squadron for his accurate navigation and bomb-aiming. All of them were senior NCOs, trained over the years in their individual jobs and by general consent among the top men of the squadron. The navigator, Jackie Axford, married, and the wireless-operator and front gunner, Leading Aircraftman Rex Orland, were both regulars. Their collective professionalism was no surprise to Wilson – it was no more than he had come to expect from his Iraqi days.

During April, Gray and his crew were given a brand-new Wellington 1c as their own machine – L7791. Wilson told Hugh: 'It's like having a new toy.' Hugh visited Feltwell during the Easter holidays and was

Rex Orland, with 'Dolly' Gray (above) wearing a parachute harness. (Cyril Orland)

given a ride in a Wellington. It was a tremendous thrill to feel the atmosphere and try out the turrets his father had described to him.

Back at Eton he received sobering news. 'We lost two machines over Stavanger last week. Gerry Gordon, who piloted you, tall, erect, dark, was one of them.' For Hugh, still only fifteen, it was hard to believe. 'Another was Squadron Leader Bradford, whom I dearly loved. This is for your eyes only.' Wilson and his crew had taken part in the same raid but had been frustrated, like most of the others, by the weather.

This was the time of the Allied débâcle in Norway. It forced a debate in the House of Commons which threatened to topple the Chamberlain government, and Wilson, hurrying from Feltwell to London and arriving and speaking in uniform, made a spirited defence of his old friend. 'The Prime Minister and certain of his colleagues have been accused of lack of foresight.' He went on to ask, with conscious irony: 'Are there any of us in this House who have always been right?'

He was at his most spell-binding on the subject of criticism of the way the war was being run. 'I wonder how many of those who have spoken today on Norway – a subject of which I have some knowledge – realise the difficulties of the weather. Will the weather hold? What is the visibility? Where is the warm front and where is the cold front? Upon these subjects we have heard nothing.

'Those who have seen active service know well that the problems of war are always a gamble with rain, a gamble with cold, a gamble with fog and mud and dirt and squalor.' Coming as he did straight from the air battle, he had his audience transfixed. But his eloquence on Chamberlain's behalf was in vain. On 10 May came the German *blitzkrieg*. The Phoney war was over, and the Chamberlain government fell.

That night 36 Wellingtons, Wilson's among them, were sent to bomb the airfield at Waalhaven, near Rotterdam, 'which German parachutists had captured earlier in the day', as Wilson explained to Hugh, 'after which German airborne troops landed on it'. It was the chance the bomber crews had been waiting for. '*Der Tag*', wrote Wilson, 'had come'. The hangars were blazing and there were big fires in the town, so big they dazzled us and it was some time before we found the target.'

Gray and Brown descended to 1,500 feet and waited until a flare dropped by another machine illuminated the target. After shearing off to gain height they descended at 280 mph before settling down on their chosen line. Their first bomb went wide, but their second fell well within the airfield. They turned away for a second run.

'This time', recorded Wilson, 'we dropped seven bombs in quick succession. I saw a burst of flames which lit up a great troop-carrying plane, it heeled over and seconds later burst into flames, which showed five smaller machines, close by, that must have been seriously damaged. I fired a few bursts from my machine-gun, hoping they would pierce the hides of the German sentries.

'Gray made one more turn, climbing to 4,000 feet and descending rapidly to 2,000 before releasing the last of our twelve 250-lb bombs. We had done our job.'

Next day, Saturday 11 May, Lady Wilson arrived to spend the week-end, staying with the local rector, and they visited Sarah at Westmere. On the Sunday they went to church at 8 am after which Wilson sat down and wrote to Hugh. 'We shall go again at 11.30, then a sandwich lunch in the woods nearby.' It sounded idyllic, and war or no war it was spring. 'Then, I hope, dinner together, but I may be flying off again to bomb something else.' Not so idyllic. Gray, however, was also enjoying a week-end off and he had earlier been joined by Nan and the two children in rented accommodation at Methwold, a tiny village near Feltwell. He was running a small car, and since they too were regular churchgoers, and the Wilsons were staying at the Rectory, the two wives met.

37 Squadron was not called upon again until the *Luftwaffe* bombed Rotterdam three days later, on 14 May, after which the War Cabinet finally allowed Bomber Command to attack oil and rail targets east of the Rhine. The fortunes of Gray and his crew, in what was intended as the first blow in the much-vaunted Bomber Command's strategic offensive against Germany itself, were vividly described by Wilson.

'We crossed the coast at 6,000 feet and were soon at 12,000 feet with the thermometer just below freezing point. Lightning flashed from the clouds over Belgium. I kept a sharp look-out for enemy aircraft. Conditions were favourable for them; we were silhouetted against the moon and a clear sky.

'Again and again in the next half-hour searchlights got us, but seemed unable to hold us in their beams. After two hours we were over the Ruhr.

'For half-an-hour we nosed around looking for a hole in the clouds which would show us our target. At last we turned sadly back. A burst of heavy ack-ack in front of us showed that we were observed.

'At last Gray saw a bridge across the Meuse. We were at 4,000 feet. We dived to 1,000 feet, and Brown was ready – but again the searchlights foiled us. We could see nothing, and, careful to obey orders, we did not bomb blind.'

That was still strictly forbidden.

'Nothing was left but to find a good *autostrade*. This we succeeded in hitting from less than 1,000 feet. Then up and home, but not before we got a red stream of tracer within 20 or 30 feet of my turret. I gave them 500 rounds from each of my guns and they stopped.'

Next morning Churchill, newly installed as Prime Minister, visited Feltwell to see how this inaugural strategic raid, of which so much was hoped and even assumed, had fared. It had been a total failure. But Churchill and Wilson had a chance to compose their differences. 'You and I have not always agreed,' said Churchill, 'but today we are comrades.'

Wilson told Hugh: 'The war is coming very near and getting hotter. I am flying a lot.' Willie Merten still tried to restrain him from flying as often as the younger men, but Wilson insisted. His efforts to fly with other crews when his own crew were stood down, though, Merten was still able to stop.

Nevertheless he was flying every alternate night over Belgian territory now occupied by the Germans. Dutch resistance had now virtually ceased. And as the *panzers* advanced, the abortive attempt at strategic bombing was abandoned for the moment, German lines of communication nearer the battlefields becoming the targets for all Bomber Command aircraft – Blenheims and Wellingtons, some 50 of each.

Wilson described his next raid in letters to Sarah as well as to Hugh. 'We were over Belgium on the night of 17/18 bombing bridges round Namur. My pilot, Gray, did very well – got a direct hit on a bridge and knocked out a span. We then bombed a railway bridge and it began to blaze. Our machine and several others came back with some holes in it, but no losses.'

On the night of the 19/20, 37 Squadron were out again over Belgium, south of Namur this time, bombing bridges and roads. 'I am not sure how much damage we did,' he admitted to Hugh. 'It was in a gorge, hard to get down to, with a good deal of ack-ack and machine-gun fire. One of our pilots was wounded. One very persistent searchlight was in range of my gun, also a nest of machine-guns where flashes were clearly visible. I "hosepiped" them for several seconds and was cheered by a voice on the inter-com: "Good, Sir Gunner! A very pretty pattern right round them!"'

The German advance was gathering momentum and none knew it better than the Wellington crews. 'On the night of 21/22 I was bombing

Aachen, railway marshalling yards west of the town. One of our machines failed to return. (Don't tell your mother this.) We sustained lots of hits, but all our twelve 250-lb bombs exploded in the right places. The searchlights were marvellous to look at, very blinding, but we hit the target all the same.'

Meanwhile he had a letter from Sarah. She was wearing the air-gunner's brevet he had sent her. 'Have you done any more bombing over Belgium? It sounds rather exciting yet very awful really. Thank goodness you weren't shot down! What luck you received no real damage and no one was hurt. Have you been over Westmere yet? If you do, don't forget to wobble your wings like you said you would, so that I'll know it's you.' (He had said 'waggle'.)

To Hugh he wrote: 'I think of you and Sarah even when I'm in a rear turret. I'm so glad you know what a rear turret is like.'

Crossing the Channel with the home-based force almost daily – but always in darkness for the Wellingtons – in an effort, as he feared, to stem an inexorable tide, he had no illusions about the way the war was going, and he felt the media were deceiving the public by pandering to what he called 'the childish optimism of the ignorant.' He could see disaster coming all too plainly. 'We are still not working hard enough: still playing about with peacetime rules. We have not begun to win. Germany has gone far on the road to victory with increasing momentum. We can stop her only by a vast effort. I'm not even now sure that we are making it.' This was written on 23 May. Already, unknown to him, the evacuation at Dunkirk was in prospect.

Two days later, after a raid on Charleroi, his sixth mission in twelve days, he and his crew were given a day off and he hastened to London where he met Lord Dunglass (Douglas-Home), PPS to Neville Chamberlain. Dunglass took him in to see Chamberlain, now Lord President of the Council in Churchill's government. Not surprisingly he seemed distant, 'but he listened carefully to what I had to say about the tangle of peace-time regulations which made life a burden to officers and men of operational squadrons'. Having fought their way to targets it was worse than frustrating to bring their bombs back. Chamberlain could do nothing, but he sent him to see Arthur Balfour, Under-Secretary of State for Air.

Wilson was now hitting directly at some of his more complacent seniors, who seemed unable to match what was required in total war. 'There's a great deal of deadwood' he told Balfour, 'to be cleared out.' He was not talking about the lower ranks: they to him were beyond reproach. 'The strength of the RAF is in the Sergeants' and Corporals' Messes and in the barracks.' His years of social campaigning had rubbed off on him. 'There should be no direct commissions except through the ranks in time of war and every skilled and unskilled man in the Forces should be eligible.' He was especially delighted about Dolly Gray's change of cloth.

Meanwhile Chamberlain, knowing Wilson's talent as an organiser and as a firebrand, asked Sinclair to take him off flying and give him an administrative job, and Sinclair broached the idea to Wilson. But Chamberlain was told of his rejection. 'As you would expect,' he concluded, 'he did not want to give up what he was doing.' He did not altogether exclude a change some time in the future, but nothing would persuade him to desert his crew. 'They look to me,' he said.

On his return to Feltwell he found that the matter had been taken out of his hands. He had been posted to Headquarters No.3 Group as Group Gunnery Officer, a non-combatant role.

There had been many who had hinted that he must have wangled his way into operational flying in the first place, a slur he resented. There would be many more ready to accuse him of wangling his way out. So vehemently did he protest that the posting was cancelled and he was allowed to remain on the squadron.

That night – 25/26 May – despite heavy and continuous rain, Wilson's was among ten 37 Squadron crews detailed to attack enemy columns and concentrations at Soignies, 20 miles south-west of Brussels. Visibility was poor and they were forced to bomb from low level, with results that were impossible to judge. Next day the evacuation of the British Expeditionary Force (BEF) was begun.

Dunkirk now began to figure prominently in orders and communiqués. The final débâcle was near. Still hampered by the weather, the bomber crews continued as best they could to harry enemy columns as they pressed forward to cut off the Allied retreat. All too often, as on the night of 28/29, when Wilson's was one of seven 37 Squadron crews airborne over Belgium, most were dazzled by searchlights or frustrated by low cloud and smoke haze, and only two claimed to have located their targets near Menin, although numerous unconfirmed hits were registered. Returning to the UK the crews found conditions no better, only two being able to land back at Feltwell due to ground mist. One got down at Bircham Newton and the remainder at Mildenhall. .

What effect was all this air activity having? 'The bomber effort,' said the *RAF Short History*, 'was certainly as great as the Royal Air Force was capable of at the time.' Their efforts were not 'puny', as was alleged. 'Every day some fifty Blenheims, escorted or under cloud cover, attacked enemy troops closing in on the BEF. Every night an equal number of Bomber Command 'heavies' (Wellingtons) concentrated against the road approaches to the Dunkirk area, while as many more,' – aided by the squadrons still based in France – 'attacked enemy communications further back. Very little of this work could possibly be seen by our ground forces.' Hence the apparent discrepancy.

One operation, however, did earn high praise. 'This was on the afternoon of 31 May,' reported the commander of an infantry brigade, 'holding a sector from opposite Nieuport to the sea.' They were suffering a determined attack on their front – the third within twelve hours. 'The leading German waves were stopped by our light machine-gun and mortar fire, but strong enemy reserves were observed through Nieuport and on the roads to the canal north-west of Nieuport.

'At this moment some RAF bombers arrived and bombed Nieuport and the roads north-west of it. The effect was instantaneous and decisive – all movement of enemy reserves stopped: many of the forward German troops turned and fled, suffering severely from the fire of our machine-guns…'

This was a high point for the Blenheims. What could the Wellingtons do? Twelve of 37 were among those briefed for action that night, led by Willie Merten. Nine of them were concentrated on the Nieuport area, while three crews were given specific areas where enemy troops were known to be advancing. One of them was Gray's. It was their ninth attempt at penetration of enemy defences in twenty days.

For the bulk of the crews, after making landfall on the French/Belgian coast, Nieuport was not difficult to find, and attacks were sustained throughout the hours of darkness, at levels of 1,000 feet up to 7,000, numerous hits being seen in and around the town. But for the three crews briefed for the specified areas, where enemy columns were advancing, the task of identifying troop concentrations from low level, in a strange countryside, in darkness, and in poor visibility, was not only more difficult but also of greater hazard. An artillery post seven miles south-west of Dunkirk was hit, buildings housing troops were straddled, and stationary vehicles were blasted. But these three crews all met fierce opposition, and two of them were lost. One was L7791 – Dolly Gray's. With one of his crew wounded, and an engine on fire, Gray was unable to maintain height.

All that was known at Feltwell was that two aircraft were missing from the night's operations and that one of them was Gray's. The other nine, with some minor damage, returned safely. There was no further news of the missing crews, nor could any be expected, and what they might have achieved was not known. Shot down it was assumed at low level, there was a hope they might have survived. Both crews were posted missing, and their effects were gathered up within a day or so and posted to their next of kin. All anyone could do now was hope.

In fact, the news of Gray and his crew, although it was a long time before it could be pieced together, did not at first appear to be all bad. They had been shot down by concentrated fire in enemy-occupied territory. Gray had been wounded but he had survived and got the Wellington down in one piece, then been taken prisoner. It was five days before, on 5 June, he was able to take advantage of International Red Cross support to write a reassuring note to Nan.

'Darling Nan – Am lying in hospital slightly wounded, hope to be out of hospital soon. What abominable luck. Make your own decisions about staying on; don't forget to see someone about financial arrangements if you decide to leave Meth. All my love, Bill xxx.'

This tiny *Carte Postale*, addressed to his wife at the house where they had been living at Methwold, did not for a long time reach Nan, or anyone else. On 18 June Gray's father wrote to Feltwell for news of his son, asking too about his effects – he knew these included an expensive camera – and on the 28th the officer detailed for the task listed how the packages of effects were made up and how they were being transported (by train), but added: 'Unfortunately we have heard nothing of any of the crew or Pilot Officer Gray.' He went on to promise to look after Gray's car, keep it running, and do his best to sell it, warning that cars were going cheap and it might be best to hang on to it. He concluded by sending his sympathy 'in this time of strain and anguish'.

Another letter to Gray senior, on 4 July, confirmed that the packages should be there by now and added that the camera was being forwarded by registered post. This letter was from the squadron adjutant, and it ended: 'I am sorry to state that no further news has been received, but we still hope and pray that more encouraging news will reach us in the very near future.'

Gray senior now wrote to the British Red Cross, who replied on 24 July: 'Will you be so kind as to make quite certain that you have sent your son's correct number, as we have, on our records, a Pilot Officer reported missing who has a different number to the one you quote.' Gray senior had quoted his son's number *as an airman*, 560136: that had been his number for fourteen years. But on commissioning a month earlier his number had been changed to 43166. This discrepancy added to the family's frustrations.

For Dolly Gray, then, for the few who knew, the news was mixed. He was hurt but had survived and was optimistic of recovery. But he was worried about his crew, whose fate was known to some, but not to him.

In fact, he had not been the only survivor. Although 'Bomber' Brown, probably in the act of releasing the bombs, had been killed outright, Gray at some stage must have given the order to bale out. One man, Jackie Axford, the observer, was believed to have jumped. He broke a leg but survived. Meanwhile Rex Orland, the wireless operator, the only man uninjured, was trapped by his legs at the radio. The Wellington was hit and fire was spreading, but before the flames could take hold, Orland and Gray were freed by German troops.

What about Arnold Wilson? Orland at least knew the answer. 'They (the Germans), after releasing me, went to the rear of the plane to free Sir Arnold, but he too was trapped.'

Tail-end Charlie, in a Wellington, was reckoned to be the most vulnerable place to be, but it was a position where the occupant often survived in an otherwise disastrous crash. The danger of being trapped, too, had been foreseen by Wilson, and he had insured against it. But this time, sadly, his foresight had been in vain. Ground fire had drenched the Wellington, and the rear turret had not escaped. Either Wilson had been mortally hit or he had been knocked out. 'Freeing him proved impossible,' says Orland. 'Although the Germans could see him, they were pretty certain he was already dead.'

Orland continued: 'None us of are quite sure of exactly what followed, but we think that at that point the ammunition, fuel etc. began to explode from the fire in the plane, so that all ran for cover to a nearby ditch. 'We knew very little about Jackie Axford, except that he too was safe but injured, through baling out too close to the ground. He too, having been taken prisoner, was in hospital.'

Dolly Gray, too, was still in hospital, though not – according to his letter – seriously hurt. Given the chance to pen something to his wife, he had inevitably done his best not to alarm her further. In fact, it seems that he was fighting for his life. The truth was revealed in a letter to his father, written by Jackie Axford from hospital on or about 9 June, but not forwarded by *Kriegsgefangenenpost* for several weeks. This is what Axford wrote:

'I deeply regret having to write this letter informing you that your son, Alfred, 'Dolly' to our crew, passed away at Cambrai, France, on the 9th of June.

'I was the observer on your son's aircraft when we were shot down, but I was hit and unconscious before we crashed and did not know the true facts until a few days ago, when our wireless operator, Rex Orland, arrived here.'

He says nothing about baling out, but some confusion between one crew man and another was perhaps inevitable.

Shot down 14 miles from Dunkirk, inland, by A/A, your son stuck to the controls, the aircraft was badly damaged, and he himself was wounded in the legs. He managed to level out before crashing in flames. We were all thrown clear except the second pilot, killed I think on impact. Dolly was taken to Arras and thence to Cambrai – we were separated.

Rex (Orland) was sent for on the 8th and spent a good while with your son who seemed fairly comfortable but greatly worried about his wife and children and the rest of the crew. He had a relapse during the night and Orland spent the last few minutes with him in the morning before he passed away. His last words were about his wife, children and family, but Rex cannot remember word for word. The two of us seem to be the only survivors and we owe our lives to Dolly, our crew were together about seven months and like one happy family. Hoping I have not put this too awkwardly, deepest sympathy to Mrs Gray and yourself from us both and other squadron members here.

Gray's was not the only 37 Squadron aircraft lost in that period, although the Wellington lost with Gray on the night of 31 May disappeared without trace, presumably lost over the Channel. What happened to Gray and his crew was at least capable of reconstruction,

After receiving the news of Rex Orland's safety, his mother corresponded with Lady Wilson and Nan Gray (who soon returned to Cumberland), and also made contact with 'Bomber' Brown's wife. The latter explained that she had been to a spiritualist medium and was convinced that her husband was alive, although wounded. Eventually it was confirmed that he was buried side by side with Arnold Wilson, near the north-eastern corner of the church at the tiny village of Eringham, inland from the Dunkirk beaches. Dolly Gray was buried at Cambrai.

His was clearly a crew of outstanding merit, a loss that the embryonic Bomber Command could ill afford. He had developed into the model senior NCO and pilot officer of pre-war years, looked up to by all, keen to be given and always entrusted with the toughest tasks. His crew too were exceptional: he had attracted the best.

Jackie Axford and Rex Orland survived the war and were repatriated in 1945. Axford carried shrapnel in his spine from that day until his death in 1978. Orland died in an RAF Association Home for the Disabled in 1981.

Dolly Gray's friendship with Arnold Wilson was a matter for pride on both sides and contact by the wives was maintained through correspondence for many years.

Supported by family and friends, Nan Gray, still only twenty-four, proved herself to be the paragon her husband had promised. Capable, mentally strong, and a wonderful manager and mother, she even taught her boy Ian to box. He and his sister Eileen were an indispensable help in compiling this account, as indeed were Hugh and Sarah (née Wilson) and Ann Pennant (née Carver). Through Ian and Eileen I have been able to reconstruct Gray's meritorious career from the access I was granted to personal correspondence and Service records.

Posterity was to accord Arnold Wilson the striking and unexpected accolade of great social reformer, based on the many Bills he tried to introduce into Parliament in the 1930s. For his pursuit of comprehensive welfare legislation he was seen as a successor to the great Sidney and Beatrice Webb, and as the precursor to William Beveridge, whose wartime reports on social insurance and full employment were to form the basis of the Labour Government's welfare legislation in the later 1940s.

A full-length biography, entitled *Late Victorian, the life of Sir Arnold Talbot Wilson*, by John Marlowe (Cresset Press) appeared in 1967.

Other posthumous achievements included the book he was working on in his spare time at Feltwell, *South West Persia: A Political Officer's Diary*, and Volume II of *Workmen's Compensation: the Need for Social Reform*, his second collaboration with Professor Herman Levy, both published in 1941. The first of these threw further light on the relationship that developed between Rose Wilson and Eileen Gray. A copy of the book, inscribed 'Mrs Gray and her children, from the Author's wife,' signed Rose Wilson, ended: 'In memory of the Spring, 1940'. That was a special memory, when they had met so happily in the Norfolk village of Feltwell.

On 28 November 1942, two and a half years after Wilson's death, the London *Daily Express* gave the credit for the imaginative Beveridge Plan, recently announced, to none other than Sir Arnold Wilson. Under the heading 'What more can Sir William say?' they declared:

'Sir Arnold Wilson was popularly regarded as a reactionary right-wing politician. But now we are beginning to recognise that he was

Sir Arnold Wilson. 'A pretty fearless independent thinker.' (Hugh Wilson)

a pretty fearless independent thinker. There seems little left for Sir William Beveridge to say.'

Wilson himself had covered the entire spectrum in the 1930s. His name, it is clear, should always be coupled with that of William Beveridge. History will accord him his rightful place in the nurturing of social conscience in Britain prior to Beveridge. But for Dolly Gray, and the members of his crew, and others who were lost in that tragic period, it should be remembered that Eringham, a village and commune only 10 miles south-south-west of Dunkirk, where Wilson and 'Bomber' Brown are buried, was within striking distance of the beaches from which 338,226 Allied troops escaped to fight again. This puts into perspective the modest but not insignificant part these and other – mostly regular – RAF airmen played, often forgotten, in what Churchill described as 'The miracle of deliverance at Dunkirk.'

CHAPTER THREE

Pilot Officer W.J. Edrich – The Daylight Boys, Summer of '41

Flattened low on the water, tucked in as close as he dared to the leader, wing-tip to wing-tip, the new pilot officer – he was older than many at 25 – was feeling an exhilaration that swamped all other emotions, even those pre-war highlights – and reverses – that had come his way as an international cricketer. It was unbelievable that here he was at last, after the long months of frustration, training, and preparation, bombs at the ready, speeding towards the enemy coast in a Blenheim Mark IV on a daylight raid. It was 7 June 1941.

Low flying had never bothered him. He'd always loved it. It never failed to give him an illusion of speed and security. 200 knots wasn't much by Spitfire standards, but for Bill Edrich, with the sea racing by 30 feet below him, it seemed scorchingly fast. Surely no one could catch them. There was security, too, in the knowledge that at this height the enemy's radar scanners were powerless to track them.

Flying in formation, too, was something he revelled in. It had been drilled into him that it was the stragglers who got picked off by enemy fighters. He feared these fighters even more than the risk of collision. A minor impact with a similar plane flying on the same course at the same speed was something from which he believed he might recover. If that was wishful thinking – well, it sharpened the thrill.

Also part of the thrill was the knowledge that he was a raw pilot officer, on his first operational trip, flying No.3 to the leader, Squadron Leader Peter Simmons, a man he greatly admired. Peter was at the other end of the scale, on the last trip of his second tour.

Ahead of them lay a white screen of fleecy cloud, stretching from about 600 feet right down to the water, and it occurred to him that

Peter might have to turn back. The density of that cloud, he gauged, might be enough to break up all but the closest formations. But he knew his man. Simmons wouldn't want his last trip to be a wash-out. He'd be sure to press on, and he tucked in even closer.

In that moment of reflection he had noticed that the No.2 in their formation, the chap on Simmons's right, had got slightly above him, and a little behind. He might not last long if they were attacked. Almost certainly, they would lose him in that cloud.

Who was the pilot? He hadn't had time to get to know him. But he had exchanged a few words with the navigator. That afternoon they were booked to play cricket for the Station against a local village team. If they got back all right.

Bill Edrich had joined the RAF in 1940, for much the same reasons as most of his colleagues. All had wanted to fly, and all had looked for an active part in the war. For most, life in the RAF looked preferable to life in the infantry. Most of them felt – as Bill did – that such qualifications as they possessed would be best suited to training for aircrew, pilot if possible, and that this would make their fullest possible contribution to the war. All had resolved that life with all its faults was something worth fighting for.

Many of course, like Bill, had found themselves out of a job. For him, first-class cricket as he knew it was over, presumably for the duration. He didn't feel that his sacrifice – if that was what it came to – was any different from anyone else's.

He had had to use a little subterfuge to get in when he did. To that extent he had played on his name. The flying schools were overloaded, and after waiting several months for his call-up he had learned from a friend that the quickest way into aircrew was to join the Physical Fitness Branch and remuster. It sounded chancy, but he did as he was advised. As soon as he registered at RAF Uxbridge he was grabbed for a game of cricket. That evening the station commander, a keen cricketer, asked him to let him know if he wanted anything. 'Yes,' ventured Bill, 'I want a transfer to aircrew.' He was on his way within 48 hours.

His flying training went through almost without a hitch except for one false alarm, when he was issued with tropical clothing. South Africa was what he hoped for, with the chance to renew the many friendships he'd formed during the 1938-39 Test Match tour. Old hands told him it was more likely to be Canada, despite the tropical kit, but they were all wrong: he was posted to Cranwell. 'I never did get the chance,' he says, 'to wear that boat topee.'

At the end of his course he was commissioned, and soon afterwards operational training followed on Blenheims at Upwood. There he acquired a navigator, Vic Phipps, a Londoner, and a wireless operator/air gunner, Ernie Hope, from Lancashire. They were bound for a Blenheim squadron in No. 2 Group, Bomber Command, and on 21 May 1941 they reported to 107 Squadron at Little Massingham, in Bill's home county of Norfolk.

An RAF truck met them at Massingham Station and took them to their respective Messes. The party consisted of three Blenheim crews, all sergeants apart from Bill. The sergeants were dropped first, and then the truck turned into a broad drive, at the end of which stood an imposing manor house. This, for the next seven weeks, was to be Bill's home.

As he walked into the spacious hall he could hear the sound of voices and the clink of glasses, and for a moment he hesitated. Up to this moment he'd been a pupil, the lowest of the low, though with many hands ready to guide him. Now he was a squadron pilot, about to take a serious part in the war. Was he up to it? What would the other fellows be like? Had he got what it takes?

A door opened and the squadron adjutant – he introduced himself as Tony Richardson – plied him with questions. Had he eaten? Were the NCOs in the party fixed up? Anything he needed? He learned that his welcomer was a peace-time journalist, later to be the author of several war books. His greeting was unmistakably friendly. As soon as accommodation had been fixed he said: 'Come and have a drink.'

He learned that the squadron had mounted a very successful low-level raid on Heligoland earlier that day. Eight Blenheims had set out, and seven had returned. If there had been any gloom about the missing crew, it had apparently been dissipated.

He was introduced to the squadron commander, Wing Commander Lawrence Petley, 'Petters', it seemed, to almost everyone. Dark-haired, square-jawed, and of medium build, he seemed of thoughtful disposition, reserved and unassuming, but, as with Richardson, unmistakably friendly. More extrovert was the man introduced to him as his new flight commander, Peter Simmons, tall and colourful, his DFC ribbon, a rarity at that time, startlingly bright against the drab blue of his battle-dress. It was Simmons who took him on one side and told him what would be expected of him in the next few days.

He soon realised that his training days were far from over. Practice formation flying, low-level practice bombing, crew training, flying discipline, and general familiarisation would absorb all their time for a fortnight or more. Their impatience to get started was being sensibly restrained.

After a couple of beers the Mess began to thin, so Bill excused himself and went to his room. He was doubling up with a navigator named

107 Squadron at Little Massingham, June 1941. Pilot Officer Edrich is at top right, Laurence Petley, seated in the centre with Pete Simmons on Petley's right and Tony Richardson second from Petley's left. (Simon Parry)

Harry Pearse, with whom he had struck up a friendship at Upwood, where he had been on instructor duties. He found that Pearse had already got himself selected for Petley's crew.

In the middle of this familiarisation period Bill was selected to play for the RAF in a one-day match against a Rest of England side at Lord's. He went to see Petters somewhat shame-facedly, hardly expecting to get permission so soon, but Petley gave him the day off. Vic Phipps and Ernie Hope were not cricketers, but with Bill allowed to fly the squadron 'hack' – 'M for Mother' – down to Hendon as an exercise, they were glad enough to go with him for a day out in London. In the event they probably had a better day than Bill, who only scored 6 and 1 run and failed to take a wicket.

In 1938 he'd scored a thousand runs in May. Now it was 2 June and he'd hardly handled a bat. Plenty of practice – but of a different kind. He was glad enough of all that practice when, three days later, he learned he was on stand-by for his first operational flight.

Churchill himself, with the Chief of the Air Staff, Sir Charles Portal, and other members of the Government, visited their parent station at nearby West Raynham that same day and the whole squadron was assembled to meet him. Wearing a light grey suit and carrying an unlighted cigar, he mounted a set of servicing steps and addressed them.

'43,000 civilians have been killed in air raids on Britain in the last twelve months,' he began. 'My promise that the RAF would retaliate by day and by night has not yet been fulfilled. I've come personally to explain the importance of the special tasks you'll be undertaking in the next few weeks, when our operations are likely to have a major impact

Ernie Hope, Bill's gunner, gets married. Vic Phipps, the navigator, is to the left of the bride and Bill Edrich on the right of the groom. (Alan Hill)

on the outcome of the war.' He went on to list some unpalatable facts. German intervention in the Middle East was turning the war against us in that theatre. 'Germany must be forced to move her fighters westwards. We will attack targets in the West which Germany will have to defend, and sometimes, to lure the *Luftwaffe* into the air, you will be escorted by large numbers of fighters. Our purpose will be to relieve pressure on other fronts, and to ease the stranglehold on our lifelines.' He concluded: 'I am relying on you.'

This eve-of-battle harangue from the PM himself certainly raised morale. But Bill, sitting in the cockpit of his Blenheim next morning, with the engines ticking over, waiting for the signal to go, dare not analyse his feelings. He'd been impatient to make a start, and so too, he knew, had Vic and Ernie. They'd been flying together for three months and they were beginning to need something to show for it. But as the moment approached, these impulses evaporated. For his part, Bill was left with the uncomfortable feeling that he was just another freshman pilot, on the threshold of a new experience, setting off into the unknown.

Some of the old hands on the squadron had exaggerated the dangers, just to tease them. Others, partly perhaps to reassure themselves, dismissed 'ops' as a piece of cake. This left Bill apprehensive, but also in a curious way, elated. There was only one way of finding out the truth about what lay out there beyond the Channel and the North Sea, and about oneself. He was about to take it.

In the little cottage attached to the Nursery gardens on the edge of their satellite airfield – which was all the squadron boasted as a headquarters – they had learned that a large and heavily defended enemy convoy, on its way from Hamburg to Rotterdam, was moving down the Dutch coast. There were two big ships in the convoy, both carrying important war cargoes, according to Intelligence, and these would be their primary targets. Nine crews were briefed to attack – in three 'vics' of three.

At last Peter Simmons gave the signal and they began to roll forward. Vic Phipps was sitting next to Bill for take-off, Ernie Hope behind him. Peter did a circuit of the airfield to give the others time to form up and they headed for the coast at 500 feet, dropping down to 30 feet over the sea. Soon their way was barred by that fleecy white curtain of cloud.

Simmons held his course, climbing almost imperceptibly. They were still below 100 feet. Soon they were enmeshed in cotton-wool cloud, flying on instruments. Bill had no real experience of cloud formation flying – it was something they just hadn't practised – and it frightened him. Did Simmons really mean to press on? Bill realised he had not only to trust his own altimeter but Simmons' as well; he was immediately terrified of flying into the sea. Edging in even closer, he determined not to lose contact. All he could see was a dark smudge in the cloud which was Simmons' wing-tip. He was nearly tempted to give up. Twenty minutes must have passed, and he was still hanging on, concentrating more fiercely than ever before – and his concentration had always been a strong point. Then quite suddenly the cloud thinned and he could see the whole of Simmons' Blenheim from wing-tip to wing-tip. A moment later they were through the cloud and visibility was about two miles. He followed Simmons back to wave-top level, and they were flying so low that the surface of the sea was rippled by their slipstream.

There was no sign of the No.2. Could they have lost him? No – he must have turned back. There was no sign, either, of their other two formations: it looked as though he and Simmons would be attacking alone. He guessed this would not deter Simmons. Two minutes later, as Vic moved down into the Perspex nose, he heard him shout over the inter-com, 'There they are!'

Strung out in front of them like beads, about two miles distant and slightly to the north, he could see the silhouette of perhaps a dozen ships. This was it.

They stayed at low level until they were about a mile off. Then, as Simmons zoomed up to perhaps 250 feet, he broke formation and followed him, pulling in the full boost lever for maximum speed of 240 knots for the attack.

The two big merchantmen stood out from the others, one in the centre of the convoy and the other to the rear. He thought they might be between 5,000 and 6,000 tons. Typically, Simmons went hurtling after the one in the centre. He went for the one in the rear. He thought his was the larger of the two.

A five-starred rocket floated up from one of the ships, no doubt challenging their identity. They'd been seen.

From Bill's angle, he was bearing down on the rear merchantman in a shallow dive, skidding and jinking to put the gunners off their aim. But the fire was getting accurate. A flak ship was having a go at them from over to port. With a fixed front gun, he couldn't bring any answering fire to bear.

'Ernie! Look after that flak-ship!'

He heard the clatter of Ernie's guns above the engine noise, and glancing to the left he realised he was right on target. But they were now flying through a terrific barrage from the merchantman, and as the tracer squirted up towards him his instinct was to duck. He couldn't help it. He was experiencing a strange sense of claustrophobia, trapped in the goldfish bowl of the cockpit, feeling that if any of those rising balls of light hit his windscreen his whole world would explode and disappear in some abrupt feat of legerdemain.

Now he was coming within point-blank range, and he pressed his own gun-button, letting the tracer hose all over the ship. After two or three seconds of this he felt that if the gunners weren't dead already they would be taking cover. Yet all this was subsidiary to his main obsession – to time his run so as to sling his bombs into the hull of the ship.

The superstructure was floating up towards him at terrific speed and he shouted to Vic, 'Now!'

Vic pulled the contact across the switches and their four 250-lb bombs dropped away simultaneously. He held on a moment longer, to be sure they'd gone. The deck of the merchantman filled his windscreen and he thought they must crash into her. For some reason the Blenheim was hanging awkwardly to the left. He pulled back viciously on the stick and at once she responded, and with a prayer of thankfulness he zoomed upwards, just clearing the masts.

'Get down!'

The climb had taken them to 300 feet and Vic, fearing fighters, was begging him to get down on the water. He pushed the nose forward hurriedly, weaving as he did so to avoid the flak, still heading northwards. Another minute or so and he judged they were out of range, so he turned to port and set course for home.

In the turn they got a good view of the ship. She was labouring under a billowing cloud of flames and smoke, an almost exact replica of the ship attacked by Simmons, which was listing as well. Vic was jumping up and down in his seat, but Bill knew that Ernie, in the turret, was the only one who could actually have seen the bombs fall. There was no reply from him on the inter-com. Had he been hit?

'Vic! See if Ernie's all right.'

Vic's reply silenced their fears. 'I can see him moving! He's all right.'

Bill suddenly remembered he was supposed to join up with Simmons for the return trip, but having split up for the attack, he could see nothing of him. Yet the curtain of cloud they had passed through on the way out would make an ideal refuge, and soon he was back on instruments at 300 feet.

Ernie then called him up. He had been busy clearing his guns. Bill asked: 'Did you see the bombs hit?'

'Yes – two undershot, but the other two must have hit.'

'You didn't actually see them?'

'There were only two splashes on the water. And you saw the ship.'

Glancing at his altimeter, Bill was horrified to see that in the excitement he had allowed his concentration to wander and they were right down on the water. Sick with fear and self-disgust, he yanked back on the stick and pulled up.

'Christ! What the hell's happening?'

'It's OK now. Too bloody close to the water.'

In the same instant the engines spluttered and coughed. What could have happened? They still had over a hundred miles of water ahead of them. But within seconds both engines picked up smoothly. There must have been a momentary hiatus in the fuel feed, through his ham-fisted flying. But all was well.

When they landed back at Little Massingham they found that quite a lot of rudder was missing, which explained why they had hung to the left during the attack. But the Blenheim would take a lot of punishment, and Bill's faith in the type – and especially the model he was flying, V5529, was confirmed. He was never quite so happy in any other machine.

At the interrogation which followed, the two crews were able to corroborate each other's claims. For leading this highly successful attack on his last trip, Simmons was awarded a bar to his DFC.

They learned now what had happened to the other crews. The other vics of three had run into patches of dense fog and had turned back, but even of those six, one had been lost. And of their own No.3, nothing more had been heard or seen. The losses rather dampened their spirits.

For Bill, he was pondering that ghastly moment when he had so nearly flown into the sea through faulty instrument flying – or had it been sheer inattention? He was left wondering what had happened to the missing two. They had been as inexperienced at that sort of low-level formation flying as he was – he had found it scary enough himself. On balance, though, he felt that between them they had made a positive response to Churchill's appeal.

The loss of their No.3 meant that the station team was one short for the game that afternoon. They managed to find a replacement. They played on the private ground of a local landowner and they beat the village after an enjoyable game. Bill can still remember one straight drive he made over the elms for six – and the delay while they looked for another ball! He made 67.

In the here-today-gone-tomorrow atmosphere of squadron life in wartime, says Bill, he adapted well. Like most of his colleagues, he saw parties as the necessary antidote to the neuroses of anxiety and stress.

These parties were largely Stag: women certainly came into their lives, but their impact was mostly superficial, and few lasting attachments were made, anyway among the officers.

The real buttress to morale came from Mess life and the feeling that if the other fellow could take it, so could you. When there were losses they simply closed ranks.

Another source of strength was regimental pride. They were 107 Squadron, the daylight boys, and their fiercest rivals were the other Blenheim squadrons, doing the same job. Each squadron liked to think it was the top squadron, and during Guest Nights the rivalry came near to the physical.

Every month one station in the Group would hold a Guest Night, to which the other stations would be invited, and the horseplay was liable to get out of hand. Bill remembers finishing up one night at the bottom of a High Cockalorum scrum – a massed pick-a-back battle between squadron and squadron – and the neck injury he suffered (ignored at the time) was still giving him trouble nine years later.

More domestic were their visits to the Crown Hotel in Fakenham, about eight miles from their base. There the three attractive young daughters of the proprietors, 'Pop' and Mrs Myers, were nicknamed 'The Crown Jewels'. The girls put on gramophone records and invited them to dance, and when it got past closing time the police turned a blind eye.

One evening in mid-June (1941) Bill was invited to the home of a Norfolk farmer with whom he had played cricket before turning professional. One of the guests was Paddy Bandon, the Earl of Bandon, an extrovert known throughout the RAF quite slanderously as the abandoned earl. Paddy Bandon, who was then station commander at West Raynham, was a group captain. Bill was still the rawest of acting pilot officers.

There were five people in the party, and after dinner they played poker. Paddy's laugh could almost be heard back at West Raynham, but Bill had not forgotten that he had a dawn take-off to look forward to, so when it got to midnight he began to get fidgety. But Paddy brushed his protests aside. 'I'll take you back when I go. I've got my chauffeur with me. It's all buttoned up.' So Bill had no choice but to stay.

It was after three o'clock before Paddy decided it was time to go. Paddy drove him straight to the Operations Room at West Raynham to see if the trip was still on.

'Got it all buttoned up?' he asked of the ops. room controller. This, Bill found, was his favourite expression.

'Yes, sir, it's still on.'

Paddy turned to Bill. He still had to get back to the satellite. 'Take my car, go back to Massingham and wake the buggers up. Off you go.'

It was all typical Paddy Bandon. He would be the driving force at West Raynham, as Bill knew, for the rest of the day. 'Lucky I have a strong constitution too,' he thought. The loss of a night's sleep didn't bother him.

They took off at dawn on what was their first 'Circus' operation. This was a new type of action that had been foreshadowed by Churchill on his visit ten days earlier. The pressure was very much on the Blenheim squadrons that summer. Britain still stood alone, the whole of Europe lay under Nazi domination, and Hitler could concentrate his *Luftwaffe* where he pleased, with disastrous results for our Middle East armies. No. 2 Group's task was to force Germany to defend targets in the West and hope to ease her stranglehold.

The night bombers in this period were having scant success, and exposing the Blenheims over enemy territory in daylight without fighter or cloud cover had become suicidal, so the Circus operation, mounted against targets in occupied Europe, within the range of fighter escort, became the chosen expedient.

Compared to the tensions of unescorted low-level flying in close formation against shipping and other perimeter targets – their normal occupation – Bill found Circuses almost fun. Their escorts were so attentive that they rarely had to bother about enemy fighters, targets were interesting and easily identifiable – power stations and chemical works – and their main preoccupation was the flak.

He was one of only two pilots from 107 to make the rendezvous with the Spitfires on the first Circus, after which their squadron commander, the pensive, reticent Laurence Petley – 'Petters' – took special care to ensure the second was a success. They bombed Le Havre from 12,000 feet, succeeding in straddling the docks and the refuelling basin, and Petters was satisfied that they had redeemed themselves.

On both these operations Bill's plane was hit by flak, and for their third Circus he was rested. As they lost two crews from 107 on that show, plus two nasty forced landings, Bill was lucky to be out of it.

For their fourth Circus Bill's regular aircraft, V 5529, in which he had such confidence, was still under repair after the beating it had already taken, and he had to take a strange machine. It shouldn't have made any difference – but he was unhappy from the start. Nothing seemed to go right, and when a fuel tank suddenly showed empty he decided he'd had enough and turned back. It was the first time this had happened to him, and to see the others go on proved a psychological blow – feelings of doubt, indecision, and guilt overwhelmed him. Had he been justified? His return implied a criticism of the ground crew, and when the trouble proved to be nothing more than a faulty gauge, he knew he should have gone on.

Bill, although not one to dwell on his own actions and reactions, recognised that the line between an intelligent and reasonable prudence and a reluctance to engage the enemy that bordered on cowardice was a difficult one to draw. How much more must this be true for the leaders.

Standing orders to abort when unescorted, in the absence of adequate cloud cover, often left crews with mixed feelings. Briefed and keyed up for action, they felt let down. An undeniable relief at living to fight another day left a residue of uneasiness, even remorse. What constituted adequate cloud cover? At what range from the target did it become scarcely more dangerous to press on than to turn back?

Often formation leaders were placed in a dilemma. Press home your attacks to the limit or the war will be lost. Turn back if it looks recklessly hazardous; losses are not easily replaced. Sooner or later there was bound to be a showdown.

When, on 22 June, Germany attacked Russia, Britain had a powerful ally at last, but it was Russia now who faced Hitler virtually alone. Churchill's reaction was to call even more urgently for an intensified effort. Day after day the Blenheim squadrons stepped up their Circus raids, and on the afternoon of Thursday 27 June the crews of 107 Squadron were ordered to fly over to another 2 Group airfield, Swanton Morley, for a special briefing. Ten crews were selected, Bill's among them – one as reserve – which meant the usual three vics of three. The rest were stood down. Petters was 'in the know', and he told the crews: 'It's rather more important than the average operation.' The show-down they had all expected was about to come.

There was to be a special briefing at Swanton Morley, where they were to be joined by another ten crews of 105 Squadron, under the Australian Hughie Edwards. The target was a tough one all right – Bremen, the second largest port in Germany. Petters was to lead. It was to be a bold attempt to step up the daylight offensive. They would be beyond the range of fighter protection, but were to keep well clear of the shipping lanes off the Frisian Islands, evading the German fighters known to be based there, and pass to the south of Heligoland before turning to make a landfall west of Cuxhaven. They were then to skirt east of Bremerhaven before making a dash for Bremen itself. They would be over German territory for about 150 miles, an unprecedented daylight penetration in June 1941.

Hughie Edwards won the VC for the Bremen raid on 4 July 1941. (IWM)

There would be an effort to soften up the target overnight with raids by Whitleys and Wellingtons – the only 'heavies' yet available – but the order specified that overall success depended on the daylight raid. Vital as the raid was regarded, as a gesture to the Russians, if the Blenheims were spotted or intercepted before they hit the mainland they were still to turn back.

Bill found he was No.2 to Petters in the leading formation. The inference was clear: if Petters were knocked out, Bill would take over. He would be in the lead.

At 4.30 next morning they were all sitting in their machines. They taxied into position before switching off and waiting for first light.

'Start engines!'

Within a few minutes all engines were running except the starboard on Petters' machine. Bill was parked right next to him and he could see they were having trouble. In the half-light of dawn he saw a fellow officer running across towards him with a message from Petters. 'You're to take off as planned. You're to lead, Edrich. Petters will try to catch you up and take over on the way.'

Seconds later, off they went, Bill in the lead. It was the first time he'd been at the head of a formation on a real show and he felt good. It was his eleventh operational flight. By 1941 Blenheim standards he was a veteran.

During a circuit of the airfield, Ernie Hope called to confirm that all the other aircraft were moving into formation, eight in all. There was still no sign of Petters.

Setting course at once for Swanton Morley, where they were to meet Hughie Edwards and 105, he soon saw that they were circling the airfield already. They immediately attached themselves to 107. With an 'All OK!' from Ernie, Vic gave him the course for their departure point, Cromer.

Crossing the coast, Bill throttled back slightly and took the whole formation down to less than 50 feet, where he levelled off and settled on course for their first turning point. Soon there was a shout from Ernie.

'There's a plane chasing us! Looks like a Blenheim!'

It was a Blenheim, all right. Was it the reserve, or Petters? Soon it was recognised as Petters, and as he overtook, Bill made room for him. Again his feelings were mixed. He'd been thrilled to be leading, on such an important raid. Yet he felt relieved, too, at having the responsibility taken from him.

They dog-legged round the Frisian Islands, and after nearly two and a half hours in the air they reached their main turning point and followed Petters south-east across the Heligoland Bight. The danger of a chance encounter with German fighters was increasing now, and Bill tucked in closer and shot a glance at the rest of the formation. They seemed to him to be dangerously spread-eagled. Some crews were having difficulty in keeping up and others were clearly unused to tight formation flying.

'What are those ships up in front?'

Bill was too preoccupied with Petters' starboard wing-tip, but he was aware of several ships on the horizon. To see them at this low level meant they must already be close. He was not surprised when they opened fire.

Beyond the ships the sky looked ominously clear. They were opposite Cuxhaven now, perhaps 50 miles from Bremen, and any element of surprise was gone. Soon every fighter in North Germany would be after them. They had expected to have to fight their way out, but to fight their way in as well, with scant cloud cover, looked suicidal. All this, and the slack formation flying, must have been in Petters' mind as he turned the formation round and headed for home.

To say what precisely one would have done as leader, when one doesn't have the responsibility, was impossible. Most crews hated getting this far and turning back. Hughie Edwards said afterwards that having got so far he thought he might have gone on, but he added that he couldn't be sure what he'd have done in Petters' place. For the rest of them, Bill included, there wasn't a man in the formation who didn't think Petters was right.

After landing back at Little Massingham they trooped straight over to the cottage which housed their tiny ops room and headquarters, and there the adjutant, Tony Richardson, was standing with the telephone in his hand. He called out to Petters: 'Sir – the AOC's on the line.'

Everyone was feeling glum, and the chatter that normally accompanies a debriefing was strangely absent. All eyes were on Petters as he took the receiver. They saw his face blanch, then tauten in a mixture of anger and humiliation as he listened to the voice that no one else could hear.

In that silent ops. room they were watching their leader being torn off an almighty strip. They did not need to hear the words. Their leader was being accused of a failure to press on. Cowardice. They knew that in Stevenson's mind they were all tainted with it. Watching Petters, and remembering how nearly the leadership had fallen to him, Bill wondered again what he himself would have done had he remained in charge. In that moment he imagined himself, like Petters, arraigned before the entire squadron by a contemptuous AOC.

'If that's what you think,' they heard Petters say, 'we'll do the whole bloody show again this afternoon.'

No one doubted that he meant it. Nor did they doubt that Stevenson would have sent them. They also realised the political pressures he was being subjected to, by the government, by his seniors. All they could do was hang around until they heard their fate. When it came, it had the ring of anti-climax. They were to fly up to Driffield, a bomber station in Yorkshire, that afternoon and await further orders.

Petley led them up to Driffield, but he was ordered not to fly on the subsequent operation. Perhaps Stevenson saw the injustice of that dressing-down and feared that in his resentment Petley might be suicidally rash. Petley himself, in his reserved, introspective way, gave no sign.

At Driffield they learnt that the first six Halifax four-engined bombers ever to operate against the enemy were to raid Kiel next morning. The Blenheims were to support them with a daylight raid on Westerland, the fighter airfield on the island of Sylt. Sylt was renowned for its formidable defences and 2 Group's job was to create a major diversion, drawing off the fighters from the Halifax raid.

The role of decoy was not popular, but the station commander at Driffield did his best to cheer them up. He told the crews it was no accident the raid had been timed for midday Sunday. At that time, he promised them, the German fighter pilots, creatures of habit, would be enjoying a pre-lunch lager. This inspired planning, as the Blenheim crews rated it, with heavy irony, was nullified when the operation was postponed until Monday.

They took off at ten o'clock next morning, seven of them, leaving Petley and one other Blenheim – unserviceable – behind. A New Zealander, 'Zeke' Murray, was leading, and they followed him at extreme low level for the entire North Sea crossing, 360 miles, relying on dead reckoning and on what drifts the navigators could get from the wave-tops. Bill was No.3 to Zeke in the leading vic, with a box of four behind them, and the long crossing at low level demanded intense concentration. Bill's back began to stiffen up and he found it impossible to relax.

At length, straight ahead of them, they could make out the outline of Sylt, flat and featureless, a bleak panorama of deserted sand dunes. So far as they could tell they hadn't been seen. Lifting over the dunes, they crossed the narrow extremity of the island, ten miles south of the central bulk. Soon they were over the sea again, between island and mainland, and as Zeke turned and headed north they followed. At once the flak guns began sparking off at them, to the left from the island, to the right from the mainland, and straight ahead from the causeway connecting the two.

With gun-flashes illuminating the scene, and water thrown up on all sides by shell bursts, Bill had never seen such a hail of metal before, but like the others he just had to fly through it – the plumes of water too. He shut his mind to it, concentrating on Zeke's port wing-tip to his right. In close formation they might present a better target, but he hoped the heavier guns would find it difficult to range them at such low level. All his experience so far had convinced him that to lose formation over the target was fatal.

They were manoeuvring now, approaching line abreast for the bombing run. With 11-second delay fuses everyone was anxious to be clear before the bombs exploded.

Suddenly Bill caught a glimpse of a Blenheim from the box of four behind him. It was like a wild duck that has just been hit and is about to drop. When he shot another glance it was gone. He was hardly aware of crossing the causeway, but he knew that seven of them had begun the bombing run, and now there were four.

When they turned to port for the airfield the flak thinned out a little. Few were able to pick out a target – they were disorientated from the pasting they'd sustained. The picture was so much more confused than the 'stills' they'd studied at briefing. They just dropped their bombs on the biggest buildings and hared off out to sea.

Now they strove to get back into tight formation before the fighter attack that they knew must come. In his mind's eye Bill knew where Zeke was, and he slid back into position on his left. He saw another Blenheim zoom erratically into the No.2 position, and then a fourth, intent on catching up, moved in to port and astern. Soon they were back in a box of four, keeping low so as to show nothing but their top camouflage to any pursuing fighter.

Four of them had apparently got away with it, and no one seemed to be chasing them. When they were 100 miles from Sylt, Bill got Vic to light him a cigarette. He had barely inhaled it when he heard a shout from Ernie.

'Snappers!'

He'd forgotten the fighters at Terschelling on the Frisian Islands, but Ernie hadn't. He said there were four, apparently Bf 109s, hurrying towards them. Zeke too had seen them, and he turned coolly away to the north, drawing them away from their base. Their range was thought to be limited. But they hung on.

Zeke's gunner, on the voice radio, took control, directing the fire-power of the four Blenheims, and they began to put into practice the tactics they had rehearsed so often. Under attack, by fighters of superior speed, their best defence was reckoned to be to turn into the direction of attack, making it difficult for the fighters to get a good stern view.

Zeke led them into this manoeuvre at once, but the enemy pilots didn't fall for it. Two of them took up position to the port rear, two to the starboard rear, and as the port pair attacked with cannon and machine-gun, and the Blenheims turned left to make them overshoot, the starboard pair automatically fastened on their tails.

'Bandit port five o'clock, half a mile. Hold it.....Hold it.....Fire!'

The gunners were answering back. When Ernie opened up the Blenheim juddered, and Bill sniffed the stench of cordite. Ahead he could see the water bubbling and foaming as the enemy bullets churned up the sea. Zeke's gunner was good, and it was only his precise and timely instructions that gave them a chance, either in the opening attack or the more scattered attempts that followed. The gunners couldn't match the fire-power of the 109s, but four Blenheim turrets, switching from target to target, kept the Germans at arm's length.

Bill could see spluttering little spurts on the metal surfaces of others in the formation and knew the same thing was happening to him. One shell burst with a little pink explosion behind Zeke's port engine nacelle, leaving a jagged hole, and fluid streamed down his fuselage and sprayed off the tail. Then Ernie called Bill.

'My guns have packed up.'

It was the same for all four Blenheims. Their guns had either jammed or they were short of ammunition. Four badly mauled Blenheims were left with evasion as the only hope. Three of the 109s were giving up the chase. But the fourth was coming in for the kill.

The pilot was approaching from the port rear. There was no way of shaking him off. Reassured by the absence of answering fire, he came in closer. The Blenheims were sitting ducks. Yet he did not fire. As he overtook them, Bill looked straight up into the pilot's face. His exasperation was unmistakeable. He too had run out of ammunition – or his guns had jammed. With a despairing shrug he turned away south.

Bill called Zeke to suggest he switch off his port engine, which he did, reducing his speed, but the others closed in and escorted him home. Nothing was ever more welcome than the sight of Flamborough Head. They landed singly, Zeke being one of two to crash-land. Soon they were grouped round one of the wrecks, talking excitedly about the trip, wondering what happened to the others.

While they were doing so, a lone Blenheim, recognised as one of their formation, staggered in over the field. They knew they had lost three machines on the run in, reducing their attack from seven to four. Of the three that were missing, one was piloted by a sergeant named Leven. One of the others had slewed into Leven, chewing up his ailerons and flaps on one side. Somehow Leven had regained control. This may have been the plane Bill had seen. Leven had kept straight and level by holding the aileron in the vertical instead of the horizontal sense, but it had been such a strain that he had borrowed a leather belt from his navigator and between them they strapped up the controls. He had then skipped from cloud to cloud and eventually got back to Driffield. He got an immediate award of a DFM.

'Are all your trips like this?' asked the bomber crews based at Driffield, highly impressed.

'Most of them,' they said, laconically.

None of the Blenheims was strictly in a fit state to fly back to base, but here Bill confessed later to a breach of discipline. He had a date that night in Massingham, and he wanted to keep it. Vic and Ernie, too, had their reasons for getting back. They argued that their beautiful V.5529 had got them back and forth – or forth and back – across the North Sea. They reckoned it would take them back to Massingham. Bill asked Petters, who was still technically in charge, for his OK, but he looked right through Bill. 'You haven't asked me,' he said. A nod was as good as a wink, and they went.

Back at Little Massingham, Bill put in for some leave. He and his crew had done twelve trips. Better try and get a break before the thirteenth.

Bill spent a week at Symond's Yat in the Wye Valley, with the friend he had hurried back from Driffield to see, walking over the wooded hills and generally enjoying the tranquillity of the valley. For a few hours the hectic life of a low-level bomber squadron seemed impossibly remote. But it ended all too soon, and Bill was on his way back by train, wondering what he would find.

He had to change trains at Gloucester, and he bought an evening paper. The headline that caught his eye transfixed him. 'Successful daylight raid on Bremen.' He read on breathlessly. He felt he was reading his own obituary. The raid they had all attempted ten days earlier had been repeated. There followed a highly colourful account of how fifteen Blenheims had attacked the docks and other industrial targets at low level. He was to find out later about the losses. Only one of the six Blenheims of his squadron had got back to Massingham. One of those shot down on the way in was Petley. Deposed from the leadership, he had loyally followed Hughie Edwards of 105 and had been seen to crash in flames over the target.

Petley's navigator, Harry Pearse, had been Bill's room-mate. He was missing too. And there were others. For leading this raid, Edwards was subsequently awarded the VC. He told the surviving crews that it was the squadron's VC and he was simply the person presented with it.

When Bill got back to Little Massingham, the Mess that had always been so full of life and personality was silent and empty. 'I'm afraid there's no one from the squadron here,' said the Mess sergeant. 'We lost nearly all the officers on the Bremen raid. Those who are left have moved over to West Raynham. I'll lay on some transport for you.' Bill went to his room to collect his things.

When Bill got to West Raynham he found he was one of the few who still had a serviceable aircraft and a fit crew, and he was lent at once to No.21 Squadron at nearby Watton for what he was told was a special raid.

Fortunately he had friends on 21 Squadron from training days, and they made him welcome. The squadron commander, Wing Commander P.F.Webster, known as 'Tom', after the famous cartoonist, was a powerful personality who inspired confidence. Only a week or so earlier he had led 30 Blenheims in a raid on Rotterdam harbour which had developed into one of the most destructive strikes of the war. Some 40,000 tons of enemy shipping had been claimed sunk or damaged, and the dockside and warehouses had suffered too. The Germans had been caught napping and not a single Blenheim had been lost.

Bill met up with another old friend in Denis Graham-Hogg, who had just been promoted to flight lieutenant. He'd been a pupil on Bill's course at Upwood, and he owed his rapid promotion to the high loss rate in 2 Group. Tall, slim, fair and a lively soul, he loved flying and was obviously booked for a great future. His presence made Bill feel at home.

Soon, at 10.40 next morning, they were all on their way towards Cherbourg in four vics of three at their usual low level, twelve Blenheims, to meet up with a Spitfire escort off Beachy Head. Five miles from the target the Spits broke off, and the Blenheims went on the attack.

Bill's position was No.12, on the extreme right, and he was a bit squeezed for room, but he opted for a large dockside warehouse and dropped his bombs on that. Soon they were beyond the docks and speeding over the hinterland, waving back at French civilians in fields and gardens. Bill spotted a German gun-crew running to their gun and he shouted to Ernie. 'Let them have it!' Bill didn't see what happened but they weren't fired at. He did a starboard turn and soon they were over the sea again, joining up with the other Blenheims. Their escort was circling above them, shepherding them home.

Meanwhile 107 Squadron was taking shape again at West Raynham after its mauling at Bremen. The new squadron commander, Wing Commander A.F.Booth, had been a flight commander on 105 under Edwards and had taken part in the Bremen raids. Meanwhile Bill found he'd been promoted to flight lieutenant, jumping one rank completely.

Booth led them for the first time next day, on a shipping strike off Holland. The Germans had begun positioning innocent-looking 'spotter' vessels several miles out from the coast to supplement their radar warning, and Blenheim crews were ordered to eliminate them where possible. Bill attacked one with bombs and machine-guns and left it wallowing in the water, but in doing so he lost contact with the formation. When he got back to base he found that the main convoy had escaped serious damage but that their new CO had been shot down. Senior rank conferred no benefits of invulnerability in 2 Group. Six wing commanders, according to Bill, were lost in one week.

Two days later Bill was one of six crews detached to Manston on the Kent coast to relieve 21 Squadron of their part in an operation known as 'Channel Stop'. The task was to close the Straits of Dover to enemy shipping, and with German fighter airfields just across the water, strong escorts were needed. When the Germans tried to get a tanker through, 21 Squadron suffered grievously in trying to stop them. Bill's old friend Denis Graham-Hogg, who had just been promoted to squadron leader, on his first trip as a flight commander, was among the missing. Inured as they all were to the almost daily recital of casualties, the loss of Graham-Hogg hit Bill hard.[1]

Also operating from Manston at that time was a squadron of Spitfires under the American Whitney Straight, the famous racing motorist. Their job was to go in before the Blenheims, knock hell out of the flak ships, and provide them with top cover. They too had their losses. After standing by all day, nervy and impatient, without being scrambled, by nightfall they resolved on a party.

Paddy Bandon was down at Manston on a visit and he joined them. No one was more fun on a party. Whitney Straight's boys had been down at Manston for several days, and although they'd caused a beer famine locally, they thought they knew where to find it. The whole

---

1. It was not known until some time later that Graham-Hogg had survived and was now a prisoner in Stalag Luft 3. He was not one of the 50 escapers murdered on Hitler's orders, and he survived the war.

party, 601, 107, and Paddy, and of course Bill, led by Straight, raced off down the country lanes in an assortment of cars and vans requisitioned quite improperly for the occasion, but they found the relaxation they were looking for.

Bill, too, was a great party man, slotting in enthusiastically – a characteristic, in the post-war years, that was to get him into trouble. Getting back to his hotel room in the small hours in the middle of a Test Match was to scandalise some, but it never affected his flying or his cricket. He needed the relaxation. This was one reason, he always believed, why morale remained high. Frequent high-spirited parties were a feature of squadron life. He certainly had a sympathiser in Paddy Bandon, and that evening Paddy drew him on one side and told him in confidence that he was being promoted to squadron leader and posted to 21 Squadron as a flight commander. He was to replace Denis Graham-Hogg. That was the way of it that summer.

The night after the party Bill was awakened from a deep sleep by an explosion. Manston was under continual attack at that time, and thinking it was a stray bomb he turned over and went to sleep again. Next morning at breakfast he was joined by Bunny Harte, their new CO, a South African who had commanded one of the training flights when he was at Upwood. 'I'm afraid you lost your aircraft last night,' he told Bill, 'one of the night fighter boys swung on take-off.' That was what had woken him up. Both aircraft were a write-off and the pilot was killed.

For Bill, it was a stark reminder of what Paddy Bandon had said last night. Throughout his time on 107, he had regarded his aircraft as a kind of talisman. Now he had no further need of it.

Next day he was posted to 21 Squadron at Watton, also in Norfolk, to take over 'A' Flight. He'd gone from pilot officer to squadron leader in 19 days.

He found the squadron very much changed. 'Tom' Webster had been rested, and there was a new CO, Wing Commander Kercher, and two new flight commanders, Dick Shuttleworth and Bill. Kercher he never got close to, but Dick Shuttleworth became probably the best friend he had time to make in that crowded summer. They were quite unlike both physically and in flying experience. Where Bill was short (five foot six) and compact, Dick was over six foot and a great big bear of a chap. And whereas Bill had comparatively few flying hours but had been through the 2 Group mill that summer, Dick had been flying long hours on convoy and anti-submarine patrols in the Atlantic but had no low-level experience on Blenheims. He'd applied for a job with more action, but Bill felt that posting him in as a flight commander in 2 Group was too much like throwing him in at the deep end. He resolved, so far as it lay in his power, to break him in gently.

Bill's resolve was strengthened by the fact that he was such a delightful fellow. He had recently got married, his honeymoon had been curtailed by his posting, and he had got permission to live out temporarily with his wife in a local pub, a rare privilege in 1941.

Crews were always especially vulnerable on their first few trips. Time and again pilots with considerable experience of other types came to grief before they'd properly acclimatised. Once over the first few trips they had a much better chance.

As for Bill, he felt fully capable of carrying out the duties of a flight commander in 2 Group, he relished the responsibility and enjoyed it. He reckoned he had just about enough knowledge and experience to be able to pass something worth while on to his crews.

For a week or two they were fully occupied in reorganising and rebuilding the squadron. There were new crews to train and new tactics to learn. A half-sunken ship in the Wash provided newcomers with a practice target, and Bill took his crews on low-level formation flying almost daily, whipping them into shape. Careering around East Anglia at tree-top height was a thrilling experience, and the crews began to enjoy it.

Early in August, before the squadron began operations again, Bill was given a couple of days off to play cricket. There was a match at Lord's on 4 and 5 August, and Bill was part of a team representing Middlesex and Essex against Surrey and Kent. The Sexes batted first, and during the afternoon Bill joined Denis Compton at the crease. It was like old times. While they were together they scored at two runs a minute, against an attack that included Alf Gover and Doug Wright. Bill made 102 in eighty minutes.

Next day, back at Watton, they began practising – which meant dummy runs at very low level against a St Neots power station – for what was to prove one of the most ambitious and spectacular raids of the summer. All shipping strikes were to be suspended meanwhile. The flying was so intense and realistic that seven Blenheims were lost or damaged in training.

They were briefed by the station commander, Group Captain Laurie Sinclair (holder of the George Cross, for pulling a wounded gunner out of a blazing Blenheim with bombs still on board). Sinclair now told them that in pursuit of the policy of trying to draw German fighters away from the Russian front they were going to hit two sensitive targets that the Nazis could ill afford not to defend. The targets were both major power stations, housing the largest steam generators in Europe.

Fifty-four Blenheims were to take part, at low level throughout. There was to be a strong diversionary effort. There would be high-level bombing attacks by a small force of RAF Flying Fortresses on major targets, Hampdens with Spitfire escort would fly Circus intrusions, and Westland Whirlwind twin-engined fighters, although of limited range, would escort them to the Dutch coast. Finally, Spitfires would meet them in the Scheldt estuary to cover their withdrawal.

Of the fifty-four Blenheims, thirty-six were to attack the power station at Knapsack. The other 18, which included twelve from Bill's squadron, 21, and six from 82, their sister squadron on the nearby satellite airfield at Bodney, were to attack two smaller power stations at Quadrath. All were described as vital to Ruhr industry.

Kercher was to lead the 21 Squadron formation, which would form three boxes of six. Bill was to lead the port box of six and Squadron Leader Meakin, of 82 Squadron, the starboard box. Such was the planning for a so-called 'major' raid aimed at bringing relief to the Russians, all that Britain could manage in daylight in the summer of 1941.

'What a shock when we saw the map of the route!' recalls Sergeant Jim Langston. The ribbon stretched right across the North Sea and Holland and far into Germany.

They took off on the morning of 12 August (the 'Glorious Twelfth,' as someone noted) into an early morning mist, their progress unusually sluggish at first under the weight of full fuel and bomb loads. 'The leader of our box,' says Langston, 'was Squadron Leader Bill Edrich, with Pilot Officer Jim Corfield and then myself on his starboard side and three others on his port side'. At Orfordness they were joined by all the other Blenheims, also their Whirlwind escort, a fantastic sight. The Blenheims were flying in line abreast – 'I had never seen so many aircraft flying together, stretching as far as the eye could see,' says Langston. 'It was exhilarating.'

When they reached the Dutch coast the Whirlwinds retreated, and as the countryside flickered beneath them they pulled up over tall trees and church spires. The corn had ripened early and they saw harvesting in progress. 'Everyone was waving,' says Langston. 'We could see people as clearly as if we were on top of a double-decker bus.' They continued in a series of dog-legs, hoping to confuse the defences, and soon they were over Germany, with no waving from below now.

'Four minutes from the target!' came from the navigators – but still no trace of fighters. So far, surprise had been achieved. But the atmosphere soon changed. Blue flashes were sparking along a line of high tension cables stretching obliquely right and left. Someone, it seemed, had failed to clear the cables.

Bill focused briefly on a farmer, wearing what looked like plus fours, with a little group of labourers bending over a binder harvester that had apparently broken down. As they crossed the field the former looked up and Bill caught a split-second reaction of alarm and dismay as the RAF roundels were recognised.

Now they glimpsed the twin towers of Cologne Cathedral on the skyline, a short distance east of and beyond their targets. Then the tall chimneys of the power stations rose defiantly. 'There's the target – dead ahead!' – the pilots banked and swerved into the attack. They had practised the drop often enough – now they prepared to put it into effect. Each plane carried two 500 lb 11-second delay bombs, so it was essential to clear the target in quick time. Bill's box of six were going in last.

At St. Neots they had got everyone across the target in less than three seconds. That was the kind of discipline they needed now. The chimneys of the power station were forcing them up to 400 feet and more. The three Blenheim sections were stepped up slightly from front

56 Blenheims attacked the main Cologne power station at low level in August 1941. These photographs were taken from Bill Edrich's section during the attack. (IWMCH2022, 2023, 2024)

to rear. Light flak was ascending from the target area, but otherwise they were unopposed.

Kercher and Meakin flew their formations in regimental fashion, directly in front of Bill and slightly below. All they had to do was keep position. The drop was almost simultaneous and all were safely past the target when the bombs went off. Rear-facing cameras in the Blenheims were recording results. Success seemed certain. The core of the power station was in flames and the gunners reported direct hits. They saw no one hit over the target. One Bf 109 began the chase but it came under concentrated fire from the turrets and broke off.

It was every man now for himself – the quickest possible get-away before forming up again. Continuing their dog-legging, they passed quite involuntarily over the airfield at Antwerp, machine-gunning what looked like Bf 109s on the ground and claiming to have shot one down as it tried to take off. But they struck a problem soon afterwards when a thunderstorm near the estuary broke up the formation.

They were emerging from the storm when Bill asked Phipps for a course to steer to lead them to the Spitfires. Joined by other Blenheims, they sped across the shallows and mud-flats of the estuary towards the rendezvous.

Now, for Kercher's eighteen Blenheims, began the worst part of the trip. Intensive flak greeted them from the coastal batteries, but for Bill by far the greatest immediate hazard came from the huge flocks of waders which rose from the surface as they approached. He'd experienced this hazard before over the Wash, but never to this extent. Thousands and thousands of birds scattering in all directions, and several aircraft were damaged.

'Fighters ten o'clock port!'

'Spits or 109s?'

To Bill, the familiar waggle of wings from the fighter leader was the most welcoming sight ever. But the Spitfires were not alone: suddenly there were Messerschmitts everywhere. A loud explosion shook Jim Langston's aircraft, smashing the nose and depriving him of elevator and rudder control. 'Please God, let it be quick!'

Ken Attew in the turret was already dead, but Langston and his navigator somehow got out alive, to be taken prisoner. Not so lucky, even closer to Edrich, was Jim Corfield, shot down, as it later emerged, by the German ace Adolph Galland, with no survivors.

For the Knapsack formation the losses were even worse. Of the thirty-six Blenheims briefed to attack, nine were lost. They too had mostly got through to the target safely only to meet a determined fighter attack on the way out.

Jimmy Corfield. (Bill Corfield)

Twenty-five individual members of the Blenheim crews had paid for their brief exhilaration with their lives. Only eight survived as prisoners of war. Nearly all the returning Blenheims were severely damaged. Photo reconnaissance nine days later revealed that the main targets in the power stations – the turbine sheds – had not been hit. Yet it remained a daring attempt, the first deep penetration of Germany in daylight, and, as a gesture to the Russians and a morale booster for the British, the raid was adjudged a success. A blow had been struck, and two days later the personal congratulations of the Commander-in-Chief were celebrated. Leaders of the three formations of eighteen got the DSO, and of the boxes of six, including Bill, the DFC. A genuine attempt had been made to force the Nazis to defend their homeland, a pinprick no doubt in the overall strategic scenario, and even that at daunting cost. Had it been worth while? (The basis of Bill's citation is at Appendix One)

The truth was that such attacks were virtually unrepeatable. At such a loss rate the entire Group would have been wiped out in a fortnight. The best bet remained the Circus operation – probing the German defences without incurring crippling losses – and for the next No.2 Group target a German-occupied airfield in France was selected. Longuenese near St.Omer, and Bill was chosen to lead.

In the Mess beforehand, Bill was introduced by Laurie Sinclair to a Colonel G.F.Hopkins, a charming and likeable little man who was involved in the formation of the Airborne Division. 'Will you take 'Hoppy' with you tomorrow?' asked Sinclair. 'Show him as much flak as possible.' It seemed an odd request, but 'Hoppy', as everyone called him, wanted first-hand knowledge – flak was something the airborne troops would have to get used to. Bill knew that almost wherever he crossed the French coast they would see flak, but the requirement was to find a concentration of it yet endeavour to keep out of trouble.

After rendezvousing with the fighter escort in glorious sunshine they set off across the water. Bill chose a point south of Boulogne, where he knew the batteries were active but in his experience inaccurate. Cap Griz Nez looked so peaceful that Hoppy, sitting on a bucket seat beside him, looked at him quizzically; but then the action started.

Bill went through his usual corkscrew evasions and black puffs surrounded them. The Blenheim bucked once or twice and Bill began

Laurie Sinclair, GC. 'I want you to show this chap some flack!' Bill duly obliged. (IWM CANII2)

to regret the course he'd taken. He glanced at Hoppy, to see how he was taking it, and was amazed to see him grinning excitedly, darting quick little glances in all directions so as not to miss anything. He gave Bill the thumbs up, then they were through the worst of the coastal flak and nearing the target.

Ten miles from St.Omer, at 12,000 feet, they began their bombing run, but then the black puffs started again and Bill changed his mind. 'We'll do a shorter run,' he told Phipps, 'I'm going to avoid this lot if I can.' It might be fun for Hoppy, but Bill had seen enough flak for one day.

Next day Hoppy presented him with a silver pencil inscribed 'W.J.E. from G.F.H., Aug.16th 1941. It was one of Bill's proudest possessions. Sadly Hoppy was killed in the Sicily glider landings in 1943.

The other type of operation the Group still specialised in was the shipping strike, and this was Bill's favourite. He loved the low flying; and then there was the hunt, the seeking out of their prey. They often searched in vain, and when they made a sighting and gave chase it became doubly thrilling, and Bill forgot his fears.

It was on one of these anti-shipping strikes that Bill had a new hazard pointed out to him by the fighter pilots of No.11 Group, who were escorting them. An extract from the Group Fighter Intelligence Report read: 'The sea-coloured camouflage on the top surface of the Blenheims was so effective that the first we saw of them was their wakes on the water.' They urged them not to fly so low. 'Do you realise,' they asked, 'that the wake you leave on the water can easily be picked out by fighters overhead?' This delighted Bill: 'Wakes on the Water' was a new and fanciful alliteration that appealed. Whatever they said, he would always prefer to be low down: he would take his chance on being seen from above.

On 26 August they were briefed to strike at a southbound convoy believed to be on its way to Rotterdam. They were to intercept off the Dutch coast opposite Ijmuiden. They took the usual bomb-load, four 250-pounders, descended to the usual 30 feet, and aimed slightly north of the estimated position, before turning south parallel with the coast, which they could dimly see.

Soon they sighted first one small ship then another, and slightly to starboard the main convoy. Bill manoeuvred his vic of three into an attack from the landward. They might even be mistaken for the *Luftwaffe*. The two smaller ships astern were clearly flak ships, guarding the rear. Bill elected to go for these ships, clearing the way for the second vic of three, led by Dick Shuttleworth. This gave them the juicier targets. This was Dick's first taste of this kind of action and Bill wanted him to do well.

Bill chose the first flak ship, eased back the stick to give height in the dive, and pulled in plus 9 boost to give maximum speed. As he pushed the nose forward again he saw a coloured Verey light floating up towards him, challenging him, and his answer was to open up with his front gun and continue in the dive.

The black and white diagonal markings which were characteristic of German flak ships became so sharply delineated that he could almost smell the paint. He pressed the bomb release button four times in rapid succession and then pulled up.

There was no flak at first, but as they pulled away the tracers overtook them, racing past like a blizzard. Once clear, Bill did a half-turn to starboard, and looking back he saw the ship already going down, bow first and stern up. Between them they must have got a hit below the waterline.

They had opened up a path for Shuttleworth and the other two Blenheims, but not without cost. No.2 was forming up again, but No.3 was plunging towards the sea, his port wing a flaming torch. Not much chance for them.

The other three Blenheims all attacked merchant ships in the main convoy and all reported hits. That night, at a party with the 82 Squadron boys at Bodney, Bill had one of his most cherished compliments. It came from a Canadian pilot named Frankie Orme, in Shuttleworth's formation. 'Billy boy,' he said, 'we'd follow you anywhere!' It was pretty late in the evening, and by then, as Bill admits, the beer was talking.

Kercher then went on leave and Bill was left in charge of the squadron. Orders immediately came through for a major raid next day. No. 21 Squadron were to supply six Blenheims for a low-level do on Rotterdam harbour. The same operation order specified that Bill was not to fly. Shuttleworth was to lead. Bill didn't like this at all. In the first place, as the man in charge he felt he should be leading. Second, he didn't think Dick had anything like enough experience to lead the squadron on such a hazardous do. He was worried, too, about the raid's whole conception. The tactics to be employed were too much a repetition of Tom Webster's successful raid six weeks earlier. The Germans would be ready.

He couldn't do much about the choice of target or even the tactics. They were laid down by Group. But as acting CO of the squadron he felt he should have some input, especially about the leadership. Laurie Sinclair was a man he could talk to and he dropped in at station headquarters for a word. He told Sinclair his fears. Could he possibly get the orders reviewed? Sinclair shook his head: 'Quite impossible.' 'If it has to go,' said Bill, 'let someone lead it who's inured to it.'

'Who do you suggest?'

'I'd feel very much happier if I could lead it myself.'

Sinclair had expected that. But the orders about Bill were clear and he countered at once: 'Shuttleworth has to start leading some time.' But he saw Bill's point about this particular raid. 'I'll get through to Group and see if they'll allow you to go.'

When Bill got back to his office the phone was ringing. 'I'm afraid it's no good,' said Sinclair. 'They won't let you go.'

Bill's worst fears were confirmed. Only two Blenheims got back and one of them was badly shot up, with the rear gunner wounded. Amongst the officers, only one got back. His supper remained uneaten.

Late that evening Bill was having a brandy in the Mess and trying to pull himself together when the squadron adjutant reminded him that Dick's wife was staying at the Crown Hotel in Watton. Would Bill go and break the news to her? Bill said he would if the adjutant would come with him as far as the hotel foyer, for company. He accepted it was a one-man job. There followed, for Bill, one of the saddest nights of his life. Dick's wife was very brave. She had already sensed the worst and was actually packing when he entered the room. She asked him if he would drive her to Dick's parents at Wroxham, and this of course he did.

At about two o'clock that morning he found himself ringing the doorbell of the house. As soon as Dick's father saw him he knew what had happened. Mrs Shuttleworth senior took charge of Dick's wife – though she must have been equally devastated – and Bill watched while Shuttleworth senior poured two large whiskies. 'You probably need this,' he said, 'as much as I do.'

It was a bleak and silent drive back to Watton. Next day Bill discovered why they hadn't let him go on the raid. He'd been posted to group headquarters, to a staff job. His tour of operations was over. The move was probably well judged. Apart from one week's break he'd been flying on operations the entire summer. He was one of the few to survive.

For many years afterwards, the months of May to August, comprising the English summer cricket season, were to be the highlights of Bill's life. But they could never approach the drama, the pathos, the endeavour, and the comradeship of that summer of 1941.

CHAPTER FOUR

Jimmy Ward – Kiwi 'Sprog' Pilot – How and Why He Got the VC – July 1941

The young sergeant pilot from New Zealand, on leave in London, was not enjoying the hero-worship he was getting. He looked ill-at-ease. Puzzled and embarrassed by his overnight celebrity, he was doing his best to look unconcerned. But beneath a veneer of natural good manners he looked bewildered. The news that he was to be awarded the Victoria Cross had shocked and amazed him. He couldn't see what all the fuss was about.

His school-boyish modesty was suddenly a fault. In a Press interview, asked to give his account of a war story that had hit the headlines, he played down his part in the action so effectively that he nearly deprived himself of the award – the highest honour of all.

He did not know it, but doubts about the award had been raised elsewhere, at the highest level. All honours and awards – and particularly for a VC – were subject to the closest scrutiny. When such an award was recommended for a young man whose sole operational experience was confined to a handful of sorties as second pilot, attached for training and familiarisation to an experienced crew, the scrutiny was doubly severe. (At his operational training unit he had been allotted his own crew, but he had not yet been thought fit to take charge of it.).

At the age of twenty-one, James Allen Ward had been serving an apprenticeship as a schoolmaster in Wanganui, North Island. When war was declared he immediately applied for training as a pilot. By the time acceptance came through he had begun his teaching career, but he abandoned it at once and enlisted. He started elementary flying training in July 1940, completed advanced instruction that year, got his 'wings' and was promoted to sergeant. In January 1941 he sailed via Canada for England.

He had always wanted to fly. His favourite hobby as a youth had been aero-modelling. Normally of placid, equable temperament, he had the small but compact physique of the games player; rugby, tennis and swimming were the sports at which he excelled. In England he mixed easily with young men of his own kind, though they were soon aware of his love for his native New Zealand. He was looking forward immensely to being captain of his own crew, a team who had already joined him for operational training at his Wellington OTU at Lossiemouth, Scotland.

Exposed now to all the hullabaloo of sudden fame, he felt timid and inarticulate in the sophisticated company into which he had been thrust. It wasn't that he hadn't enjoyed his leave. Deprived of his daily companions, he had nevertheless enjoyed it. London, in that summer of 1941, was pulsating with life as only a great capital city, reprieved from threatened annihilation, can be. Fêting, adulation, publicity, theatres, restaurants, tourism – all had filled his days, and sometimes half his nights. Everyone had wanted a piece of him. Especially the New Zealand authorities. They wanted him off operational flying and back in New Zealand as a magnet for recruitment, but he would have none of it.

'Jim Ward,' said his navigator, Joe Lawton, 'received a great deal of publicity after his award – and hated every minute of it.'

A return one day to New Zealand, to his family, to the forests and the mountains, the mists and the legends, was the most desirable of all things. But not before he had done what he came to do. And there was his squadron, No.75 (New Zealand) Squadron, with its Maori motto, 'Ake Ake Kai Kaha' (For Ever and Ever Be Strong). Even more important was his crew: they would be depending on him, and eventually his request to rejoin them was granted. 'Between ourselves,' he admitted, to the well-meaning hosts who were treating him to a farewell dinner on the last night of his leave, 'I want to get back to the boys.' The comradeship of squadron life was both refuge and reassurance.

One more night in that luxurious bedroom overlooking London's river, one more breakfast in London's most famous hotel, and it would be back to the familiar, uncomplicated landscape of East Anglia, back to the tensions and excitements of wartime flying. That, and his own sense of duty, had protected him from temptations elsewhere. Even so, tonight he had the fidgets. Now that it was all settled, he was impatient to get back. He reached for the only palliative he knew, a smoke. The chap sitting next to him at the dinner table offered his lighter and he flicked at it with his thumb.

The lighter had been over-filled. As Ward flicked at it a second time the petrol that had only moistened his fingers the first time now ignited. A tendril of flame clung to his fist. He stared at it uncomprehendingly. He was seeing something else, something remembered from his sub-conscious. He passed out. When he recovered consciousness he was back in his room and the hotel doctor was bandaging his hand. He realised what had happened, and he began to laugh at his foolishness.

But the doctor knew the background, and he didn't think it was foolishness. A lad whose nerves were in that state was surely not fit for operational flying. He needed a rest. 'I'll write a note for you to take back to your unit,' he said.

Ward and his crew had been posted to No. 75 Squadron, based at Feltwell in 3 Group, in the Fenlands, on the Norfolk/Suffolk border. But to start with, on 14 June, his twenty-second birthday, Ward was detailed as second pilot, as an initiation, with a veteran crew for a raid on Dusseldorf. The squadron commander, the fatherly, beak-nosed Wing Commander Cyril Kay, was also a New Zealander. He had originally served in the RAF but was now in the RNZAF. Always known as 'Cyrus', he was punctilious about giving 'sprog' pilots straight from operational training a chance to learn their trade. Being entrusted with the life and career of this youthful Kiwi, he chose his senior flight commander to put him through his paces. This was Squadron Leader R.P.Widdowson, Reuben Widdowson, or Ben, a Canadian from Winnipeg in the regular peacetime RAF. Only four years older than Ward, he had served in the Middle East and India and was a lifetime older in experience. Naturally reserved, and with a crew of exclusively senior NCOs, he tended to keep to himself.

The partnership proved a congenial one, and in the next three weeks Ward continued with Widdowson for another six sorties, Essen and Cologne being among their targets. Kay, presumably advised by Widdowson, certainly avoided rushing him. Quite the reverse. Then on 7 July Ward and his hitherto mostly unoccupied crew were at last allotted a brand-new aircraft of their own, Wellington L7818, R for Robert, which was given a brief night-flying test. One can imagine their excitement after this long wait, while their pilot, as it seemed, had been flying over Germany almost daily. But on the same day, after the new Wellington had been prepared for action, it was given to someone else

– to flight commander Widdowson! Perhaps Widdowson got it through *droit de seigneur*: or perhaps, since a heavy raid was planned on Munster – a longer trip – the baptism of Ward and his crew was deferred. Anyway, Widdowson and his crew took R for Robert, and Ward was again appointed to go with them as second pilot.

There were two more New Zealanders in the crew, navigator Joe Lawton and rear gunner Allan Box. Lawton was a clerk from Auckland who had already distinguished himself: only four weeks older than Ward, his navigational skill and courage had been recognised by the award of an Air Force Cross. Widdowson said he was the best navigator he'd ever had. Lawton admired Widdowson in turn for his coolness in escaping searchlights and flak, and envied him his magnificent Delage motor, in which he – very occasionally – accompanied him to the pub.

Allan Box, youngest of all at nineteen, also came from Auckland. The radio operator, Bill Mason, came from Stamford, Lincolnshire, and the front gunner, Titch Evans – inevitably 'Taffy' – was a Welshman from Llanelli. The aircraft was still the original and much-loved Wellington IC. Its unorthodox system of geodetic construction, fabric-covered to reduce weight, and devised by Barnes Wallis, endowed it with exceptional resilience. It soon showed a unique ability to shake off combat damage and keep flying.

The twin-engined 'Wimpey' was a sizeable aircraft for its time, with a wing-span of 86 feet and a length of 61 feet three inches, nearly as big as the four-engined Lancasters and Halifaxes that were soon to replace it. With its distinctive cigar-shaped body, its latticed side-windows and its two power-operated gun-turrets, front and rear, it became a familiar sight over southern and eastern England in those early war years – not to mention over Germany. A high tail-fin, and a small cupola or astro-dome half-way along the top of the fuselage, completed its silhouette.

For the night of 7/8 July 1941, Bomber Command were putting up forty-one Wellingtons from their East Anglian bases, ten from Feltwell. The target was the industrial areas of Munster, to the north of the Ruhr, 300 miles from their base, and they were to attack individually. The briefing, after lunch on the 7th, by Cyrus Kay, was unexceptional. They were to climb to their operational height of 13,000 feet, cross the English coast north of Aldeburgh, then the Dutch coast north of Ijmuiden. Moonlight was expected to assist map-reading. Photographs of the target area were studied at briefing and areas of heavy concentrations of flak and searchlights – mainly on the Dutch/German frontier – were specifically marked. Take-off was not scheduled until

23.10, which meant a long wait, so after a spell in the crew room preparing their maps and charts, Lawton and Ward were among those who went to bed.

At 11.10 pm on 7 July the heavily laden R for Robert took off from Feltwell. Each aircraft carried a full bomb load of over two tons, so the climb to operational altitude was slow. The night was fine and clear, there was no cloud, and there was sufficient light from a rising moon to map-read – until the glare of the searchlights blinded them. They got through the most heavily defended areas but still had fifty miles penetration of the Third Reich before they reached their target.

The Wellington was not equipped with dual control, and Ward stood in the centre section below the astro-dome, watching out for enemy activity. Munster was smaller and more compact than most German cities Ward had seen from the air, making it easier than usual to identify target areas. Fires were already burning near the aiming points, and dummy fires north of the target did not deceive them. Searchlight activity was desultory, and it was not until Ward had dropped their illuminating flares and they had begun their bombing run that they became aware of medium and light anti-aircraft fire.

Lawton, in the nose, aimed the bombs, and Ward, from the astro-dome, took photographs and observed hits on a railway south of the target. Factories and buildings stood out in Braille-like relief and a warehouse seemed to crumple and collapse. Numerous fires littered the industrial area. As they left the target and turned for home Lawton moved back to stand next to Widdowson. A terrific conflagration, which they took for a gas-works, was visible half-way to the Dutch border. Nights like this seemed empty and dreamlike, strangely unreal, too good to be true. They were taking part in the most dangerous activity of the war, yet this part of Germany seemed as dead as a small country town. It seemed they were getting away with it.

They were half-way across the Zuider Zee at twenty-past two in the morning, still at 13,000 feet, when the illusion of solitude and tranquillity was shattered. There was no warning. One moment the expanse of inland water beneath them, twenty miles wide, was a silvered lake of fairy-tale beauty, the next it held the immediate threat of a watery grave.

The hail of cannon shells and incendiaries that tore into the Wimpey hit them from nowhere. The German fighter, choosing the blind spot under the tail, soared up unseen from underneath, fired a concentrated burst and broke away before anyone could react.

Nineteen-year-old Allan Box, swinging his turret from side to side continually to search the arc his view commanded, saw the tracer splashing towards him and felt a searing pain in his foot. Before he could manoeuvre his guns the enemy plane vanished into the night, no doubt to prepare for another attack. It was a twin-engined aircraft, of that he was sure, probably a Messerschmitt Bf 110. But he had totally lost sight of it. Now the German pilot would be turning back into the attack, bent on administering the *coup de grace*.

The first shell hit the main spar inboard of the starboard engine, between the engine nacelle and the fuselage on that side, close to the wing-root. The fuel tanks were located outboard of the engines, three on each side; but the fuel in each tank was piped independently to a collector box in the bottom of the fuselage, enabling each tank to be isolated and the fuel supply as a whole to be balanced. But the fuel balance pipe on the starboard side had been cut, and the escaping petrol had ignited. The torn fabric where the shell had passed through the wing had caught fire.

Fed by the leaking petrol, the fire was rapidly gaining a hold. If they couldn't extinguish it quickly, it would spread across the entire starboard wing. Already the wing on that side was vibrating alarmingly, and the cockpit was filling with flames and smoke. The hydraulic system, too, was damaged, and the bomb-doors swung open, slowing the speed and changing the trim. Mason tried to raise base on the radio but could get no joy from his transmitter. Widdowson, shouting instructions, soon realised that the inter-com was dead.

The German pilot, seeing the bomber on fire, came in for the kill. But the Wellington's sudden loss of speed confused him and he overshot. Even now Box saw nothing of him until he broke away, but as he did so the German exposed the belly of his aircraft and Box got in a long burst at point-blank range. He could see from his tracer that his aim was good. Flame spurted from the German's port engine and he went into a steep spiral, with the damaged engine still emitting dense black smoke.

After the initial blaze-up in the wing of the Wellington, the flames from the leaking pipe settled into a strong jet four to five feet long which gushed out and blew back along the wing, scorching everything in its path. With petrol-soaked fabric as tinder, there seemed no way of containing the fire. Sooner or later it would jump the engine nacelle and spread to the tanks. Then the whole plane would blow up.

Widdowson, desperately hoping somehow to reach land before ordering a bale-out, still held his course. A forced landing in enemy-held territory looked the best he could hope for. He turned to Ward, now standing beside him. 'Tell them to put their chutes on! Stand by to abandon!'

'What will you do, skipper?'

'Head for the shore! See if you can put that bloody fire out!'

Box, far away in the tail, could just about distinguish the shadowy figure of Ward as he made his way aft from the cockpit. He saw Lawton and Mason reaching for their parachutes, and he released his own from its stowage and clipped it to the snap-hook on his chest. Fearful of the fire, he kept his gaze away from it, lest it impair his night vision. They were now an illuminated target.

Lawton and Ward kept hacking at the fabric, trying to get at the fire. Wrenching a fire extinguisher from its stowage, Lawton pushed it through the hole they'd made, pressed the plunger, and squirted it at the fire. The jet was fierce but the airstream was fiercer, and the precious liquid scattered back along the fuselage, splattering on Box's turret. Unscrewing a vacuum flask, Lawton jerked it at the flames in vain. Caught in the airstream, it splashed harmlessly short of the fire.

'How's it going?' Widdowson was still holding on, hoping to get above dry land.

'It's no worse at the moment. But it's still burning.'

Widdowson could not easily resign himself to being a prisoner for the rest of the war, but the fire seemed about to consume the entire wing. Yet baling out when they were still over water seemed suicidal. What else could they do?

'Is there any way you boys can reach that fire?'

Jimmy Ward, odd man out in the crew, on his final 'fresher' flight, somehow felt it was up to him. And an idea, far-fetched and hare-brained, was forming in his mind.

Lying loose on the floor of the fuselage was a canvas cockpit-cover. It wasn't supposed to be there, but Widdowson sometimes used it as a cushion. It could be manhandled, with an effort, and it was dense enough to smother the fire. That meant jamming it into the hole where the pipe was leaking. And that meant getting out on the wing. Gathering up the cover, he said matter-of-factly to Lawton: 'I think I'll just hop out with this.'

'That's impossible,' said Lawton. 'You'd be blown straight off.'

'It's worth a try.'

'Then you'll take your parachute?'

'Too much wind resistance.'

'You're not going without it.'

Lawton's will was equal to Ward's. And Ward, an inexperienced lad in an experienced crew, hesitated.

'O.K.?' demanded Lawton.

'O.K. then.'

Lawton went forward to tell his skipper. Shocked but anxious to help, Widdowson called: 'I'll throttle right back.'

Lawton and Ward worked out a plan of action. Lawton seized the crash axe from its stowage, and the two men began cutting handholds and footholds from the astro hatch down to the wing – something that would have been impracticable in any other type of plane. A length of rope, normally for use with the dinghy, was then freed, Ward temporarily removed his parachute, and Lawton wound it round Ward's waist and secured it.

Helped by Lawton, Ward clambered up and lifted the hatch. It was only two and a half feet wide, and was impossible to climb through with the parachute pack clipped to his chest. Hands gripping either side of the ring of the hatch, he pulled himself up until his head and shoulders were buffeted by the airstream. Widdowson throttled back as far as he dared, and the crippled Wimpey lumbered along at little more than a hundred miles an hour. Even so, as he emerged the blast made him gasp. Eyes narrowed, scalp tingling, he reached down for Lawton to hand him first his chute, which he clipped on, then the cockpit cover.

Recovering his breath, he took stock, head poked through the hole, planning his next move. Tucking the cockpit cover under his left arm, he supported himself with his right wrist and drew his legs up until they were suspended across the top of the hatch, using his left elbow to steady himself. Then he swivelled his legs to starboard prior to dropping down on the wing. Feeling with his toes for the wing-root, several feet below the hatch, he found he couldn't reach it.

There was only one answer to that. His whole plan depended on the geodetic construction of the plane, and the pliable fabric of the skin. Kicking the steps they had already begun with his flying-boot, he planted his right instep on one of the aluminium struts, forced the heel of his boot hard against it for support, and then lowered his left leg until he could feel the wing-root firm under his foot. Soon, still clutching the rim of the hatch with one hand and steadying himself with the other, he was precariously established on the wing.

The battering he was getting from the gale forced him to pause. He was suddenly conscious of the noise. Engines and airstream were combining to produce a fortissimo of sound that blunted his eardrums. While he was working his way out of the hatch he had hardly noticed it. Now it was as though someone had turned the volume up to full power.

When he had considered the problem inside the aircraft, the distance between the fuselage and the fire had seemed relatively insignificant, easy to span. Now it looked like a chasm, four or five feet to traverse.

And the leaking pipe was even further away, behind the engine nacelle. Four, five feet – it was nothing. That's what he had told himself. But to reach as much as a foot, he had to release his grip on the hatch, get down on his belly, cling like a leech to sections of the torn wing, and worm his way across. If only he had both hands completely free! But the cockpit cover was an essential part of the plan, and as the gale threatened to tear it from his grasp he hugged it to his body in a vice-like embrace.

The fire was spreading. Soon it might arc across the engine nacelle. Or another fighter might get on to them. There was no time to waste. Holding on with one hand, he kicked two holes in the fabric outboard of the wing-root for his feet. Two of the holes made by the cannon-fire were in roughly the right spot, and this helped. Getting his feet well dug into the holes, sufficient to support him briefly, he prepared to let go of the hatch.

It was like standing on the edge of a cliff in a gale. The next gust might throw him off. But having got this far he would sooner go on than turn back. Throwing his weight forward against the blast, he plunged face down on the wing, pinning the cover under his body and clawing with both hands into the torn fabric. His grip was firm, and there for a long moment he stayed, clamped into position, panting with fear and relief.

Lawton was still releasing the rope inch by inch. Ward was nearly there. He still had to stretch another two feet out from the fuselage to reach the fire, and he needed to find or fashion more holds. But as soon as he tried to move, the gale found the gap under his body formed by the parachute pack and lifted him up. He felt his arms being torn from their sockets, his fingers were numb, and he had lost his precious handholds. Then he felt his body being thrown back. The parachute was preventing him from flattening his body on the wing. Yet it now seemed his only chance of survival.

The rope round his waist was of dubious value. He doubted if it would sustain his weight. He saw himself pirouetting on the end of it, crashing into the tail-plane and knocking himself out.

He was winded now by the shock of a fresh impact. He had been thrown not against the tail-plane but back against the fuselage. Crouching there in bewilderment, his feet still caught in the geodetics, he clutched at the astro-hatch with his free hand and miraculously made contact. Lawton had tautened the rope, he still had hold of the cover, and he hugged it instinctively and held on.

The flames from the leaking pipe seemed no better. He would try again .

The natural and unnatural forces that were pitted against him had drained him of rational thought. The task he was attempting was insect-like, and it was with insect-like persistence that he continued it. For a second time he forced his body down on to the wing, secured handholds, and resumed the task of working his way towards the fire. As he came behind the starboard propeller he was fiercely buffeted by the slipstream, and once, as he tried to transfer his grip, he thought he was going. But he still inched his way crab-like towards the fire.

Holding on with his left hand, he dragged the cover from underneath his body with his right and dumped it into and over the blazing fabric, choking the flames. But then the wind caught one edge of the cover and nearly dragged it off. He held on to it grimly. The fabric was only smouldering now, but the leaking pipe still looked menacing. Somehow he must stuff the cover into the hole and finally throttle the flames. That meant moving even further out from the fuselage.

The effort of clinging to the wing against the gale had exhausted him and his muscles ached. Rallying for a final effort, he squirmed still further to the right, seeking a new hold, stretching his body to the limit. Then he pushed the cover forward and stuffed it into the hole. He had done it! He had put out the fire! But as he took his hand away the cover loosened, ballooning out of the hole.

He was just in time to crush the air out of it, and with the last of his strength he stuffed it back where he wanted it. The fire for the moment seemed quenched, and this time he thought the cover would stay. But when he took his hand away, it ballooned as before, evading his grasp, and as he scrabbled it swirled out of reach. Box, in the rear turret, saw it billow past him like a sail.

There was nothing more to be done but work his way back. That might be the hardest part. Throwing his weight forward to get down on the wing had been tricky enough. But now he had to set himself for the return. Again he was exposed to the full force of the gale.

It occurred to him that most accidents, in the mountains back home, happened on the way down, when the climbers relaxed. He had to guard against that. No longer hampered by the cockpit cover, he was making steady progress, using the same handholds and footholds as before. Once, as a fierce squall assailed him, he paused. He was only aware of it sub-consciously, but all the way back along the wing, Lawton was steadying him on the rope. Now, as he pressed his body against the fuselage and reached up to grip the hatch, the support he had was crucial. Hauling himself up, he somehow got his shoulders wedged near the top of the hatch. As he struggled to free himself, Lawton reached up and grabbed him.

A photo taken immediately after the raid reveals the holes that Ward punched through the Wellington's outer skin to use as hand and foot holds. (Bowyer)

There was still an occasional flicker from the leaking pipe, but the danger of a conflagration seemed to have passed. Yet, for the crew, the crisis seemed no more than postponed as Widdowson, having turned parallel to the coastline when they reached it, headed the crippled bomber for the North Sea, preferring a possible ditching to capture.

They were losing height rapidly now, but Bill Mason got his radio working again and got a distress message off to base. That would give them a chance of being found if they ditched. Taffy Evans jettisoned the front guns and ammunition, Allan Box did the same in the rear, and everything loose was thrown out.

Having been so long away from the navigation, Lawton used his sextant to check their position before giving Widdowson a final course for base. Ten miles off the English coast there was an alarming eruption from the starboard engine, but it died down as suddenly as it had come.

It took them one and a half hours to cross the water, and when overhead Feltwell Widdowson called the Controller. 'We've been badly shot up. We don't want to mess up your flare-path, but we've got no flaps or brakes and our bomb-doors are drooping. But we've got to land.'

The Controller, with other returning raiders to attend to, directed Widdowson elsewhere. 'Make for the long runway at Newmarket. You'll have plenty of room there.'

Widdowson had no hydraulics, but he managed to pump the undercarriage down, using the emergency system, and he came in to land at a good pace. They overran the runway, ran through a wire fence and finished up in a hedge; but they suffered no further injuries. Widdowson's (and Ward's) brand-new R for Robert, however, was a write-off.

When the story of the flight was told, the squadron, station and group commanders all recommended Ward for the VC, and the Commander-in-Chief of Bomber Command endorsed it. But in that press interview, Ward's apparent modesty did not go unnoticed. The Awards Committee were sceptical. Ward, it was said, had been helped by the navigator. He had had a rope tied round his waist for security, and he had worn a parachute. The night had been calm and a parachute descent and the launching of a dinghy would not have been difficult. Also it appeared that the engine cover had blown out of the hole almost as soon as it was inserted. Finally they cast doubt on whether Ward had extinguished the fire at all. It might have subsided anyway.

Air Vice-Marshal Philip Babington, head of the Awards Committee, was against the award of a VC. He pointed out an anomaly in the awards system: for other ranks in the RAF, there was nothing between the VC and the DFM. He proposed what he called a super-DFM, corresponding to the CGM (Conspicuous Gallantry Medal) in the Navy and the DCM (Distinguished Conduct Medal) in the Army. The RAF had no equivalent, and the Ward case emphasized this.

What the AOC, Air Vice-Marshal Jack Baldwin, thought of this was revealed in two foolscap pages of acidulous description of what Ward had done, of what might have happened to him, and of the state of the aircraft on its return. The matter was referred to the Chief of the Air

A dinner in the Airmen's Mess for Ward. The CO (centre), Ward, Box and Lawton to his right, Widdowson to his left. (IWM CH3225)

Staff, Sir Charles Portal, as final arbiter, and on 26 July 1941 he gave his verdict.

> This is a very difficult case.
>
> Much as everyone admires the kind of courage displayed by Sergeant Ward on this occasion, I must say that I think the VC should more often be given to a man who displays exceptional valour in getting himself into greater danger, (rather) than to one who shows great bravery in getting out of the desperate situation which is latent in all operations.
>
> The first type knowingly raises the odds against himself in the pursuit of his duty, whereas with the latter type of case the motive of self-preservation may sometimes dominate the situation.'

It seemed clear that he agreed with Babington, and he took the point that the RAF had no equivalent to the CGM, an award which, as a result, was introduced in November that year. However, his final sentence reeked of a *volte face*, presaged as it was by the classic get-out pronoun: nevertheless.

That was how the CAS conceded the point. 'Nevertheless,' he wrote, 'as Sergeant Ward volunteered from among his six comrades to perform an act of the greatest bravery, which saved their lives and the aircraft, I agree that he should be recommended for the VC.'

Two months later, on 15 September 1941, Jimmy Ward, now with his own crew, took part in an attack on Hamburg. It was only his second sortie as a bomber captain. 159 aircraft were sent, including 12 Wellingtons from 75. There was clear weather over the target, searchlights were working in cones, and flak was heavy. Despite strenuous efforts to escape from the beams, as later recorded by the survivors, Ward's machine was mortally hit, and fire broke out and spread so rapidly that he ordered his crew to bale out. Two of them, the navigator and the wireless operator, are known to have baled out successfully and been taken prisoner. When last they saw Ward, he was still at the controls, and he fell to his death with the rest of the

An artist's impression of Ward's heroic deed as published in the Illustrated London News. (C.E. Turner)

VICTORIA CROSS WON TWO AND A HALF MILES ABOVE THE SEA: THE HEROIC FEAT OF SERGEANT J. A. WARD.

crew. He is buried in Hamburg.

There were always pilots who stayed longer at their controls than they might have done, and Ward was only one of many. Frequently it was an act of sacrifice, unwitnessed and unrecorded, but typical of the corporate responsibility of so many bomber pilots. Only when it could be attested by witnesses – as, for instance, with Middleton and Bazalgette, as recorded in Chapter 8 – could it qualify for a VC. But if there was ever was any doubt in anyone's mind about the VC for Ward, it was surely silenced now.

Jo Lawton's career provides a poignant contrast between those who survived the war and those who didn't. Eight months before that dramatic episode with Ward, Lawton had already been severely wounded on an earlier tour, on 38 Squadron at Marham. He had been lying on the bomb-aimer's panel during a raid when he was hit. From September 1940 to May 1941 he was recovering in Ely Hospital, and he had only recently returned to operations when he joined Widdowson.

After completing his tour with 75 Squadron he was commissioned and he returned to Marham, this time as Navigation Leader. Then in 1942 he was posted home to New Zealand, where he flew in Hudsons, Venturas and Transport Squadrons in the Pacific. After the war he was made Chief Navigation Officer of Air New Zealand, and he had amassed nearly 20,000 flying hours before what he calls the 'necessary exalted age' brought retirement in 1974.

As a contrast in fortunes, Jimmy Ward never received his decoration at the hands of the King. By the time of the investiture at Buckingham

Sergeant James Ward VC.
(IWM)

Palace he had been reported missing.

What happened to the letter addressed to the medical officer at Feltwell, written by the Savoy Hotel doctor, recommending a period on rest?

In the train back to Norfolk after his leave, Ward found the note in his pocket. The incident of the cigarette lighter had been an isolated reaction. He had had no other symptoms. Determined to get on with the job he'd come 12,000 miles to do, he screwed it up and threw it out of the open window.

CHAPTER FIVE

Reg Howard– Aussie Rear-Gunner – The Man Who Wouldn't Die, Middle East, September 1942

The windows of the operating theatre looked straight down at the Nile. The man being wheeled into the theatre had been rushed to the 15th Scottish General Hospital, on the outskirts of Cairo, for urgent brain surgery. Still fully conscious despite his wounds, he had overheard enough to know that his chances of survival were slim.

It was eight o'clock in the morning, and the hot sun of a Cairo summer was already beating down relentlessly outside. Yet the operating theatre, chilled by a German air-conditioning plant, struck deliciously cool.

The hospital had been completed three years earlier, in 1939, and the theatre was modern and well-equipped. Entrance hall, changing rooms and theatre were lined throughout with pale blue tiles that lent an ethereal glow. The conventional padded and adjustable operating table, the instruments on the instrument table, and the anaesthetic machines, gleamed with polished steel. A faint odour of disinfectant reached the patient as he was wheeled in, enhancing the purity of the atmosphere, deepening the sense of peace and tranquillity already induced by sedatives.

Waiting for the patient were five of the medical staff – two orderlies, the theatre sister, the anaesthetist, and the surgeon. Surgeon and anaesthetist were members of a neurosurgical team which had served through two Libyan campaigns. They had travelled back and forth across the Western Desert in advance and retreat, forward to Benghazi and beyond, back to Sidi Rezegh and Tobruk, and then, narrowly escaping capture by the advancing Afrika Korps, falling back on Cairo. Rommel's victorious drive for the Nile had at last been halted, but Egypt was still under siege. Alamein was yet to come.

Major Peter Ascroft, surgeon, R.A.M.C. in wartime, but in peacetime a Middlesex Hospital man through and through, winner of the Gold Medal at London University in 1931, and formerly a house surgeon to Professor Sir Hugh Cairns at the London Hospital for specialist training in brain surgery, he was thirty-five, slim and five foot ten. Although unmilitary in appearance and manner, he nevertheless took military service seriously, swotting up his basic knowledge of map-reading and navigation, enabling him to lead his surgical team out of Tobruk when it fell, negotiating the notorious Qattara Depression without getting lost. An amateur botanist and photographer, he was a specialist who saw the dangers in specialisation and never lost sight of the patient as a whole.

His anaesthetist, Major Robert Cope, was thirty-two. Young as they were by the standards of their profession, they had more experience of head surgery than any other operating team on the Allied side.

The patient had been admitted exactly an hour earlier. Since then a blood transfusion had been given and X-ray pictures had been taken of the track of the missile that had penetrated his brain, locating the many bone splinters and metallic fragments that remained. From these X-rays, and from his own clinical appraisal and that of his colleagues, Ascroft had made his estimation of the patient's injuries and planned the operation he would perform.

As anaesthesia was induced by drip pentothal, the patient's last conscious thoughts were inevitably of the events of the precious day, 17 September, 1942. Despite the damage to his brain, his memory of these events, as Ascroft's gentle interrogation had elicited, was extraordinarily clear.

Reg Howard, twenty-seven-year-old Australian rear gunner, of No. 38 Wellington Squadron, Middle East Air Force, had woken up that morning with a premonition. He couldn't think why. On the previous night, 16 September, they had attacked an Axis convoy bringing arms and supplies across the Mediterranean for Rommel – and missed with both the torpedoes. That, for Flying Officer Lloyd Wiggins, Howard's Australian pilot, was a personal affront. That convoy would now be safely in Tobruk harbour. After lunch today they were due to return to the Canal Zone from their advance base at Gianacles, near Alexandra. Howard could sense Wiggins' frustration – but in the light of his premonition he welcomed the break. There would be nothing to fear today.

Howard turned over in his camp bed in his tent on the landing-ground perimeter, swished at the flies that had bothered him since sun-up, and tried to get back to sleep. It was no use, and he reached for a cigarette. Tired after last night's longish flight, he stayed in bed all morning, and it was lunchtime when he heard the reconnaissance Maryland fly over – he recognised the characteristic blurp of the Pratt and Whitney Twin Wasp engines. Soon he learnt that the Maryland crew had brought news of another Axis convoy. They would be held back for a strike tonight after all.

Howard felt his stomach turn over. He quelled the reaction with sham optimism. 'That'll be one more trip in the log book,' he said to his tent companion, Jack Giddy. 'Then I'll have only three more to do.' He had completed 180 operational hours and needed 200 for a rest – perhaps even a return home.

He and Giddy were both wireless-operator/air gunners, and they were both North Coasters, too, from the same part of New South Wales. They had done six operational flights together, then split up, on the principle that this would improve the chances of one of them getting back home to tell the tale. Since then Howard had volunteered to fly with anyone who needed a gunner, to get his ops in quickly. Now he was nine ahead of Giddy.

'You'll get yourself knocked off,' said Giddy.

'I want to get them over.'

This morning Howard would dearly have liked to go sick, but he still had enough self-respect – or too little guts, he wasn't sure which – to do it. He had a basic contempt for those who wouldn't have a go, but he had developed a ready sympathy for those who tried and found themselves wanting. He had had his fair share of minor misdemeanours, pre-war and wartime. In civilian life, when a seaman/steward, he had once stowed away in the wrong ship, and in the Service, 'absent without leave' was the usual charge. He passed no judgements on others and respected those who'd lost their nerve and said so. That took guts too.

Howard knew himself well enough to know that whatever came up for today he would have to go. He sensed he was booked for trouble, but couldn't face the humiliation of backing out. He couldn't talk to anyone about it, not even Giddy. It wasn't a topic for conversation. He was single and his next of kin was his mother, so he sat down and wrote to her.

'I'm going to take a crack,' he told her.

Howard was no hero, and he had a pretty elastic conscience, but some of his early operational flights had left him feeling slightly unsatisfied, even guilty. There were periods when he had seen little action, but the hours had mounted up just the same. That had all changed, though, when he started flying with Lloyd Wiggins. Wiggins, from South Australia, might not be the most skilful pilot on the squadron, but he was a great operational flyer. Howard, secretly fearful of his quiet dedication, had taken to him straight away.

Wiggins was one of those pilots who often seemed to be in need of a spare gunner. Either they got hurt or they went sick. Fair-haired, athletic, a tee-totaller and non-smoker, he was a disciplinarian who would have been shocked if he'd known that Howard got through a packet of twenty ration cigarettes per flight. But Howard, cut off from the rest of the crew in the rear turret, was a chap who knew what he could get away with.

Less than a week earlier, on one of their rare bombing flights, they had blasted the dock installations at Tobruk. Wiggins had begun with a dummy run to absorb the geography, dropped one 1,000-pounder on a second run and then come back and dropped another on a third. 'That's three ops for the price of one,' complained Howard. 'Three chances of getting knocked off.'

'The taxpayer paid for those bombs,' said Wiggins. 'He wants his pound of flesh.'

'Fuck the taxpayer.'

But Howard loved him for it. 'Mad bastard' was what he called him, under his breath; but he wouldn't let him down tonight – or any other night.

When the Maryland crew sighted the convoy it was about a hundred miles from the North African coast, heading for Tobruk, with about 180 miles to cover before it reached port. It was a sizeable convoy, according to the sighting report, of three merchant

Lloyd Wiggins – the 'mad bastard', according to his tail gunner. He was awarded a DSO for sinking Rommel's last tanker. (IWM CH 14576)

A Wellington launches a 'tin-fish' in practice. (IWM CM5036)

The splash as the torpedo enters the water – launched at 60 feet and at 120 knots. (IWM CM5037)

vessels ranging from 3,000 to 8,000 tons and two destroyers. One of the destroyers was a large one – possibly a small cruiser. They were steering south-south-east at about eight knots and they had an air escort of three Junkers 88s. Clearly it was an important convoy, vital to Rommel's hopes of breaking through to Cairo.

Because of their slow speed, which made them far too vulnerable against fighters in daylight, the Wellington crews had developed a technique of dropping their torpedoes at night. When there was a moon, they dropped from the dark side into the moon path. Otherwise they dropped flares for illumination. But first the target had to be re-located, and for this purpose a special squadron of Wellingtons was formed carrying radar. They also carried bombs and flares, providing a useful load.

There would be a moon tonight, and an early take-off was ordered. The crews of the radar Wellingtons, four of them, were briefed to take off soon after six o'clock, at intervals, to allow the sand to settle. Six torpedo Wellingtons, Wiggins and his crew among them, would take off at suitable intervals half an hour later. It would be daylight when they left, but darkness would fall as they flew to the target area, and before they reached it they would be homed on to the convoy by their radar comrades. By then the moon would be up.

Wiggins' aircraft was R for Robert. In these torpedo Wellingtons the front turret had been removed to save weight so that a second torpedo could be carried, and they were denied use of radar for the same reason.

Wiggins' navigator, Ralph Wagstaff, from Stevenage, was the only Englishman on board. Like many a pilot and navigator, the two men were inseparable. They were known as Wiggy and Wags. The second pilot, Lea Croll, was a Canadian. The second gunner – the gunners shared the radio duties – was another Australian, Sammy Thickens.

Howard had been in the turret the previous night and so it was his turn on the radio tonight. But he liked to see what was going on and he much preferred the turret, where he would also have twin Browning machine-guns to hit back. He hated the thought of being confined in the middle of the fuselage tonight, with this premonition hanging over him. Sitting there at the radio, hearing the flak and machine-gun fire tear through the fabric, smelling the cordite, listening to the shouts on the inter-com, and seeing nothing, could be terrifying. His fear was nothing like so great when he could see what was happening.

'Do you mind if I take the turret again, Sammy?'

'It's my turn.' Thickens preferred the turret too.

'I'll do two on the trot for you.'

Two torpedoes being loaded on to a Wellington of 38 Squadron. The front gun turret has been removed to save weight. (Simon Parry)

Thickens argued, but when he realised Howard was set on it he gave way. When they boarded, Howard went back to the turret.

Wiggins took off at 18.50, circled over the vineyard on the airfield perimeter and headed out to sea, flying a north-westerly course until they were out of sight of land. He came down low over the sea to keep under the enemy radar, then turned west, straight into the setting sun, shaping a course for the convoy. The sea was smooth and the sky cloudless, and Howard fired a short, rackety burst from the turret, churning up the blue water so Wagstaff could estimate their drift.

The Wellingtons flew to the target area singly. It was impossible to make a concerted attack at night. After two hours the light began to fail, and Wiggins climbed to 6,000 feet for more economical cruising. They were safe from shore-based fighters now.

It still didn't get completely dark. The sky was brilliantly starlit, and soon the moon would be up.

The four specially equipped Wellingtons, sweeping the surface of the sea with their radar, located the convoy just before ten o'clock. Its composition was unchanged – three merchant ships and two destroyers.

They had reached position 33°.15′ North, 23°.43′ East, on a course of 170 degrees – about a hundred miles from their haven, still aiming for Tobruk. The sighting report was picked up on the radio in the torpedo Wellingtons and they changed course fractionally to intercept.

There was no point in stealth now. Radio silence had been broken, the convoy knew it was being shadowed, and the destroyers began to dispose themselves to protect the merchant ships, anticipating torpedo attack. The radar Wimpeys lurked in the area, keeping out of range.

'There they are!'

Wiggins and Croll were the first men in R for Robert to glimpse the dark shapes on the water. Howard, rotating his turret excitedly, could see nothing until Wiggins turned and began a wide circuit, assessing the picture, biding his time.

'G for George is going in!'

One of the other torpedo planes had reached the target ahead of them, and Thickens, at the radio, heard G for George signal that it was about to attack. He called Wiggins. They couldn't pick out the other Wellington, which was flattened low on the water on the dark side. But they could see the curtain of multi-coloured flak that the destroyers were putting down. That was something they would all have to fly through.

For a brief instant they saw G for George silhouetted against the moon path as it broke away. It looked as though they were getting away with it. A long pause – and suddenly there was a dull red glow on the water.

'It's a hit! It's a hit!'

The glow flickered and went out, but they were certain one of the torpedoes had struck. The vessel had survived for the moment, though, as all three ships were still there.

Meanwhile Wiggins had turned into position for his own drop. 'Hold on to your hats! The big one's ours!'

'You would, you mad bastard,' thought Howard. He had forgotten his premonition, the adrenalin was flowing, and he was enjoying himself. But as he swung the twin Brownings to get the feel of them, and clipped his parachute to his chest for protection – they would be too low to bale out – the sweat was fresh on his brow.

At the radio, Sam Thickens was sending his attack report. 'R for Robert going in.'

Above the convoy, one of the radar Wellingtons began its bombing run. The ships were under attack from above and below.

Picking out the 8,000-ton merchantman, Wiggins dropped down to low level, 60 feet above the glassy water, and manipulated his throttles until his speed was steady at 120 knots. If his height was wrong his torpedoes wouldn't run true. Nor would they function if his speed was too fast.

A recurring weakness with aerial torpedo work was the difficulty of estimating distance over water. 1,000 yards looked horribly close, and many torpedoes were dropped out of range. Wiggins was determined to get in close tonight. The briefing had stressed the importance of the convoy to the land battle, and his own experience the previous night was fresh in his mind. He was sure he had come within the recommended range, yet he had missed with both torpedoes.

Wellingtons aiming torpedoes at night were forced to attack independently, not in formation, for fear of collision. But their ability to carry two torpedoes doubled their threat. If the first torpedo was dropped from 1,000 yards and the second from 800, they formed a bracket which gave a much better chance of getting a hit. As the vessel under attack manoeuvred to avoid the first torpedo, it risked running into the second – which, to further confuse, would actually reach the target first.

It was essential to aim well ahead of the target, to allow for deflection. And as Wiggins settled down on his torpedo run, the zigzagging of the merchant ships, and the desperate efforts of the destroyers to offer them some protection, left him in a perfect position to drop at the 3,000-ton vessel. Since no one else seemed to have attacked it, he maintained his heading.

The curtain of fire had become more desultory as the ships began zigzagging, and Wiggins, coming from the dark side, thought he hadn't been spotted. The target vessel practically filled his windscreen, and the coloured lights were rushing past his shoulders, but he held on.

He must have been inside 800 yards when he dropped his first torpedo. Almost simultaneously, his Wellington was hit. Wiggins was totally blinded as the cockpit, illuminated for an instant by an incandescent light, became flooded with white smoke. An armour-piercing bullet had severed the main electric cable, rendering all systems ineffective. At the same time it had set the signal cartridges alight in the rack behind. The Wellington was on fire.

Because of the cable breakdown the second torpedo wouldn't release. All communications systems were cut off. Wagstaff, Thickens and Croll rushed to extinguish the fire while Wiggins fought to regain control. Still half-blinded, Wiggins' immediate concern was to stay airborne. His carefully planned breakaway to avoid the destroyers had to be abandoned. Howard, looking down from the turret, saw that they were heading for the big destroyer. He was sure it was a cruiser. As they passed over the top it looked the size of a battleship. They were so low he could pick out individual figures manning the guns.

The warship was at last disappearing under the tail of the Wellington when there was an explosion like a great splash of water right outside the turret. For a moment Howard thought they were down. Then fragments of the exploding shell, one of them the size of a cricket ball, struck him with sledgehammer force. The front part of the turret disintegrated, pieces of Perspex beat into his face like rain, one huge piece of shell forced its way through 40 yards of parachute silk before coming to rest against his breastbone. His shoulder was dislocated and his spine bruised, and he slumped to the floor. These, however, were not the worst of his wounds.

Bludgeoned by the impact of the explosion, lying sprawled crazily across the turret floor, Howard was clutching desperately at his skull in an involuntary gesture. It was sheer self-preservation. A piece of jagged metal nearly half an inch in diameter had entered his head through the right eyebrow and passed straight through the frontal lobe of the brain, coming out two inches inside the hairline and tearing a rough-edged hole in the top of his flying helmet. He could feel something oozing through the top of his skull, and the entry wound was leaking a sticky liquid. He supposed it was blood.

Despite these terrible wounds, which he realised instinctively he could hardly recover from, Howard did not lose consciousness for more than a few seconds. When he opened his eyes the coloured lights of the tracer, red and green and yellow, were still streaming past his shattered turret. He tried to extricate himself but the turret was jammed.

The flow of blood from the entry wound in his head terrified him, and he began trying to drink it, thinking confusedly that he was losing too much to survive, that this way he might retain enough to live. He tried to stand up in the shell of his turret, but his legs collapsed and he crashed back to the floor, lying sprawled over the pedals with the night air cooling his wounds and reviving him. His mind was a kaleidoscope of distorted images, sounds and sensations, an accelerated montage, and through it all, weakly and without hope of being heard, he called for help.

Forward in the cockpit, the chaos was not yet resolved. The starboard engine had been hit and was running roughly, there were several other holes from machine-gun fire, and one incendiary bullet had started a fire in Wagstaff's navigation bag. These fires were quickly dealt with, and when the smoke had cleared and the starboard engine had settled down, Wiggins sent Wagstaff back to check on the crew.

To Wagstaff it seemed at first that the turret was intact and that Howard was probably all right. But Lea Croll shone a torch past the 'dead man's handle' – the lever for operating the turret from the fuselage in emergency – and although he was as tough as most men he swayed into a near faint at what he saw: a gory unrecognisable monster drinking his own blood.

Wagstaff and Thickens wound the turret to the fore-and-aft position and between them they got Howard out. Croll went up front to relieve Wiggins, by which time the others had got Howard forward to the bed in the fuselage. His right hand was clamped over his skull in a vice-like grip and their combined efforts failed to move it. They desisted when they saw the white matter, like toothpaste, oozing through.

Howard, a Roman Catholic, had only one thought: he was going to die, and he wasn't in a state of grace. Wiggins gave him two shots of morphine, but he still didn't pass out. He moved his hand briefly while they bandaged his head, but otherwise he kept it clamped there. Sam Thickens gave him a cigarette, and from then on he smoked continually, sucking in the tobacco in great puffs that consumed cigarette after cigarette. In his own rough-and-ready way he made his peace with God and prepared to die.

It was quite a pleasant sensation. The combination of the shock, the pain, the loss of blood, the morphine, and the nicotine, induced a hallucinatory calm. But he never stopped smoking, and he talked for most of the time.

For nearly three hours Howard lay on the bed while Wiggins coaxed the damaged Wellington back to base. Howard's life clearly rested on a thread – none of the crew expected him to last until they landed. No one, they thought, could possibly survive such a frightful head injury. But as they circled Gianacles, with the second torpedo still on board – the only way to dislodge it would have been to throw the aircraft about, and they dare not expose Howard to that – he was still smoking and talking.

Croll plugged the signalling lamp into the 24-amp battery and flashed an SOS. 'Seriously injured man on board.' Wiggins made one of his smoothest landings, and the ambulance was there to meet them.

'Poor bastard – he's had it.'

'That's what you get for volunteering.'

Howard, now apparently unconscious, heard them writing him off.

Treatment of Howard's injuries was altogether beyond the simple M.I.Room and Sick Bay at Gianacles. He would have to go to Cairo, but the M.O. doubted if he would survive the trip.

'Suppose we fly him there?'

'It's a chance.'

Ninety minutes after landing at Gianacles, Wiggins and his crew, taking the least damaged of the machines that had operated that night, were airborne again. Forty-five minutes later they landed at Heliopolis, on the outskirts of Cairo. The duty physician at the RAF Hospital at Heliopolis decided at once to transfer Howard to the Head Centre at the 15th Scottish General, alongside the Nile.

Pushing aside the ragged walls of the missile track with his instruments, Peter Ascroft saw that the shell fragment had passed through the frontal lobe adjacent to the falx – the section of the brain which runs from front to back and separates the two parts. By a

The official squadron report of the incident. (Royal Australian Air Force)

ME.
2527

No. 38 Squadron,
Royal Air Force,
Middle East.

26th September, 1942.

Sir,

Damage to Wellington A/C R.F.862 by enemy action on operations, Night 17th/18th September, 1942.

Crew:-   Captain   AUS.407541 F/O R.L. Wiggins.
         2nd Pilot   R.10452 Sgt Croll. A.
         Observer.   -   F/O Wagstaff, R.E.
         W/Op A.G.   R.402861 Sgt.Howard. R.P.
         W/Op A.G.   R.401255 Sgt.Thickens. S.

    I have the honour to submit a report, further to my signal F.B.A.268 dated 19th September, 1942 on damage done by enemy action to Wellington aircraft HP.862 and a casualty sustained by a member of the crew.

2.   The Captain F/O J.R. Wiggins. R.A.A.F. and a crew of one other officer and three N.C.O.'s were detailed to carry out a torpedo attack on enemy shipping from Gianicles.

3.   The aircraft took off from that landing ground at 18.51 hrs 17.9.42. and a sighting report led the Captain to a position 35° 15 N., 23°39 E where a convoy consisting of two Merchant vessels and three destroyers was found.

4.   An attack was made but when turning away from the drop, a 5" bullet entered the nose of the aircraft, severed the electrical wiring, rendered the W/T equipment unserviceable and ignited a Verey Cartridge in the Navigator's Cabin. The pilot was completely blinded by the resulting smoke but turned away and heavy A.A. fire from the target vessel and escorting destroyers was encountered.

5.   The Rear Gunner No. A.402861 Sgt Howard, was badly wounded in the head.

6.   Without I.F.F. and W/T it was decided to set course for Gianacles rather than Heliopolis, where a safe landing was made.

Distribution:-
B.P.S.O. (4 copies)
H.Q.R.A.F. M.E.
301 Group Advance 248 Wing

I have the honour to be,
    Sir,
Your obedient Servant,
    Sgd. ? Wing Commander, Commanding,
               No. 38 Squadron. R.A.F.

miracle the falx itself was unpunctured. The tract through the frontal lobe was about a centimetre wide. Working up to five centimetres into the brain, Ascroft removed numerous bone and metallic fragments from the area near the track of the missile. There was still a lot of bleeding from the blood vessels in the brain, and this Ascroft stemmed by the use of silver clips and by heat coagulation. Some troublesome bleeding of a branch of the front cerebral artery was also controlled with a clip. All this was done with surprising speed. He inserted antibiotics into the track leading through the brain, then drew the exit wound together with some difficulty and closed and stitched it.

Howard's other injuries were then dealt with temporarily. After the operation his pulse was rapid but of fair volume and his condition was not unhopeful when he was returned to the ward.

An hour later, when Ascroft made his first post-operative examination, Howard was still unconscious, and he did not respond when Ascroft shouted his name. Ascroft feared some degree of paralysis. The pulse was tending to rise, which was a bad sign.

By nine o'clock the following morning Howard seemed to be responding, but many of his reflexes were still absent. He was dangerously ill, that was all too apparent, and by eleven o'clock he was less responsive. He did not react at all to a pin-prick and his pupils were dilated, which suggested fresh bleeding in the head, causing brain compression. He could not keep his eyes open and he made no response to requests other than feeble movements of the lips.

'I'm afraid he's had it. It won't be long now.' That was one of the opinions expressed at Howard's bedside. Unconscious though he was, the words penetrated. He struggled to prove them wrong.

All day he was anxiously watched. The crisis had come.

At four o'clock that afternoon he spoke and asked for water. Slight as such an action might seem, it betokened a dramatic improvement. Next morning, forty-eight hours after the operation, to the great delight of Ascroft and Cope and the surgical team, he got out of bed to wash.

Reg Howard remained on the 'Dangerously Ill' list for a fortnight, then 'Seriously Ill' for some time: he was on a long road to a recovery that could never be quite complete. The 'motor' areas of his brain were undamaged and he escaped any form of paralysis, but memory and temperament were subtly affected. He was classed as permanently medically unfit for further service, unsuited to occupations requiring concentration and excessive noise or stress, guaranteeing him a pension. But over the years a recurring restlessness and instability complicated his life. His memory, more than anything, let him down – but not his memory of that night in the Wellington turret or the hours that followed. As though etched by the passage of the shell fragment, that remained vividly clear.

By his instinctive protective action Howard contributed decisively to his escape. 'If you hadn't held your brains in as you did,' said Ascroft afterwards, 'we'd never have been able to save you.'

Howard lived on, despite handicaps that he learned to live with, for another fifty-eight years; the Department of Veterans' Affairs in Canberra giving his date of death as 11 July, 2000. He was in his eighty-sixth year. He would have stood less chance of a protracted survival today than he did all those years ago, in the hands of that overworked surgical team. Their experience of battle casualties was unique.

The convoy the Wellingtons attacked was certainly damaged, but reconnaissance next day seemed to indicate that all three merchant ships had somehow limped into harbour. The work of these and other anti-shipping squadrons, however, was to prove fatal to Rommel's hopes, and the *coup de grace* came five weeks later, aptly enough off Tobruk, at the hands of Wiggy and Wags.

Howard of course was not present when, on 26 October, three torpedo Wellingtons of 38 Squadron were briefed, at their advance base at Gianacles, for an attack on a tanker. Rommel was still desperately short of oil, this raid came right in the middle of the Alamein battle, and three tankers, two small and one large, had been assembled and had left Crete, bound for Tobruk. The Germans were making a last-ditch effort to save the Afrika Korps. The two smaller ones had already been sunk by bombing,

Professor Peter Ascroft, RAMC. The brain surgeon who used his brains to escape from besieged Tobruk and later saved Reg Howard. (U.C.L. Hospitals NHS Trust Archives)

but the big one had got through, anyway to within sight of Tobruk. That too would be heavily bombed as soon as night fell, so it had not yet put into harbour. A dusk attack by torpedo Wellingtons was chosen to surprise them.

During the day a fourth Wellington was sent up from Suez to join them – piloted by Flying Officer John Stancomb – but it missed the trip. Stancomb was prepared for the normal night take-off, but on arrival he was told: 'You're too late! They took off half-an hour ago!' Stancomb's disappointment was tempered by what he heard had been said at the briefing. 'This tanker is so important that it doesn't matter if not one of you gets back!' He could imagine how well that would have gone down. He decided he could live with the frustration. It was his twenty-first birthday.

Anyway Wiggins led the attack through a stiff barrage from shore batteries and a fierce but belated reaction from the crews of the escorting destroyers. The ship's crews were caught napping at last light and were actually hanging out their washing on the decks as the Wellingtons, at 60 feet and 120 knots, sped between them. The strike was brilliantly successful and all six torpedoes hit the tanker. Rommel himself is said to have witnessed the carnage from the cliffs above Tobruk, watching the final extinction of his hopes, while Monty himself was so thrilled that he sent his deputy, Air Marshal Tedder, to present the leading pilot, Lloyd Wiggins, with the DSO and his navigator, Ralph Wagstaff, with the DFC. They were told they had shortened the war by three weeks, and perhaps by very much more. Rommel, minus the oil, was forced to retreat.

And Peter Ascroft? As Professor P.B.Ascroft he held the chair of surgery at the Middlesex Hospital for five years after the war. But his wartime experiences, although they gave him unparalleled opportunities, had left their mark. In 1952 he resigned from the chair at the Middlesex through ill-health, and he died in 1965.

His greatest moment, perhaps, came at the time of El Alamein when, working on penetrating head injuries only, he and his team worked for thirty-three hours without rest, operating, as always, on friend and foe alike.

Ascroft's colleagues all speak of his hatred of war, yet it was the war that brought his greatest fulfilment. For his anaesthetist, Professor Robert Cope, to whom I am hugely indebted for the medical details of this account, the same applies.

'Occasionally, in wartime,' said Bob Cope, 'a doctor's life is blessed with incidents where a degree of recovery is achieved that seems almost miraculous, especially when the patient is young'.

'That was the great joy of war surgery.'

How Bill Stannard Swapped a Seat on a London Bus for a Chariot of Fire – May 1943

The aim of the German fighter pilots was deadly. As Bill Stannard, tail gunner in a Lockheed Ventura bomber of No.457 (NZ) Squadron, moved forward to pull his wounded co-gunner clear of the mid-upper turret, his grasp closed around limbs that would never move again of their own volition.

George Sparkes, a fellow Cockney – a diminutive five foot three – was dead.

Stannard called his pilot, Stan Coshall, on the inter-com, his voice hoarse and attenuated. 'Hello Cosh. George has had it. Are you all right up front?'

There was no reply, and he began to make his way forward. Then he saw that between him and the cockpit the whole of the radio cabin – the area he had recently abandoned when the shooting started, to man the tail guns – was ablaze. He had no way through to the cockpit. He was completely cut off. There was only one more thing to be done. Get out as soon as he could.

His exit door was just forward of the mid-upper turret on the port side. His parachute was stowed by that door. But as he stepped forward to get it, the flames mirrored his movement, advancing menacingly towards him. He was looking straight into the luminous heat of a furnace. Tantalisingly, he could see his parachute safely in its stowage, clear of the fire. Sparkes's parachute was there too, so in effect he had the choice of two. But as the heat drove him back he had no chance to reach either.

He had to quieten that fire, and he looked round despairingly for a fire extinguisher. There wasn't one this far aft. Christ, he thought, I've had it this time.

Stannard's plane was one of twelve that had been on their way to bomb a power station at Nazi-occupied Amsterdam, on a low-level daylight strike. Their role was to create a diversion, to provide some support for a squadron of Douglas Bostons that were to attack the main target, the Royal Dutch Steel Works at Ijmuiden, on the coast north of Haarlem. Leading the Venturas was Squadron Leader (NZ) Leonard Trent, with Flight Lieutenant Arthur Duffill as his deputy. For those looking ahead to D-Day, the steel works was an important fringe target, and this was to be a major 2 Group effort, with strong fighter protection.

Similar attacks had been attempted the previous day by colleagues, but success had been modest. Headquarters, after hours of indecision, had resolved to try again. The result, for the air crews, had been a day of uncertainty.

The crews had been briefed early that morning for a raid on the docks at Flushing, They had been about to clamber into their machines when they were called back. An alternative target was mooted, then that too was scrubbed. Finally, soon after midday, the crews were brought back for an early lunch and a fresh briefing. This time they were told of the diversionary attack on the power station. They were also given news that it was hoped would be a morale-booster. 'The raid is also intended as encouragement for the Dutch Resistance. Dutch workers have been organising labour strikes, in defiance of the Nazis.' The crews made of all this what they could.

The majority of the Ventura crews were New Zealanders, but there had been continual dilution due to casualties and some all-British crews had been substituted. These were mostly typical of wartime aircrew volunteers. Stan Coshall, Stannard's pilot, had been a librarian at the Bodlean.

What of their aircraft? The twin-engined Ventura, slow, clumsy and elephantine, was based, like the Lockheed Hudson, on a pre-war airliner. It was known to be totally unsuited to daylight operations over enemy territory, hence they'd been given a powerful escort.

At Methwold, in Suffolk, where Stannard's squadron, 457, had recently moved from Feltwell (another 2 Group base), the crews dubbed their bulging, obese machines 'Flying Pigs'.

Stannard voiced the general feeling of apprehension. 'I don't like this. I don't fancy this at all.'

Stannard had really wanted to join the Navy, but they weren't taking people 'only for the duration'. He had lost his father in the Navy, killed in the Battle of Jutland, but he wasn't prepared to sign for five or seven year terms. He had a job to go back to. Apprenticed to W.H. Smith and Sons at their printing works in Stamford Street, he had spent several years doing casual work on different newspapers before getting a permanent job with the *Daily Telegraph* in 1936. He didn't think the war would last five years, let alone seven, and he hoped to be back in Fleet Street long before then.

At the age of nineteen he had begun to take flying lessons at the Brooklands Flying School, but he couldn't afford to keep them up. Now, at twenty-nine, those days seemed a life-time ago. Recently, visiting a friend in Eltham, Kent, travelling on the top of a No.21 bus, he happened to pass a big pub called *The Yorkshire Grey*. Alongside it was a dance hall, which had been taken over as an RAF recruiting and medical centre. On impulse he got off the bus and went in. 'How old are you?' was their first question.

'I'm twenty-nine now. I'll be thirty in two or three months' time.'

'You're a bit old, aren't you?'

'I don't think so.'

'Why do you want to join the Air Force?'

'I did have some flying lessons, ten years ago.'

'What do you want to be?'

'A pilot. I want to fly. I'm not going to walk to war if I can ride.'

The squadron-leader bloke, as Stannard called him afterwards, had a twinkle in his eye. But he told the recruit what he was up against. 'The limit for recruiting pilots is twenty-six, twenty-eight for others – navigators, wireless operators and air gunners.' But he hinted that these limits were not entirely rigid. At twenty-nine he might get in as an air gunner. 'Are you willing to try for that?'

'Yes.'

'Do you know anything about radio?'

He did. Radio and electrics had always interested him. 'OK. Go through there and have a medical.'

Two months later he began radio training, first at Blackpool, then at Yatesbury, on Salisbury Plain. Then, arriving at an operational training unit at RAF Upwood with a bunch of trainees, he and the others sorted themselves out into crews. That was when he joined Stan, Rupert, and George.

It had been late on a perfect Spring afternoon – 16.44, 3 May 1943 – when the thirty-three-year-old Leonard Trent led the first Venturas off the Methwold runway. Already it had been a long day and, almost at once, one crew reported a lost escape hatch and were forced to abort.

Ahead of the Venturas there had been an error in timing. A formation of Allied fighters – there would be arguments about whose they were – had appeared over Flushing thirty minutes earlier than intended.

Bill Stannard and crew. Rupert North (centre) and Stan Coshall (right).
(G.J.Zwanenberg)

Venturas of No. 487 Squadron – 'The Flying Pigs'. (Bowyer)

Alerted by their appearance, four formations of German fighters, some 60 or 70 strong, two formations, of FW190s to deal with the Spitfires and two formations of Bf 109s to attend to the bombers, were assembling. Oblivious to the ambush, Trent and the Venturas pressed on.

Their plan had been to fly for the first thirty-three minutes at low level, with the intention of delaying detection. With an escort of nine squadrons of Spitfires and North American Mustangs, they were then to climb to their bombing height. But the timing error had been calamitous.

The first swarm of German fighters flew directly over the top of the bomber formation, then dived into the attack, firing at the Spitfires as they came. As they flashed past the Spits they carried on in the dive and came up under the Venturas.

Spitfire Vs were the only mark slow enough to escort Venturas, and they could cope with the 109s, but they were no match for the 190s. As the British pilots strove to head off their German counterparts, the Ventura crews found themselves stranded.

'There's a Jerry coming in from the port side! It's a 190!' The call came from Sparkes in the mid-upper turret.

'There's another coming up from underneath!' This was from Stannard, training his guns from his sub-astral view below the fuselage.

Ordering the formation to close up, Trent carried on doggedly. Wearing a steel helmet over his leather one, as was his practice, learnt in the early days flying Fairy Battles in France, he was better protected than most. But what followed, for the whole formation, Trent included, was a short, desperate struggle, then annihilation.

In Stannard's plane the navigator, Rupert North, a bank clerk from Penrith, moved aft from his bomb-aiming post in the nose to join Coshall in the cockpit directly the plane was hit. Stannard, peering through the erupting flames, could just make out North's compact figure standing next to Coshall. North's instinct was the same as Stannard's, to find a fire extinguisher to control the fire, and he went to grab one from the rear of the cockpit.

Both the men in the front were cut off, like Stannard, from the exit door. But pilot and bomb-aimer had an emergency escape route. They could jettison the cockpit hood and climb out through there. Now, as North moved towards the fire extinguisher, he saw Coshall reach above his head to release the hatch. When the hatch flew off it sucked the flames with it. It was North, facing aft, hand outstretched towards the extinguisher, who took the initial blast. He had kept his helmet on, also his gloves, but he was badly burned in the face and wrists and his battledress was alight. Fortunately his parachute pack, which was lying on the seat beside Coshall, was masked by his body.

The otherwise methodical North had no time to clip on his parachute. Grabbing it by the canvas handle, he stepped up on the seat and was instantly propelled by the firestorm straight through the roof. Stannard heard the thump as North's body collided with the cupola of the mid-upper turret. But North kept a grip on his pack.

The draught that swept the fire forward had two significant effects. For one man, librarian Stan Coshall, it spelt immediate and fatal asphyxiation. For the other, Bill Stannard, it spelt a respite, even the possibility of survival. His parachute pack might now be within reach.

The heat from the flames still forced him to cover his face with his gloved hands but he was able to move cautiously forward. In the gaps between his spread fingers he could see his pack, still in its stowage, already charred but not actually on fire. He grabbed at it as at a lifeline. He tried to keep one hand free to protect his face, but he would need both hands to fasten the clips to his harness and open the door. As he fumbled blindly, some involuntary change in the aircraft's attitude reversed the tide of the firestorm, sending it roaring back with voracious appetite down the tunnel towards him.

Forced to retreat from the exit door, still without his parachute, he was driven to seek a dubious shelter aft in the tapering cone of the tail. Somehow he would have to kick an escape route in the Perspex bowl of the tail before the flames engulfed him. But as he moved further aft, he saw his parachute pack burst open, spilling the folds of silk in singed bundles around him. Bending down to scoop up the crenellations, he was swamped by a blast of heat of such intensity that he abandoned the billowing silk and fled past the vertical elastic ropes that supported his guns into the farthest recesses of the tail.

He had only another few seconds, perhaps half a minute, before the fire would devour him. If only the plane would crash before that happened. But it still seemed to be flying strongly. He didn't care about dying. It was the thought of being burnt alive that he shrank from. Crouching with his back to the starboard side, feet pressed against the port side, he kicked frantically at the metal panel opposite.

'Come on, damn you!'

The metal structure proved unyielding, and he could no longer reach the Perspex panels. He was doomed to die in the fire.

The fuselage itself was burning now. Rivulets of molten metal were trickling down the inside shell, as though some unseen hand were running a blow-torch round outside. Droplets were falling on the butts of his guns like solder. The process of liquefaction so fascinated him that he almost forgot his own imminent cremation. He was almost being cremated already.

Suddenly everything went black, then coruscated into a bewildering, starry canopy. This was it all right. Then a flicker of consciousness returned. Dimly he realised there had been an explosion. Stunned and deafened, he found himself squinting into a powerful, all-pervading light. It was a moment before he recognised what it was. Blue sky and bright sunshine. The whole of the Ventura forward of his gun position had broken away at the point where the metal had melted and was diving away from him to the left, trailing an immense torch of flame.

He was perched precariously in an aerial bubble – the severed tail unit. There was about ten feet of it in all, and he himself was sitting scarcely more than a step from a drop of many thousands of feet. Yet such was the apparent stability of his new conveyance that he felt no trace of vertigo. All he cared about was that the flames that had been about to engulf him had gone.

Relief at this timely miracle transcended all other emotions, surging through his veins like an elixir, while the cool, rarefied air soothed like a balm. He was still going to die, nothing could alter that, but death was something commonplace and he had no fear of that. His mood was one of exaltation: nothing else mattered except that he wouldn't now be roasted alive. Sooner or later this strange remnant of an aeroplane would hit the ground and that would be it. It was a fate that had always been on the cards ever since he joined up. But he had no regrets. He had wanted the Navy – he had been six years old when his father was killed – but in those early days of the war they would take him only as a regular. And he had really enjoyed flying with Stan, Rupert and George.

He had done twenty-two trips with them when they were sent on leave. These were the times when you wondered how long it could last. 'I've got a premonition,' he told his Fleet Street colleagues, 'that I won't be back.'

'You'll be back all right.' But he had known.

It hadn't worried him. Everyone stuck his neck out once too often at this game. He had accepted it with Cockney fatalism. Yet he still felt elated at his escape. He began to take note of his situation. He was comfortably wedged in an egg-shell cavity, and the tail-plane, with its twin rudder fins at either extremity, was keeping his chariot stable. He could feel no movement at all, no sense of falling, and his overriding impression was of an ethereal peace and tranquillity, spiritual in its serenity. Compared with the tortures of hell he had suffered a few moments ago, it was unbelievably merciful.

The horror of those moments still paralysed his mind, blunting his senses and inducing a petrified calm. But he could hear the soughing of the airstream around and above him, gentle as a zephyr, and see that the vehicle in which he was poised so grotesquely was slowly revolving, like some aerial lighthouse, illuminating each point of the compass in turn.

Suddenly he glimpsed the sea, with the flat Dutch coastline running north and south, straight as a rule. He was only four or five miles inland, and he wondered if he might drift out to sea. He reckoned that he must still be about 5,000 feet up. Then the flat fields of Holland filled his horizon, again as though on a turn-table. If he came down on land, at least someone would find him. Then they would know what had happened.

Thoughts of his past life intruded but little. His only concern was for his mother.

They had always been close. She had brought up five children on a war widow's pension, three of them girls, the youngest born six days after Jutland. Once he had felt bitter about it. Then the second war came, and here he was.

Now, with the tail fins still acting as stabilisers, the truncated tail-piece was falling like a sycamore leaf, sometimes haphazard and erratic, but mostly in a flat lazy curve that revealed no hint of acceleration until the ground drew near. Eventually he found he could focus on landscape detail, picking out canals and rivers, then dykes, villages and farms. His chariot had given the illusion of floating, independent of gravity, yet he had known that this could not last.

Because he was looking into the distance and not straight down, he did not realise that the ground was coming up to meet him apace, that the fatal collision could be only seconds away. He was still squatting there comfortably in his makeshift eyrie, arms folded, legs crossed at the ankles, when oblivion came.

The tailplane had come down in the parkland of a sizeable mansion at Bennebrook, five miles south of Haarlem, four miles inland. In the middle distance a long column of smoke marked the spot where the bulk of the Ventura had gone in. The gardener at Huize Bennebrook had seen the mid-air explosion and watched the two sections come down. So too had the villagers of Bennebroek. To them the tail seemed certain to hit the house. It actually crashed into the tops of a group of tall trees that sheltered a wall. As it hit the trees it kept its flat trajectory till the end.

The watchers' attention had been riveted on the tail section as it rotated gently, losing height in a sort of slow motion – or so, for a long time it seemed – until at last its true speed of descent became dramatically apparent. Then came collision with the tree-tops.

The battle that had raged overhead had moved on and the gardener hurried across to investigate. So did two of the villagers. They saw someone staggering out of the tail, terribly burned and covered in blood. He seemed to be calling to someone. 'Cosh – Rupert – Where are you?' Totally disorientated, unable to grasp where he was, he was out on his feet.

When the tail unit hit the tree-tops Stannard was thrown from his hide-out, leaving him totally vulnerable to the forces of gravity. But the elastic suspension cords that supported his guns had twisted round his neck and were choking him. He fought to tear himself loose – and remembered no more. In fact, when the wreckage fell through the branches to the ground, he was suspended briefly by the gun-cords and was lowered gently before being thrown clear. He knew nothing for the next few minutes.

He was still barely conscious when the two villagers, anxious to help, accosted him with words of reassurance. 'I am a friend of you,' said one: but neither they nor Stannard could make themselves understood, and with the village mayor a known collaborator, and German soldiers swiftly commandeering the wreck, Stannard was taken into the house. When his brain cleared he was sitting in the drawing-room of Huize Bennenbrook and a doctor was bandaging his hand. From the wrist down, all the flesh had come away and he gazed with strange detachment at the tendons.

He had been wounded – without realising it – in both legs and the forehead, either in the dogfight or by exploding ammunition during the fire, and he was badly burned in the face. But he was alive.

An elderly woman was leaning over him. It was Miss Willink van Bennebrook, owner of the house. 'Would you like a glass of wine?'

'Thanks very much.'

It was then that he began to take in his surroundings. Also in the room was a slightly stouter woman who turned out to be the housekeeper, and a man in a bowler hat. Even in his confused state this struck him as incongruous. The man had all Stannard's escape kit spread out on the floor. From the attitude of his host he soon gauged who it was. The bowler hat must have been a figment of his imagination. It was the Gestapo.

There was no chance of escape, and in any case he knew he was booked for a long stay in hospital. Later that day he met up with Rupert North and learned how North had parachuted into a field of tulips in full view of a German patrol. He too had been terribly burned, far worse than Stannard, and after interrogation he was wheeled into a hospital in Amsterdam with wounded Germans for company and smeared in grease and encased in bandages, earning the playful nickname in the ward of 'the mummy'. But his interrogation persisted, and he was accused of being a spy. Under some provocation he stuck to number, rank and name, and he heard a German in an adjacent bed say, in an approving voice, something like 'moral ist gut'. Eventually they were moved to a hospital in Frankfurt.

It was exactly two years before Stannard and North were repatriated at the end of the war. Meanwhile, much of the story of what happened that day to their comrades had filtered through to them in prisoner-of-war camp. First the deputy leader, Arthur Duffill, with both engines on fire and two crew wounded, was forced to turn back. He only escaped because the *Luftwaffe* pilots thought he was finished. Two others who were following him were quickly shot down. Twisting and turning, but sticking to their bombing run, three more were shot out of the sky, then another two. That left Trent and two others. Trent had dropped his bombs and shot down one of his attackers when he suddenly realised he was alone: his was the last of the Venturas still flying. Next moment an explosion blasted the controls out of his hands and he was shouting at his crew to jump. Only he and his navigator survived.

For 487 (NZ) Squadron, this was its blackest day. The Spitfires had taken out three of the German fighters, but they lost two themselves, including the Canadian ace Wing Commander H.P. 'Cowboy' Blatchford, who had stuck to the Venturas to the bitter end, but failed to make it back across the Channel. At one point, foreseeing disaster, he had tried to turn the Venturas back, but his R/T calls were not heard.

What did their sacrifice achieve? The Bostons got through to the target more or less unscathed, losing only one, and bursts were seen on the steel works, but the cost had been too great: an entire Ventura squadron annihilated, and of the 44 crew-men, only a handful survived. 'Everybody is dazed by the news,' said the squadron record. 'A better set of boys could not be met in 30 years.' Five weeks later came better tidings: the Venturas were to be replaced by Mosquitoes. 'Good-bye,' said the record, 'to the Pigs'.

Traumatic as it was for the air crews, the effect of such losses on the ground crews could also be devastating. One young newly-trained armourer, who had been at Methwold only a short time when the raid took place, wrote to say that he never got over it. 'I can remember the anguish we all felt when we knew so many of our crews were lost. It was the first time I had felt personally affected by the war, and although in the forthcoming years I lost other friends, I never felt quite the same again.'

In Stalag Luft III, Leonard Trent later took part in the Great Escape – but was discovered early on and brought back into custody. The recapture saved his life. 50 of the 76 who escaped were later murdered on Hitler's orders.

When the full story of that disastrous raid was told, Trent was awarded the Victoria Cross. There were no medals for Bill Stannard, and there was no one to corroborate his story anyway – or so he thought. But fifteen years later, in 1958, he received unexpected corroboration of his incredible survival from a Dutchman, A.H.Vermeulen, one of the two villagers who had actually witnessed Stannard's final sycamore-leaf descent and had spoken to him and tried to help ('I am your friend!'). Stannard, in a semi-conscious state, had not been properly aware of it at the time. 'Who shall not remember the 3rd May 1943?' wrote Vermeulen. 'Certainly you do, and so do I.'

'Let me explain.

'I was on leave for three days (I was a male nurse) when we were warned that there would be an air battle between English bombers and German Focke-Wulf fighters.

'The sound in the distance was like thunder and became stronger and stronger and after ten or fifteen minutes we could see the approaching bombers and fighters about 15,000 to 20,000 feet high. Then suddenly there was smoke, then flames pouring out of the fuselages of several aircraft, and especially one right above our heads still burning......then an explosion, burning pieces falling, smoke and.....one single piece, the tail of that aircraft rotating in the air length-ways, slowly losing altitude; down, down, lower and lower and then.....a soft smash in the tree-tops, and silence......

'I have seen this stressful explosion, the down-coming tail-end of the aircraft, the burning and exploding airplanes, in my memory for over fifteen years.'

After all that time he'd been shocked and amazed 'to read an article in the Dutch magazine *De Spiegel* by a contributor, to see *your* picture, because I saw and met you only a short time after your unbelievable landing in the trees behind the house named 'Huize Bennebroek'.

'I recognised you instantly and remembered your face as well as all the facts as though it happened yesterday. You were never out of my mind and several times I said to my wife after the war was over: "Now, how to contact that pilot? Is he living or did he die in Germany?" (Stannard was not of course the pilot.) But seeing the story by Mr Vandermeer, written in memory of the RAF heroes in that air battle above the Haarlemermeer and Bennebroek, gave me

Leonard Trent, VC. (Bowyer)

the opportunity to contact you and reveal that I was the man who said to you in broken English: "I am friend of you!" But I could not understand you then, and I could not express myself as I can nowadays. (Vermeulen had since emigrated to Canada, but had kept on receiving Dutch magazines.) Another reason was that the Huns were too soon on the scene to hide you anyway.

'After we helped you, we tried to get a glimpse of what was going on over by the wrecked plane – but the Germans drove us away.'

Vermeulen's letter to Stannard, inspired by the story with pictures in a Dutch magazine, concluded in a short, devout summary which Stannard was unlikely to challenge. 'You prayed to the Lord for a miraculous rescue. And I'm thankful you were saved.....and I guess you are too.....'

The chance that someone had actually seen and watched that tortuous, convoluted, death-defying descent from the heavens gave Stannard a grim satisfaction. He had floated down near Huize Bennebroek from nowhere, and now, from nowhere, as it seemed – at least from Ontario, Canada – had come this undisputed affirmation. He had scarcely talked about it before, but he could now.

Meanwhile Bill Stannard had returned to his old job in his beloved Fleet Street, to marry, and to raise a family. When I tracked him down in 1978, through the *Daily Telegraph*, he had recently retired and was living in South Croydon. He died never regretting, despite all the traumas, that impulse on the top of a London bus.

CHAPTER 7

Canadian Gunners Andy Mynarski and Pat Brophy – A Reversal of Fates, June 1944

'Would you like to be my flight engineer?'

Neither of the two men named in the title above, fellow air gunners on a Canadian Lancaster squadron, were concerned in this question, or the answer. The questioner was a lanky, six foot three flying officer pilot, distinguished by prominent ears and a North American drawl. His question was aimed at a stocky, flaxen-haired, square-jawed, non-commissioned English flight engineer, a railway apprentice in peacetime, from Guildford, Surrey, who was quickly warming to the ways of the Canucks. Physically, though, they were very much the long and the short of it. Addressed thus by an officer, the more formal Englishman banged his right boot into the concrete floor of the hangar so that it echoed, and simultaneously, to use his own vernacular, 'threw him one up'.

The pilot's arm shot forward, not up, and the salute passed without other acknowledgement. 'Shake hands!' said the pilot. 'My name's Art. We don't bother much about saluting in this air force.'

Flying Officer Art de Breyne came from St Lambert, a suburb of Montreal: he was the son of a gardener from Belgium. Like many other Quebec Canadians he was bi-lingual. And like all Canadians who had crossed the Atlantic for the war, he was a volunteer. His manner encouraged the young engineer to speak up.

'My name's Vigars – Roy Vigars.'

'How old are you?' De Breyne himself was only twenty-three, but he sensed the extreme youthfulness of his new crew-member.

'Nineteen. I'll be twenty tomorrow.'

'Great! That means a party!'

While they were talking, Vigars had become apprehensively aware of two other Canadians careering round the hangar on bicycles. More than once he had thought they must crash into him. 'See those two silly buggers!' said de Breyne. 'They're our two gunners, one tail, one mid-upper. They're mad – but we've just got to put up with them!' He introduced them as Pat Brophy, the Tail-end Charlie, a feisty kid from Port Arthur, Ontario, and Ken Branston, in the mid-upper turret, a Toronto boy. 'Come over here and meet Roy. He's going to be our new flight engineer.'

Like most Canadian bomber crews arriving in England, de Breyne's had been at full strength apart from the job of flight engineer. Completing their training as a crew on twin-engined aircraft, they had been posted to Dishforth in Yorkshire for conversion to four-engined bombers. It was for the heavy bombers, the Halifax and the Lancaster, that the trade of flight engineer was introduced. With no facilities for engineer training in Canada, Canadian crews picked up a British flight engineer on arrival at their HCU – Heavy Conversion Unit – in England.

Vigars adjusted quickly enough to an environment that was not so strange as at first appeared. Pat Brophy and Ken Branston, the gunners, certainly had their moments, with Pat sometimes, but not always, keeping the rumbustious Branston in check. The oldest man in the crew was the navigator, Bob Bodie, and he, motivated by the tourist bug, spent most of his spare time exploring places of interest within range of Dishforth.

Youngest of the crew, younger even than Vigars, and the only one married (to Leona, back in Winnipeg) – was the wireless operator, Jim Kelly, a boisterous character much given to impersonations and impressions. The bomb-aimer, Jack Friday, was a kindred spirit, and he and Kelly, with Brophy and Branston, formed a quartet who spent spare time and periods of leave together and, in Friday's words, 'were of different personality from the rest of the crew, who were attracted to other and less mischievous activities.' The mischievous activities included high jinks when on leave in London, where Brophy, after spending too long in their favourite Chandos Dive Bar, finished up in the local police station. Kelly, endowed with a sixth sense, was a barometer of crew morale: he always seemed to know when flying was going to be scrubbed. In summary, a normally colourful Canadian crew.

With the inclusion of Vigars, crew composition seemed to be finally settled. But the two acrobatic cyclists, Brophy and Branston, in their fondness for horseplay, were always exposing themselves to the risk of injury. Although the best of pals, one of their antics ended, for Branston, in a broken jaw. He loyally blamed the injury on a fracas with an unnamed third party in a local pub, but hospitalisation resulted. He would be out for at least two months.

De Breyne had to find a replacement. His search was to start, quite involuntarily, a sequence of events that was to write a new chapter in the record of achievement and sacrifice.

The man he selected was of Polish extraction, named Andy Mynarski. He was of film-star good looks, more mature than most, aged twenty-seven and engaged to a girl – Victoria Safian – back in Winnipeg. 'Quiet until he got to know you,' said Victoria. 'Then he was a lot of fun.' He had always formed friendships, and his sociable nature soon endeared him to his colleagues. 'You could always depend on Andy to come through with a joke when the going got rough,' said wireless operator Jim Kelly. 'He was a quiet chap, but he and our more exuberant tail gunner Pat Brophy made a perfect team. They soon became great chums.'

Once they started on operations, the natural comradeship that had developed between the first pair of gunners, Brophy and Branson, transferred with redoubled intensity to the second. The night the impetuous Brophy finished up in the clink on leave, it was Mynarski, ignoring those who hoped it might teach him a lesson, who bailed him out.

Their mutual regard was understandable. In mid-upper and tail turrets respectively, they were isolated from the rest of the crew, who were more or less grouped centrally. In his letters home, Mynarski often referred to this attachment. It was a friendship that was to become historic.

Mynarski was a first generation Canadian. His mother spoke very

Pat Brophy. (Bowyer)

Andy Mynarski as a cadet in Canada.
(Bowyer)

little English and he himself spoke it with a strong Polish accent. The second eldest of six children, he had left school at sixteen when his father died, to work as a chamois cutter in the fur trade, to help bolster the family income. He quickly proved an instinctive craftsman. Quietly spoken, with a dry sense of humour, and always, according to his assessments, 'willing and eager', he brought an unobtrusive steadfastness into the crew.

Although he had done no operational flying himself, Mynarski had already lost two pilots before being crewed up with de Breyne. On arrival on a squadron, new pilots did one or more trips with an experienced crew as second pilot for familiarisation before being passed ready to fly with their own crew as first pilot and captain. Twice Mynarski lost his pilot on one of these introductory trips, and twice he was sent back to HCU for re-crewing. When introduced there to de Breyne, he simply hoped it would be third time lucky – but he was taking no chances. 'I'm unpacking only my pyjamas and shaving gear this time,' he told Vigars when they got to Middleton St George, their new Durham base. 'I've unpacked everything twice before, and I only had to pack it all up again. I'm not doing it a third time.'

Mynarski did have one weakness – a phobia about the rear turret. He would never sit in it, not even on non-operational flights. There was no nose turret in these Lancasters, giving a bonus on speed, and Mynarski, with Pat Brophy's (and the pilot's) blessing, always occupied the mid-upper, half way along the fuselage. That was lonely enough, but the claustrophobic isolation of the tail turret, incarcerated behind those closed turret doors, was something he could not stomach. Alone in that revolving and uncertain platform, he lost orientation and panicked. The mid-upper was different, a part of the plane's bosom, and offering mobility. 'Back there,' Mynarski would say, 'I'd feel cut off from the whole world.' This increased his admiration for Pat Brophy, and cemented their friendship.

Brophy was commissioned, Mynarski was not, so their ranks often kept them apart. They fed in different messes and roomed in different quarters. But it made no difference to their friendship. It did, however, have one development that contradicted that half-jocular remark made by de Breyne when he first shook hands with Vigars. After a mission, or perhaps after sharing a night on the town, Brophy would clap Mynarski on the back in informal farewell, rank forgotten. At this, Mynarski would stiffen perceptibly and throw Brophy a salute. Slightly exaggerated perhaps; but his 'Good-night, *sir*,' (it was always Pat otherwise), had a hint of respect as well as mockery. Something in his Polish and Service background demanded this rare concession to formality.

Art de Breyne returned safely from his introductory sortie, Mynarsky unpacked, and after one raid in a Halifax they converted to Canadian-built Lancasters of the famous 419 (Moose) Squadron and began operating in them on 1 May 1944.

These were the weeks of the run-up to D-Day, when the bomber offensive was switched to a planned programme of raids on rail repair centres and marshalling yards in France and Belgium, the object being to spread havoc amongst the transport system and paralyse the German reaction to the Allied invasion. The obvious danger that casualties on the ground would fall mostly amongst French and Belgian civilians was mitigated to some extent by special orders for precision bombing, often from an abnormally low level. When the aiming point could not be detected with certainty, they brought their bombs back.

Three nights in succession, on the eve of D-Day and on the two following nights, they were busy attacking rail targets, and by the night of 12 June, when they were detailed with fifteen other 419 Squadron Lancasters to bomb marshalling yards at Cambrai, they had completed twelve of these 'Transportation Plan' sorties. Some time after midnight – which meant that 12 June would have shaded into the 13th – they would be approaching the target for their thirteenth mission on 419, 13th June.

The crew as a whole, in Branston's day, had done one leaflet-dropping raid as part of their training, and this counted as an operational sortie, which would make fourteen in all. De Breyne, because of his one familiarisation sortie, would actually have completed fifteen. But Mynarski was stuck at twelve. He was not, however, in the least superstitious; and on that fine midsummer evening, as they sat on the grass at dispersal under the wing of their Lancaster – UR-A, 'A for Able', KB726 – waiting for take-off, Mynarski found a four-leafed clover, picked it, and gave it to Brophy. 'Here, Pat,' he said, 'you take it – for luck.' It was a gesture that would be remembered.

They took off at 9.44 that evening and headed south-east for Cambrai, one of a total of 225 heavy bombers from 6 Group. With double summer time it was still almost daylight. The sky was beginning to darken, but apart from a little ground haze the night promised to be clear. From Middleton St George, the most northerly of the bomber bases, they had 400 miles to cover to their target.

Their flight plan called for continual changes of altitude, as a security measure, and after climbing to 10,000 feet for the long plod down eastern England they let down to 8,000 over the Channel. 'Estimated 80 minutes more to the target,' called Friday. The only comment, typically dry, came from Mynarski. 'Good. What's the rush?'

With all navigation lights now extinguished, they began to see searchlights sweeping erratically over the French coast near Dieppe. Stretched out face down in the nose, Friday watched the familiar puffs of smoke and coruscations of sparks from the coastal barrage. 'Light flak below, skipper,' called Brophy.

Suddenly A for Able was bathed in a sea of light, blinding de Breyne in the cockpit and Friday in the nose. Before de Breyne could react, more searchlights picked them up. 'We're coned!' shouted de Breyne 'Hold tight!'

He threw the plane into a steep dive, then pulled up sharply, wriggling and squirming in a series of convulsions, pinning the crew in their places even more effectively than their seat-straps. Then, as suddenly as they had been caught in the spotlight, they escaped into a darkness that seemed equally intense. 'Nice work, skipper,' applauded the crew.

But de Breyne wasn't so sure. Had they really shaken the searchlight batteries off, or were they desisting on purpose, leaving the sky clear for some night fighter that was being directed on to their radar image? They had been warned at briefing to expect fighter attack. 'Gunners, keep searching!' called de Breyne.

Once beyond the coastal defences they descended to 6,000 feet. There they got a nasty surprise – they were met by German interceptor rockets that rose to the approximate height of the plane and chased them with evil persistence. But whatever built-in homing device they may have carried, they exploded too far away to be effective.

The threat from fighters remained. Several times they saw other bombers in the stream jinking and weaving, desperately trying to fend off fighter attack.

De Breyne began a gentle descent towards Cambrai. They had 9,000 pounds of high explosive on board, eighteen 500-pounders, and an inaccurate drop could be disastrous, so to achieve pinpoint aiming they were bombing from 2,000 feet. Two of the bombs were delayed action, to harass repair work.

Cambrai was only one of the night's transportation targets. To the right of their track they saw two more conflagrations, one at Arras, the other, more distant, at Amiens. Ahead of them, Cambrai, too, was already aflame.

Jim Kelly, at the radio, picked up the group broadcast giving them the bombing wind. He passed the figures on to Friday, who adjusted his bombsight.

They were still at 5,000 feet, some way from the target, when Vigars, keeping a look-out from the cockpit, shouted a warning. 'There's a Halifax closing in on our starboard wing!' De Breyne steered to port to avoid the threatened collision, and in the next moment Brophy shouted from the rear turret 'Bogey astern! Six o'clock!'

He had caught a fleeting glimpse of a twin-engined fighter behind and below. As de Breyne began to corkscrew, Brophy whirled the turret round to meet the attack. 'It's a Junkers 88! He's coming up underneath us!' As the white-bellied Junkers, swastika vivid on its tail, streamed past Brophy's sights, German and Canadian opened fire simultaneously, triple nose cannons of the one blazing, the four Brownings of the other replying – but heavily outgunned.

Whether or not he had hit the German, Brophy never knew. What he did know was that the German's aim had been unerring. No. 2 fuel tank on the port side had apparently been hit – the tank between the two port engines. With the sudden release of petrol fumes and vapour, it would probably explode. There was a muffled crump – and the port wing burst into flames.

Yet A for Able was still flying. The explosion was milder than de Breyne had feared. But with the fuel pipes fractured, both engines on that side conked out.

De Breyne was about to roll the plane over to port to continue his corkscrew when he realised he had no power left on that side. To prevent the plane slipping into a spiral dive, he braced his feet on the pedals and hauled back on the stick. They had fallen 2,000 feet and were now about two and a half thousand feet clear of the ground. Shouting instructions to Vigars, and holding the port wing up, he managed to slow the rate of descent, bringing them back on an even keel. At the same time he realised that Vigars had heard nothing. The inter-com was dead. The plane was still losing height and speed, much too quickly for comfort, and with Vigars assisting he pushed both starboard throttles through the gate.

It was no use – A for Able was doomed. Vigars, watching the engine temperatures rise and the oil pressures fall, was reaching for his parachute. As he did so the plane gave a violent lurch, then stalled and dropped forward, falling out of the sky. With a speed of 150 miles an hour, well above any danger of stalling, de Breyne was nonplussed. Then he realised what had happened. The outer main plane had burned right through and dropped off.

What his stalling speed might be in this situation he could only guess, but he let the plane accelerate in the dive, then gradually eased the control column back until he was in a fairly steep glide. He yelled at Vigars, in the jump seat beside him. 'What's the position with the starboard engines?'

Engine temperatures and oil pressures had both reached the danger mark and there was only one decision to take. With no voice communication, de Breyne gave one more order. 'Get out fast!' In the same moment he flashed P for Parachute on the red warning lights to alert Mynarski and Brophy.

For all but the two gunners, the escape hatch was down in the nose. For the gunners there was an escape door half-way between the two turrets. Vigars, his parachute pack already clipped to his chest, jumped down into the nose, where he found the hatch already unhinged. Friday must have gone. The hatch opened inwards and it was lying loose across the aperture. Bodie was following Vigars down, but the crew could enter the nose compartment only one at a time.

Vigars now saw with dismay that Friday hadn't gone at all. He was slumped on the floor unconscious. A gash across the bomb-aimer's left eye, five inches long, told the story. As Friday had tugged the hatch open, a violent updraft had catapulted it into his face and knocked him out.

They were down to 1,500 feet now, still in a steep glide, and Vigars had to work fast. Bodie, Kelly, and lastly de Breyne himself, must all be anxiously awaiting their turn. But if I push Jack out, he thought, he's had it too. Fortunately Friday had clipped on his pack before tugging at the hatch. Vigars dragged Friday on to his back and lugged him towards the hole. Kneeling on his chest, to keep the pack solid, he pulled the ring. In the same instant he pushed him through. It was a gamble, but it was Jack's only chance. There was a danger his canopy might snag on the unretractable tail-wheel, but with any luck it wouldn't open fully until he was clear.

As Vigars prepared to follow Friday, the airstream caught the hatch cover and jammed it at an angle in the aperture, blocking the exit. Kicking at it in desperation, he felt a tap on the shoulder. 'Take it easy, Roy.' Bodie, wonderfully calm, was right behind him. Steadying himself, Vigars kicked the cover right through the hole. 'Best of luck!' called Bodie, as Vigars dived. Bodie followed.

To de Breyne, watching the altimeter unwinding at a frightening rate, yet fearing to pull the nose up, in case of stalling, the time they were taking to get out from the nose seemed interminable. Yet until they had gone he daren't leave the controls. He had no idea that Kelly, believing they were too low to jump, had delayed his exit and was somewhere behind him in the fuselage, bracing himself for the crash.

Throttling back the starboard motors, lifting the nose slightly into a gentle gliding angle, de Breyne was down to barely 1,000 feet when he crawled for the nose and jumped in turn. His relief was, mistakenly: 'Thank God we all got out!'

Seeing him go, Kelly hurried after him. Last to go – as he thought, also mistakenly – he saw the tail-wheel pass a few feet above his head. No one had any idea that Mynarski and Brophy were still in the plane.

Both gunners had seen the winking red light. Glancing inconsequentially at his watch, Brophy noted it was thirteen minutes past midnight. Thirteen again. But now to work. His turret was still angled to port, from the firing, and to escape he had to line it up fore and aft. He pressed the pedal to rotate it. Nothing happened.

The hydraulics for the turrets were powered from the port engines. That power had gone. The turret was stuck at an angle and he couldn't get out. He tried not to panic. There was an emergency exit. By cranking the turret mechanism by hand, he could swing the cupola into the beam position, at right angles to the fuselage, and fall out backwards. A life-saver. Thank God he had that alternative.

He managed to prize open the turret doors sufficiently to squeeze a hand through and reach in for his parachute. He clipped it on his chest, then grasped the emergency handle and began to rotate it. It was a manual attachment, free of hydraulic power. Unpredictably, it came off in his hand.

This was a nightmare. It couldn't be true. He stared at the useless handle, then felt for the spindle. He couldn't move it. The turret was locked at an angle and he couldn't get out. Unless someone came to help him, he was a dead man.

Up front, the cockpit had gradually emptied. In any case there was no communication remaining with the tail. There was only one man left who could possibly help Brophy. Peering despairingly back into the fuselage, the trapped gunner looked to see if Mynarski had gone.

Between the two turrets a fire had started, where the photo-flash equipment had been hit. Spilled hydraulic fluid had leaked towards the tail and the fire was feeding on it. Brophy was doubly cut off.

Mynarski had slid down from the mid-upper turret easily enough, but his route to the exit door was hindered by the fire. He was making his way towards the door. Brophy, peering through the upper part of his turret, felt the plane wallowing unsteadily and saw Mynarski brace himself against the door. That door was only fifteen feet away, but it might as well have been fifteen miles.

Against the cacophony of engines revving and the sibilance of the airstream, it was useless for Brophy to shout, but he shouted just the same. He banged his fists on the turret doors, and still Mynarski did not hear. Just as he seemed about to jump, however, he glanced towards the tail.

It was obvious that, for some reason, Brophy was trapped. The area between the two men was becoming incandescent with smoke and flame. Turning away from the open doorway, Mynarski grabbed an axe from its stowage and struggled aft. As the pilotless plane lurched this way and that, he got down on his hands and knees and crawled, forcing his way through the flames.

Brophy could see it was hopeless. 'Don't try!' he shouted, waving him away.

By the time Mynarski reached the turret, the lower part of his khaki flying suit, soaked in hydraulic fluid, had caught fire, and flames were licking up his arms. Beating them out with his gauntlets, he drew himself up and smashed the axe against the turret doors. He could make no impression. In a frenzy of exasperation, he tore at the doors with his hands.

Inside the turret, Brophy, seeing that Mynarski would be doomed too if he stayed another second, dismissed his own agony and again waved him away. 'Go back, Andy! Get out while you can. Before it's too late!'

The eyes of both men held a despairing acquiescence. For one it was the acquiescence of defeat. For the other it was the acquiescence of death. As Brophy waved him away again, Mynarski inclined his head in a gesture of anguish, then got down on his hands and knees again and backtracked through the flames, never taking his eyes off Brophy. Then, clothes now ablaze, he struggled to his feet. Somehow, despite the plunging aircraft, he drew himself up and raised his right hand in a final salute. There was no mockery in it this time. As he jumped, his lips moved as though he was saying something. Brophy felt he knew what it was. 'Good-bye, *sir*.'

As Mynarski fell away under the tail, Brophy saw his parachute open. Then, with the plane in its final plunge, he curled himself into a ball and waited for death.

That final plunge, with four and a half tons of explosive still on board, took the huge bomber through a clump of trees that tore off the scorched

Mynarski's crew. Back Row: Jim Kelly the wireless operator, Art de Breyne, the pilot. Front Row: Pat Brophy, tail gunner, Roy Vigars, flight engineer, Andy Mynarski, mid-upper gunner, Jack Friday, bomb aimer and Bob Bodie, navigator. (Public Archives Canada)

remnant of the port wing before careering on until it impacted with shattering violence in a field. With what little control de Breyne had been able to exercise in those last seconds, he had somehow avoided the village.

The impact sprang the prison-cell in which Brophy was incarcerated and hurled him clear. In those final moments he blacked out. Seconds later, wondering whether he was alive or dead, he heard bombs exploding and felt the earth tremble. Gingerly testing his arms and his legs, and feeling no pain, he could find no injury. He wasn't even bruised. The bombs had fallen some distance away and only two of them had gone off. Miraculously, he had survived.

He had suffered one unexpected loss, however, probably psychosomatic. 'When I took off my helmet,' he says, 'most of my hair came with it.' Fully mobile, he was desperate to find out what happened to the others.

Having crashed in the plane itself after all the others had baled out, Pat Brophy was on his own. He could only assume that the rest of the crew had got out. He spent the night in hiding, wondering what had happened to Mynarski. Had he left it too late?

Next morning he sighted a French farmer who turned out to be a *Resistance* leader, Pierre Cresson. After helping Cresson to blow up a railway bridge, he was hidden near Lens with six other Allied airmen, to await the moment of liberation. This came six weeks later.

Bodie and Kelly had landed close to the village of Varennes, where they were sheltered at once by the *Resistance*. Meanwhile the people in the nearest village, Gaudiempre, reported having seen six parachutes emerge from the stricken plane, one of which was trailing flames. Elucidation came all too soon, from another adjacent village. The last man to leave, landing some distance from the others, was discovered in a nearby swamp, terribly burned. Nothing could be done for him. Stitched inside his helmet was the single word: 'Andy.'

As for Brophy, none of the crew knew of his astonishing escape. They assumed that he too was dead.

Roy Vigars had somehow knocked himself unconscious, but another group of *Resistance* workers intercepted and concealed Bob Bodie and Jim Kelly, and they also recovered Jack Friday from another nearby field. Friday's head injuries were so severe though – he was unconscious for four days – that the French, after failing to enlist the help of a local doctor, decided it would be too difficult to pass him through *Resistance*

Art de Breyne. (Bowyer)

channels. They turned Vigars over to the Germans, assuming he would get medical attention. In fact he was put straight into a civilian jail in Amiens, without any medical treatment, and a week later they transferred him to Stalag Luft 7. 'From a personal point of view,' as he said many years later, 'it has always been a great aggravation to me that never to this day can I recall that vacuum period from just prior to baling out up to five days later in a French jail.'

Art de Breyne had better luck. His plan was to walk towards Paris, skirt the city to the south-east, and head for Spain. He walked all that first night, hiding in a cornfield in daylight next day near the village of Lavieville, where he sought and made contact with a nineteen-year-old farmer, Raymond Letgoquart. Raymond's family fed him and fitted him out as an agricultural labourer, and later another family near Compiegne sheltered him until he was liberated.

Bodie and Kelly had a thirty-seven-year-old French widow named Jeanne Serant to thank for their extended evasion. With the Gestapo on their trail, she kept them hidden in her chateau at Senlis-le-Sec for six weeks, despite German troops commandeering the main floor. When the Allies freed them and other evaders in Compiegne and Lens in early September, they promised to visit Mme Serant after the war.

When Jim Kelly was liberated he reported to the Intelligence Branch in London and told them that Pat Brophy must have been killed in the plane and that Andy Mynarski had died of his burns. Within a few days, visiting the crew's old haunt, the Chandos Dive Bar, Kelly was astonished to see Brophy himself walk in, instantly recognisable despite his loss of hair.

'My God!' said the amazed Kelly. 'I thought you were dead!'

'Yeah,' said Brophy, 'dead thirsty!'

It was then, in the smoke-laden Chandos Dive Bar, that, filling their glasses perhaps a little too frequently, but with so much ground to cover, Pat Brophy, hearing about Andy's burns and inevitable death, realised he was the only one who knew how Andy had lost his life – indeed given his life – in a gallant but vain effort to save *him*.

Later he gave his account to the RCAF top brass at Canada House, relating Andy's frenetic efforts to free him and the despairing eye contact when they both accepted defeat. Then he told how Mynarski, encouraged at the last by Brophy to save himself, crawled back across the burning floor of the plane before throwing him that farewell salute. It was a tale, told without embellishment, and without hope of corroboration, that was thought worthy of a VC award.

But the war was now long since over – and the story went back to May 1944, when the war was at its height. It was many months before the facts could be known and assembled and put before the RAF Awards Committee. With many other retrospective award recommendations to consider, they turned it down. But on 7 September 1946, two years and four months after the event, the Air Member for Personnel disagreed.

'Here is a man who would probably be alive today had he not, in circumstances where the stoutest heart might be excused for quailing, fought his way (past the escape hatch) through the flames of a burning aircraft and tried to save the rear gunner, at what must have been obviously the most appalling risk – and eventually at the cost of his own life. I'm bound to say that, after careful consideration, I think this deserves a VC.'

The matter was finally resolved by the Chief of the Air Staff himself. 'I agree with AMP that his wonderful example of deliberate self-sacrifice deserves the VC.'

The award duly came on 11 October 1946. Up until then, Anna Mynarski, Andy's mother, had refused to believe her son was dead – even after she learned of the finding of his helmet. She had gone on paying the premiums for his life insurance right through till then. Not until a formal ceremony in Winnipeg, when the bronze medal was pinned to her breast by the lieutenant governor of Manitoba, on behalf of King George VI, to the applause of immigrant friends, did she at last *seem* to let go.

'I keep this,' she said, 'for Andrew.' She could not really accept that he would never come back.

The Mynarski name was honoured in various other ways. The Junior High School in Machray Avenue was renamed Andrew Mynarski and a cluster of Lakes some 250 miles south-west of Churchill were named after him. Also the post-war RCAF created a Mynarski Trophy, awarded annually to RCAF stations which shone best at developing youth recreation programmes.

Impressive too was the comradeship displayed by the surviving members of the crew. They kept in touch. Art de Breyne presented a plaque to the school on their behalf, and twice they got together for reunions, Roy Vigars and his wife Ellen joining them from England in 1965. There were also individual visits to the crash site, and Art de Breyne made return visits to both France and England. But the most moving occasion came after Pierre Cresson, the Gaudiempre *Resistance* boss, visited Canada and invited these now middle-aged men to return to Gaudiempre in June 1981.

When Art de Breyne stepped off the train at Amiens he was hugged by Raymond Letoquart, the boy who had found him in the cornfield in 1944. He was now fifty-six. 'Dear friend,' he said, 'we never forget what you boys did for France.'

Bob Bodie and Jim Kelly, who had written many letters to Mme Serant, visited her as they had always promised, and were profoundly moved when she produced all their letters, tied together with ribbon. 'Look,' she said, 'like love letters!' Bob Bodie was quick to reply: 'That's what they are!'

Next day in Gaudiempre, 1,500 people – the village itself numbered only 225 souls – formed a great semi-circle around the bronze plaque that had been brought from Canada. The mayor, military brass, diplomats and local politicians, and a colour party of war veterans, sang 'Oh Canada' and 'La Marseillaise', after which Art de Breyne took the microphone.

He began by introducing each member of the crew by name, excusing and regretting Pat Brophy's absence, due to his wife's ill health. He reminded them poignantly that Andy would normally have been one of the first to jump: he had an exit door close by.

De Breyne concluded: 'Andy had to choose between his own welfare and someone else's. That was his dilemma. Yet for him, being him, there was no choice at all. He just did what he had to do.'

CHAPTER EIGHT

BAZ – A Father's Letter Earns his Son a VC – August 1944/45

'Tell me again about Ron Middleton, Jock.'

The questioner was a twenty-five-year-old pilot named Ian Willoughby Bazalgette, pronounced Bazal-jet, but always 'Baz' to his friends. At home, though, he was always 'Will', to differentiate him from his father, who was also Ian. The younger Ian, Bazalgette junior, was a flight commander on a training unit at Lossiemouth, Morayshire. The year was 1943.

The Scots gunnery leader, Douglas Cameron, who was faced with this question, had been a gamekeeper in peacetime, from Braco, Dunblane, Perthshire, always known as 'Jock'. Like Bazaljet, as he would have known him, when not calling him Baz, he had graduated, under protest, from bombing to training duties.

In the previous year Cameron had been flying in Stirling bombers with an apparently gloomy, almost morose Outback Australian named Middleton. This was the man of whom Baz had asked to know more. Moody or not, the experience of a near-lethal interception one night over Essen, when their aircraft was riddled by a night fighter and barely got home, had so galvanised Middleton, so Cameron said, that he had undergone a transformation, gaining his crew's full confidence and enjoying their friendship. Soon afterwards, Middleton, having been made a founder member of one of the very first Pathfinder Force squadrons, had been confronted with a straight but unenviable choice. 'Your navigator isn't up to Pathfinder standard', he was told, pretty bluntly, by the legendary Pathfinder recruiter Wing Commander Hamish Mahaddie. 'That means either exchanging him for someone else or being posted back to 149.'

When it was confirmed that they could move together as a crew, personal ambition clashed with loyalty; loyalty won and they went back together to 149 Squadron. It was a loyalty that was to cost Middleton his life.

They had all been near the end of their first operational tour – two of them had in fact already completed thirty sorties – when Middleton, with two more trips to do, was briefed, on 28 November 1942, for a raid on Turin. Tour-expired members of the crew, loyalty long since cemented, volunteered to stay for two more.

This time, again over the target, the Stirling was hit and Middleton was severely wounded and temporarily lost control. Two others in the crew sustained shrapnel wounds, but Middleton, having got so close, was determined to drop his bombs on the target. Hours later, after a nightmare re-crossing of the Alps, they reached the Kent coast. But by then the engines were faltering, fuel exhaustion was imminent, and the crew, under Middleton's orders, began an attempt to escape by parachute. Five of them made it, but two, possibly staying too long in the hope of helping Middleton, were recovered from the sea next day, their parachutes half-opened.

When the surviving crew, all of whom were decorated, told their story, Middleton was awarded a posthumous VC. Baz, listening to this brief account, from one of the men who'd lived through it, could only echo the words of the citation: 'Unsurpassed in the annals of the Royal Air Force'.

Baz himself had an unusual history. The family came originally from France, and were reputed to have Moorish connections. Ian senior had reached half-colonel in the Royal Field Artillery in World War One, but he had been wounded, and was now on pension. In 1918 the family emigrated to Canada and there, in Calgary, on 19 October 1918, young Ian was born.

In 1927 the family returned to England, where Baz, after spending four years at Balmy Beach School, Toronto, continued his education at Rokeby in Wimbledon. His pursuits, when he took a job in 1938 with the Rating Department of LCF and LP Properties (Key Flats), are recalled by a colleague: 'Ian was a very amenable chap, and he was always chatting up the female members of the company we worked for.' But he remained single.

Shortly before war was declared he enlisted in the RFA, but he had no military ambitions, and thought, as many did, that the war wouldn't last six months. 'Better get it over,' he told his sister Ethel. Serving initially in the Searchlight Section, he scandalised, horrified and amused his family, back at his suburban home in Sycamore Avenue,

New Malden, with mocking descriptions of guard duty in those early days, when he found himself flourishing a rifle at an intruder, and calling 'Who goes there?', with nothing up the spout to carry the matter further. When he was commissioned a year later he was still only twenty-one; but even now he saw little hope of seeing action. He applied for a transfer to the RAF, was accepted for pilot training, and went solo at Cranwell in September 1941. Fully qualified within a year, he was sent to fly Wellington bombers on No.115 Squadron at Mildenhall in Suffolk.

Before leaving Cranwell he made a significant gesture recognising his new hazards: he made a will. He had no other attachments, and he left everything to his family.

He was now flying much the same pattern of sorties as his hero Ron Middleton had done before him. For a time, indeed, they were contemporaries in 3 Group, although in different aircraft and on different squadrons. Essen and Turin were among the targets they shared. Their ways, however, parted with dramatic finality at the end of November 1942, when Middleton was killed and Baz began converting from the obsolete Wellington to the new four-engined Avro Lancaster, a progression that Middleton had once denied himself. Baz's first Lancaster sortie came on 22 March 1943.

Before he completed his 'split' tour – half on Wellingtons and half on Lancasters – he was promoted to acting squadron leader, and he already had his eyes on a Pathfinder posting. Hamish Mahaddie, who had started the war as a sergeant pilot, had by then become known in PFF as 'the horse-thief' or 'the body-snatcher'. He was habitually visiting squadrons to lecture on Pathfinder techniques and to recruit candidates, and Baz button-holed him after a lecture

Ian Bazalgette – 'Baz'. (IWM CH14911)

to appeal for a transfer. Mahaddie sized his man up and was certainly not discouraging.

Baz had already built up a reputation with 115 Squadron. His DFC citation (July 1943) ended: 'His gallantry and devotion to duty have, at all times, been exceptional and his record commands the respect of all in his squadron.' Mahaddie wanted him.

Back home on leave in Sycamore Avenue, Baz wrote to Mahaddie. He knew that picked crews were going straight from squadrons to complete a 45-op tours with the Pathfinders, and he was determined to avoid the usual 'rest' at a training unit that threatened him otherwise. He had had enough of that in the Royal Artillery.

'3 Group finished me after completing my twenty-ninth trip,' he wrote, 'so I volunteered at once. My commanding officer has kindly made the necessary contacts for me, but I thought I would try to avoid any possible confusion by informing you directly of all the details.

'I'm now on 14 days post-operational leave' – this was 19 August, 1943 – 'and I shall be ready any time from 1 September; the sooner the better. Two members of my crew have volunteered to continue with me' – he gave their names, also the name of a third – 'who wishes to come with me as rear gunner.

'It seems a considerable liberty to write to you directly, but you were kind enough to encourage me and I am determined not to be disappointed.'

Having boldly taken one liberty, he risked another. 'To put it mildly, I should appreciate it if I may retain my acting rank of Squadron Leader.'

Mahaddie's method of recruitment was to study the daily bomb plot, circulated by 'Bomber' Harris from Headquarters, which showed, through synchronised photographs, how close individual crews got to their target. Some, through lack of skill or pertinacity, never got on the bomb plot at all. Others appeared time and again. Bazalgette was one of these.

For once Mahaddie was thwarted. He was told that Bazalgette, as an experienced instructor and embryo lecturer, had been earmarked for a 'special job, for which he is badly needed'. For Mahaddie it was hands off. 'I fear I can give you no definite hope,' he told Baz. 'However, I am working on a scheme. But this is a slender thread. Please leave the matter in my hands.'

The 'special job' turned out to be a routine exchange posting with a bored flight commander on a swap for a training unit in far-off

Lossiemouth, It was a terrible let-down for Baz, and he wrote another plea to Mahaddie by return. 'Your second appeal,' replied Mahaddie, 'has steeled my resolve.' But he could do nothing for the moment. He advised Bazalgette to 'keep your powder dry', and wished him good pathfinding 'very soon'.

So Bazalgette went to Lossiemouth, and the crew members he asked for were scattered elsewhere. But every few weeks he shot off another missive to Mahaddie. 'He *plagued* me,' Mahaddie said later. 'He *pestered* me.' Although disgruntled, Baz understood the priceless value of training, and he was a popular flight commander, aware that he had something to give. He was one of those adaptable people who are naturally at ease with all kinds of people and situations. Sister Ethel remembers that when they were thrown in

Group Captain T.G. 'Hamish' Mahaddie. (IWM CH13638)

amongst adults as children, whereas others were tongue-tied, 'Ian always conversed very naturally with the parents, to their delight. He was sensitive, articulate, intelligent and very amusing, and he gave one a sense of strength.'

At Lossiemouth Baz soon made new friends, among them four other aircrew men equally frustrated at being confined to training duties and eager to get back as soon as possible to squadron life. Jock Cameron, with whom he stayed at Braco while on leave, was one. 'You've done far too much already,' he was told, 'You're not going back again yet.' Others were twenty-two-year-old navigator Geoff Goddard, bomb-aimer Ivan (Van) Hibbert, twenty-three, and wireless-operator Charles 'Chuck' Godfrey, twenty-one. All had already completed a tour on bombers, all were commissioned, and all attached themselves to Baz. With his old crew disbanded, he welcomed them. They spent many happy hours in the mess and local hostelries, where they blotted their copybook by spilling beer over some scandalised ladies. One evening they were playing a 'game' – normally confined to the mess – which entailed balancing a tankard of beer on the top of the skull. The tankard pitched forward and the ladies were soaked. Baz, it is said, so charmed the ladies that they bought the beer from then on. But it was eight months before news of a posting came – and then from an unexpected quarter.

Mahaddie had done all he could, but now a friend of Bazalgette had asked for him.

'Do you really want to get back, Jock?' Baz asked Cameron, just to be sure. 'I can't', said Cameron, 'not until I've finished this training tour.' 'You can get back fine,' said Baz. 'I've got a friend in 635 Squadron – a navigator named Cousens. He's CO of the squadron and he wants me back.' Baz had been told by Cousens – Wing Commander A.S.G.Cousens – 'We'll pull the strings, we'll get you back. With the help of Mahaddie.' There was no hesitation from Cameron. 'All right, I'm game.' Cousens actually held the appointment of Group Navigation Officer, and had done for some months. Of his expertise Pathfinder Don Bennett was later to write: 'Group Navigation Officer was one of the main appointments in the Path Finder Force, for it was on navigation above all else that our results depended.'

Baz wanted to take all his little group of friends from Lossiemouth with him. He told Cousens: 'Look, I've got to get us all back on ops.' He was talking of Goddard, Hibbert, Godfrey and of course Cameron. All were keen to come and a transfer was agreed.

The truth was that Baz, for all his officer qualities, was one of the boys. He wore his cap on the back of his head in a raffish manner, showing his hair. He had a happy disposition, always seeming to be smiling, and at Lossiemouth he was loved. The other flight commander, says Cameron, was more of a pilot's man. Baz wasn't, he was everyone's man. Many pilots were apt to treat navigators, wireless operators, bomb-aimers and gunners as a lesser breed, but not Baz. He showed an interest in every man's job – 'Let me have a go at this, how does this work' etc. And to Cameron, 'I'll come back to you, Jock, let me have a go in the turret.' In this fellowship he wasn't unique, but he was above average.

Thus Baz took with him the four crewmen he had found common ground with at Lossiemouth, and they picked up a flight engineer and a second gunner at PFF school. Returning to the operational scene with 635 at Downham Market, Baz did not neglect to make a special visit to thank Mahaddie. 'He was over the moon,' says Mahaddie. But by the time they got to 635, Baz was dismayed to find that his friend Cousens had been reported missing. Don Bennett was to mourn many of his precious Group Navigation Officers, cut down too soon, but Cousens had lasted longer than most. There was still a chance, though, that he and his crew might have survived as prisoners.

The new crew began at once to play their part in the massive attacks on German communications that were forming the essential prelude to D-Day. Baz had already graduated to the role of deputy master-bomber when a new threat emerged to the very durability of the Invasion. On 12 June 1944 the first of the so-called buzz-bombs or doodlebugs (V1s) fell on London.

For Baz it was a curious throw-back to history. His most illustrious ancestor, great-grandfather Sir Joseph Bazalgette (Bazal-jet), had changed the lives of countless Londoners in mid-Victorian times by constructing an underground drainage system, brick-built and secured with the hitherto unproved Portland Cement, which is still the backbone of the system today. It is rightly regarded as one of the great construction feats of the age. Up until then, the Thames was simply an open sewer. Bazalgette's system of pump stations, lifting the sewage down-river, together with his construction of the Thames Embankment, not to mention his bridges, make him nothing less than the architect of modern London.

With the emergence of the V1 weapon, and then the V2, the task now was not to build or rebuild London, but to save it.

Graduating to the premier role of master bomber, Baz was now assuming control and direction of heavy daylight raids on flying-bomb sites and storage depots in France. Dedicated as he was to the task, as his ancestor had been, he never became obsessive. There were other things in life. His appreciation and knowledge of music was encyclopaedic, and he might be humming some snatch of a favourite Mozart concerto as he flew into battle. His letters home were often of vivid and spectacular landscapes seen from the air, of lightning playing on the propellers in electric storms, of the majestic tranquillity of the Alps by moonlight. For spiritual comfort, his bedside Bible was well thumbed.

Off duty, he was the life and soul of the party. On leave, he would spend precious free time in the garden at Sycamore Avenue, planting roses. On duty, he was a disciplinarian. Temperaments, under the strains of pathfinding, could be volatile, but any discord would be settled at once: 'Come on, let's have it out.'

'An amazing mixture' was how sister Ethel described him. She too was a volunteer, working as a secretary for the General of the Intelligence Section, IXth American Air Force, stationed in France. One day the entire camp, including the General, were startled witnesses of a thunderous shoot-up by a Lancaster bomber. Ethel dare not guess who it might be. 'That night,' she says, 'Ian telephoned to ask if I'd seen him.'

Baz was master bomber in a daylight raid on a V1 Storage site on Tuesday 1 August when they were attacked by three fighters. Thanks to combined skill and good luck they escaped, and the only injury, a minor one, was to their mid-upper gunner, Bob Hurnall. Their faithful Lancaster, M for Mother, also suffered minor damage, but as they were due to go on leave in two or three days time, M for Mother would be repaired by the time they got back.

On the next day, 2 August, all operations were cancelled at midday because of the weather. It was a bleak day for 635, news having come through that their former CO and Baz's friend, Wing Commander Cousens, and his entire crew, were confirmed as killed in action on 22 April. A memorial service was held that day, with Baz attending.

On Friday morning, 4 August, a daylight raid was planned on another V1 Storage Site at Trossy St Maximin, 22 miles north-east of Paris. Almost incredibly, nearly all the permanent launching sites had already been destroyed by bombing in the run-up to the Invasion, but temporary sites, harder to find and obliterate, were proliferating, and hitting the heavily protected depots was proving the best antidote. Trossy had been attacked twice already that week, but it was particularly well protected and defended, and it was decided to try again, giving the job exclusively this time to the Pathfinders. Of the 61 Lancasters detailed for Trossy, 14 were to come from Downham Market.

With London still under continual bombardment – nothing like to the extent that Hitler had envisaged, but unpleasant enough (over 6,000 were killed by the V1s and another 18,000 seriously injured) – this third heavy attack was obligatory.

It did not concern Baz and his crew. Their plane was unserviceable and they were going on leave. But one of the crews listed for the trip had gone on a local flight to an airfield in Yorkshire and was delayed there by bad weather.

Although Baz and his crew had now completed 25 trips, they expected to do 45 before being rested. They had been to Trossy once and it was a tough one, they knew, but it was a comparatively short hop. Why not replace the missing crew? 'We're not going on leave until tomorrow,' said Baz. 'Let's get another one in before we go.'

There was no dissent. The master bomber and his deputy had already been appointed, so they were relieved of that duty. No one said 'Isn't it sticking our necks out?' Sticking their necks out had become part of everyday life. And it would be one less trip to do when they got back from leave.

The only dissent came from the mid-upper gunner, Bob Hurnall, at thirty-six the oldest man in the crew. His minor injury had been treated and he was out of hospital. 'I'm feeling OK, ' he insisted. 'Can I go?' But a replacement, a twenty-eight-year-old Australian named Vernon Leeder, had already been fixed. Hurnall protested, but he was too late. Aggrieved, he went down to the airfield to watch the take-off. He would stick around until they got back.

Hurnall had already done thirteen trips with Bazalgette and was psychologically welded into the crew. 'I knew Baz very well,' he says, 'he was great fun. We were a crew all together and we had a good time. He was a fellow without nerves. He liked his pint but he was very strict in the air.'

Frequently they drank with their ground crew. Development of mutual respect and trust was encouraged. Rank didn't come into it. This fraternisation was not unique. Tears were not uncommon from the ground crew when an air crew went missing.

The new gunner, Vernon Victor Russell Leeder (Russell was his mother's maiden name) was a welcome enough replacement. The squadron was probably right to rest Hurnall. Leeder, who was no beginner, had had several months' experience on Lancasters with 102 Squadron, and his posting two months earlier to a Pathfinder squadron

'Baz' and his crew. Left to right: Baz, Geoff Goddard, navigator, Van Hibbert, bomb aimer, 'Chuck' Godfrey, wireless operator, Dave Hurnall (mid-upper gunner, substituted), Jock Cameron, tail gunner and George Turner, flight engineer. (Bowyer)

was a guarantee of his quality. A trained accountant, he had engineering experience, and his prowess as a gunner stemmed from three months' camp with a Field Artillery Brigade in Australia in the summer of 1940.

The other twelve Lancasters from Downham Market were to form the spearhead force, so Baz and his crew were still in the vanguard. They took off in T for Tommy at 11.15 that morning.

Five Mosquito crews were briefed to mark the aiming point, dropping Red Star indicators (TIs) four minutes before H-hour. Four of them got through. Two minutes later the master bomber motored in towards the target. As he did so his fuselage was holed by heavy flak and his starboard elevator was damaged. The skies were clear and he readily identified the aiming point, but his control was affected and his yellow TIs fell wide of the

Vernon Leeder (National Archives of Australia)

mark. He could see that the target was becoming smoke-covered. 'Aim in the middle of the Red TIs,' he told the others. 'Bomb on the Reds.'

One minute behind came his deputy, Flight Lieutenant R.W.Beveridge, also carrying Yellows. But as he crossed the target to assess the markers for accuracy, his machine was mortally hit. Baz and his crew saw it burst into flames and plunge earthwards at full bore.

With the master bomber crippled and his deputy gone, much depended on the remainder of the spearhead force. Unless they marked and bombed accurately, the bombing centre would shift and the depot would escape. Conscious of this, concentration intensified in T for Tommy.

The sky was stippled with bursting flak as the enemy gunners adjusted their range. The target had to be thoroughly saturated to achieve maximum effect, but the spearhead faced a formidable curtain of steel.

'Aim in the middle of the Red TIs,' called the master bomber, trying to reassert control. 'Bomb on the Reds.'

Flying straight and level at 6,000 feet, Baz and his flight engineer, George Turner, a Staffordshire farmer, sitting side by side in the cockpit, and bomb-aimer Van Hibbert, a lace-maker from Nottingham, seated underneath them, could see the markers clearly. 'We're coming up to the aiming point now,' called Hibbert. 'Bomb doors open. Hold this course.'

In the next half-minute, of the twelve remaining Lancasters of the spearhead, nine were hit, none more seriously than T for Tommy. A direct hit between the two starboard engines punctured the fuel feed and cut off power on that side. Flames erupted from the wing, and operating the automatic fire extinguishers had no effect. Fuel had leaked into the fuselage, where another fire raged, while the plane wallowed alarmingly as Baz fought for control.

One man, bomb-aimer Van Hibbert, was wounded, and Chuck Godfrey went down to help him. He could see at once that his arm was almost severed. Shocked by what he saw, he half-lifted, half-dragged Hibbert back to the bed in the fuselage. Blood was pumping from his shoulder like a waterfall and Godfrey, after doing what he could to staunch the flow, gave him a morphine injection. Turner went back and plugged Hibbert into the inter-com by the bed. Godfrey at this stage was not plugged in. Together with navigator Goddard and the Australian Leeder they began fighting the fire in the fuselage. They quelled it for the moment, but Leeder, overcome by the fumes, staggered back to his turret. The fire in the starboard wing, however, remained unquenched.

With fuel tanks punctured and fuel still slopping around in the fuselage, the plane was in danger of blowing up. A general bale-out looked imminent. Yet Baz was holding his course. Taking over from Beveridge, he was now giving instructions to the force. The task at hand was no routine plastering of some giant industrial complex. It was an urgent preventive strike on an armoury of so-called Victory weapons that were intended to devastate London. These strikes against the storage depots were having more effect than anything else. Seldom had the lives of civilians at home, far from the action, depended so directly on the skill and tenacity of the Pathfinders. And above all now, on Baz.

Flight engineer Graham Turner took over the vital task of dropping the bombs, and he went down to await the signal from Baz. Soon it was done. 'I got the bombs away all right.' Then Baz found he couldn't close the bomb doors, disturbing the trim. Turner went down again to operate them manually. It seemed an interminable time before he succeeded

Their bombs were right on target. They had so straddled the depot that the master bomber, still circling in his damaged Lancaster, changed his instructions. 'Shift the emphasis to the centre of the smoke.'

The release of six tons of bombs had so altered the trim of T for Tommy that Baz was fighting again for control. Acceleration fanned the flames in the starboard wing, and they were losing precious height. The crisis drew a tense exchange between navigator Goddard and Baz.

'We'll never get back across the Channel.' .

'We'll try for the Allied lines.' They were still hoping to avoid capture.

They were now down to twelve hundred feet. Jock Cameron, in the rear turret, swung his turret round and saw that the whole fuselage was swilling in petrol and the port wing was filleted like a herring, having burned right through. He caught a glimpse of Leeder, slopping about in his flying boots, and being either air-sick, or poisoned by the fumes. The plane was crabbing drunkenly. My God, he thought, it's time I got out. Simultaneously he heard Turner's voice on the inter-com. 'Baz, we'll have to put her down.'

Always, in the air, the discipline Baz had encouraged had been followed. It had been 'Flight engineer to pilot,' 'Rear-gunner to pilot,' and so on. Short cuts were in order now. Any attempt to crash-land the burning Lancaster looked suicidal. Baz's final instructions came over the inter-com in typical measured cadences.

'Put on parachutes. Jump!...Jump!...!Jump!' And to Cameron: 'Put your turret on the beam, Jock, and bale out!' Finally to Turner, still sitting next to him: 'Tighten my straps first!' So Baz, for the moment, was staying.

As he fastened them, Turner shouted: 'Van's unconscious! I'm not sure about Vernon!' Hibbert was probably dying. He had been with Baz since Lossiemouth days and he could not be abandoned. Still less could Baz jump while in doubt about Leeder, poisoned by fumes – after being pitchforked into a strange crew. 'Go!' Baz told Turner. 'I'll try to get the others down.'

Cameron, exiting from the rear turret, was the first out, followed up front by Goddard. Turner, about to jump through the front floor hatch, was blown back into the fuselage before Godfrey's foot unceremoniously forced him out. Last out was Godfrey himself. As their canopies billowed they watched the Lancaster, still partially ablaze, bank to avoid a village before flattening out for a wheels-up landing, aiming into the distance, two fields away. The people of the nearby village of Senantes, in the Department of Oise, cringed under the low-flying bomber as it roared overhead, then recovered in time to see it come down.

Still streaming flame, it pancaked evenly and skidded for perhaps fifty yards. Then, before anyone else had a chance to get out, it exploded in a holocaust of flame.

Of the four who escaped by parachute, Chuck Godfrey, the wireless operator, landed in a cornfield. 'I could see it all,' he says, 'as I was coming down. Baz did get it down in an open space, about two fields from where I landed, but it was well ablaze.'

Aware that he was still in Occupied France, Godfrey hid his tell-tale equipment (parachute, harness and Mae West) in a convenient corn-stack. Soon a farmer's wife called him over, where he joined Goddard, who had landed nearby. The local *Maquis* and *Resistance* then took over, and for the rest of the day they were sheltered in the house of a schoolmaster. That night they were moved to the home of a local gendarme.

George Turner, the flight engineer, the last but one to get out (after being blown back into the fuselage) had wrenched his back in his 'assisted' bale-out. In a state of shock, he was immediately helped to his feet by a French civilian, who turned out to be a patriot. Turner was hidden on a farm, where he was warned to stay put.

Cameron, first out, was on the way down when he was hit by a fragment of the falling plane and the fur collar of his Sidcot suit caught fire, burning his neck. He was only half-conscious, and he thought for a moment he was dreaming. He actually reached into his flying boot and withdrew his Scots dagger, prodding himself to make sure he was alive. But he landed safely before watching the others coming down. They landed some distance away, and trying to find them, he decided, was asking to be rounded up. The Germans would have seen the crash for sure. He didn't know that the others had virtually fallen into the arms of the *Resistance*. His instinct was to find cover, and he ran for a wooded area. Then he heard tracker dogs. 'I ran like hell! It was thick forest, some miles in depth. As a gamekeeper I knew what I must do, and I looked for a stream. Thankfully I found one, and I kept in the middle of that.

'When I heard machine-guns being aimed at the undergrowth, I climbed a tree. Hiding in the fork of that tree, I could hear the Germans searching below, but they didn't see me. They passed me several times, at intervals, but in one of those intervals I got across the road and found a farm. I didn't like the look of it so I kept on. Later I found out they had a reputation as collaborators. When it was dark I stumbled into some Free French officers and they gave me the option of going with them or staying on my own. First they satisfied themselves who I was. "You'll have to take off that uniform," they said, "and if you're captured you're liable to be shot as a spy." I asked them what they were doing. "We're blowing up bridges. We're doing everything with the Free French forces." I reckoned I could prove who I was, and I would have to run somewhere. 'All right, I'll run with you.'

Gregory and Goddard were taken by horse and cart next morning to a farm at Selacourt, where the local organisation supplied them with French identification cards. Meanwhile Cameron stayed with the French officers, who had a radio and were using it to transmit. 'I also worked the wireless. On 21 August at 1400 hours we had a narrow escape. Six Germans, SS officers, arrived with lots of wounded in the house we were occupying. We hid under a bed. We remained three hours under that bed, with all our wireless equipment, and were eventually helped to escape back into the forest. I was grateful that the French go in for full-sized beds.'

Gregory and Goddard were moved again on 26 August, when they were taken to a camp in the middle of a wood at Le Saussay, Par La Haussaye, where they joined a group of sixteen aviators already there, fifteen American and one English. Supplied with food daily by the local people, they were liberated by a British tank column on 30 August, 26 days after taking off from Downham Market. By that time Turner had joined them. Cameron followed next day.

The British already knew, from *Resistance* sources, that the Germans had recovered the bodies of Hibbert and Leeder. The French wanted them left where they were, 'for a decent burial', but the Germans insisted on taking them and they were buried in the cemetery at Beauvais. The Germans, still looking for the rest of the crew, overlooked Bazalgette's charred body, still in the wreckage. Next day the people of Senantes searched the wreckage and found the remains of the pilot, still in the cockpit. They were hidden until after the liberation.

Within five weeks of the raid – thanks to the French *Resistance* and the land forces' advance – all four survivors were back in England. There, after a period of leave, they were able to study the damage reports. Sixty-six sorties had been despatched, 348 tons of bombs had been dropped, two aircraft – captained by Beveridge and Bazalgette –

were missing: but it was rewarding to read that the V-weapon storage depot at Trossy St. Maximin had been 'completely saturated with craters'. The object of the raid – to reduce the sufferings of the citizens targeted by Hitler's V-weapons, completing the throw-back to Bazalgette's ancestor – had it was believed, been achieved.[1]

Goddard, Godfrey and Turner visited Bazalgette's parents and related in detail the circumstances of their son's death. They had to accept that they had lost their youngest son, so special and so lovable, whose qualities of leadership in wartime, at the age of twenty-six, had been so widely recognised. They were inconsolable.

Ten weeks later, on 8 October, in a ceremony attended by Ethel Bazalgette from another part of France, Baz was buried in the Churchyard at Senantes, by that time liberated. 'We return to you this day,' said the Mayor, in a glowing peroration, 'this hero so beloved by his crew, this brave soldier and magnificent comrade who preferred to die rather than abandon his wounded subordinates.' (Somehow they had never seen themselves as subordinates.) 'To you, Squadron Leader Bazalgette, a Norman from across the Channel, who comes to rest at the premature end of your glorious career among your brothers, the Normans of France, we express our deep gratitude.....'

The example set by Ron Middleton, which had been such an inspiration to Baz, might now have been forgotten. But it happened that the story had achieved national publicity through a BBC report in a Home News Bulletin more than two years earlier, on 2 February 1943. A posthumous award to Middleton of a VC had already been made, on 13 January, on the evidence of the survivors.

Soon afterwards it was announced that Middleton's body had been recovered from the sea off Dover. Four of the crew, as was known, had escaped by parachute; two more, front gunner John Mackie and flight engineer James Jeffrey, who had helped the others out, left it too late. Then on 5 February 1943 another bulletin on the Six o'clock News went into more detail. On that day, 'at about. 6.15', according to the BBC report, the circumstances of Middleton's award were rehearsed again in a poignant description of the scene in the little Station Chapel close by the airfield 'at an RAF base' (it was Mildenhall, Suffolk).

'The Bomber Command Band led the cortege through country lanes to the little village church (of St.John's, Beck Row). Ahead of the

---

1. It was later established – a poignant revelation – that Trossy St. Maximin was a dummy storage site, not a V1 depot.

flag-draped tender marched forty other Australian sergeants in their darker blue. Behind came a group of senior officers and two hundred of Middleton's comrades – men of the RAF and girls of the Women's Auxiliary Air Force.' They were called girls then.

'The Burial Service was conducted by two chaplains – one from the Royal Australian Air Force, to which Middleton belonged, and one from the RAF, in which he served.

'As the casket was lowered into the grave a firing party of the RAAF fired a triple volley. The officer stood at the salute while a bugler sounded the Last Post, and then each in turn filed past the grave.'

Ron Middleton. The story of his VC inspired Bazalgette. (IWM CH8165)

No one who heard that broadcast would ever forget it. Even those who heard it – or heard of it – at second hand, found it haunting. In those days, everyone listened to the BBC radio news, and a special item running for two and a half minutes was a topic of conversation for days. No one could miss it.

It is often said that many more VCs would be awarded if someone in authority had been present to see them. Middleton was lucky in that sense, in that there had been witnesses to what he did. The same, as Ian Bazalgette senior at once realised, after meeting his son's surviving crew, applied to Will.

A war veteran himself, disabled and now in a wheel-chair, he felt an awesome responsibility resting on his shoulders. He wanted no ceremony, no buglers or Last Post. It would be too much to bear. Nothing much was said, but he could feel the pressure to do something from his son's surviving comrades. And there were his own and his family's feelings.

He was more than satisfied with the tributes that had been paid to his son in France. He knew there must be thousands of the bereaved who judged that their own loved ones merited some special award, but few had the evidence to hand as he had. And there was the example of the Middleton award. One of Will's crew had actually been present when Middleton earned it. He could not get away from that.

Will's mother's distress alone might have been enough to persuade Ian senior to draw attention to his son's action. It might be weakness not to write. It almost seemed that by writing he would be placing himself amongst those many thousands of the bereaved who felt that something more was due to them. He was not thinking at first in terms of any particular decoration. Some sort of recognition would be deserved and would give solace, especially to his wife. But as he wrote, it was borne in upon him just what he was asking. He was asking for his own son to be awarded a posthumous VC.

The realisation made him hesitate afresh. Yet that radio broadcast kept nagging at him. Did he perhaps owe some positive reaction to his family, and to Will's crew? He began an attempt to draft the most important letter of his life.

When he had drafted it, with interminable re-writes, as though his life depended on it, he addressed it to The Secretary of State for Air.

'Sir,

'A recent broadcast by the B.B.C. gave an account of a posthumous award of the Victoria Cross to a pilot who sacrificed his life in order to save his crew.

'I wish, with all respect, to draw your attention to the circumstances of the death in action of the late Squadron Leader Ian Willoughby Bazalgette DFC No 635 Squadron, Pathfinder Force, who also gave his life for the sake of his crew on 4 August 1944.'

He continued with a full account of the circumstances of the damage to the Lancaster, the fire in the fuselage, and the injuries to the crew.

'Squadron Leader Bazalgette, finding that it was impossible for the bomb-aimer and the mid-upper gunner to bale out, had the crash belt fastened round him by the flight engineer and then gave the order to the four able-bodied members of the crew to bale out, while he remained at the controls in what he must have known was a hopeless effort to crash-land the plane.

'According to reliable French eye-witnesses he did succeed in landing the plane which exploded almost immediately after touching down.'

He went on to describe how the bomb-aimer and mid-upper gunner were thrown clear of the wreckage and their bodies taken away by the Germans, and how the ashes of his son were recovered next day by the people of Senantes. He then listed the names and addresses of the four surviving members of the crew.

> 'It was by correspondence and personal interview with the first three of the above-named that the information I have given was obtained.
>
> 'My daughter who as a British civilian volunteer is employed as Secretary to the Officer Commanding The Intelligence Section of the XI American Air Force, was able to be present at the funeral.....She has visited Senantes on several occasions and states that the Mayor and the people of Senantes are loud in their praises of the manner in which the pilot avoided crashing the plane on the village, which at one time seemed inevitable.'

He ended with

> 'I have the honour to be, Sir, Your obedient servant, C.I.Bazalgette.'

The passage about avoiding crashing the plane on the village was perhaps no more than trimming (although the villagers would strenuously have denied it), but it would hardly have influenced the S. of S. for Air. It always surfaced after crashes of this kind. Self-preservation alone would dictate that a pilot would choose open ground if he could, even over enemy territory. In other respects the phrasing of the letter seemed convincing enough, but there would be sceptics, that much he knew. How would it be received, coming from a bereaved father? For all he knew the post-bags of the military authorities were over-loaded with such appeals.

In fact the letter, with the names and addresses of the four first-hand witnesses, was routinely sent on to the Squadron, 635, and from there to the Station Commander, Downham Market, and finally to the Pathfinder Group Headquarters. Bazalgette's CO did not let him down He wrote a vivid 1,000-word account of the incident, ending:

> 'Squadron Leader Bazalgette had participated in a total of 53 operations against the enemy. He always chose to play a most dangerous and exacting role, but any task, however arduous, was always carried out in a cheerful and efficient manner. His tenacity of purpose and unswerving devotion to duty always set a magnificent example to the whole squadron. He undoubtedly made

the supreme sacrifice in a heroic and very gallant endeavour to save the lives of his injured crew.'

These of course were bomb-aimer Ivan Hibbert and the Australian Vernon Leeder.

Next the station commander, appending a list of all the Pathfinder sorties Baz had flown, wrote simply 'Highly Recommended', while the AOC of the Pathfinder Group 'had no hesitation in recommending him (Bazalgette) most strongly for the award of the Victoria Cross.'

The award was duly gazetted on 17 August 1945, and the Cross and other decorations were handed to Bazalgette's mother in an investiture at Buckingham Palace on 18 December that year. His VC is now in the RAF Museum at Hendon.

Born a Canadian, in Calgary, Alberta – although he returned with his family to the UK at the age of nine – Baz's award was even more widely celebrated in Canada, where two books – *Bazalgette VC* and *Alberta Pathfinder* – have been published about him, and he is named there on countless memorials. Finally in 1973 he was inducted, with other imperishable names, into the Canadian Aviation Hall of Fame.

Jock Cameron, surviving gunner of two posthumous VC award incidents, named his only daughter Margaret Middleton Bazalgette Cameron. Geoff Goddard named his son Ian.

For Chuck Godfrey the magnet of squadron life remained strong – though a certain sergeant WAAF at Downham Market was perhaps an even stronger attraction. He went back to 635 of his own volition and completed another 36 sorties, taking his score to 99. And he married the sergeant WAAF.

CHAPTER NINE

'What the Stars Foretold' for Jack Cannon – October 1944

T he miraculous survival of a nineteen-year-old Australian air gunner named Jack Cannon, far from his Melbourne home, had its origins not in the flak-infested skies of Nazi Germany – though they would come into it – but in an old timber-framed house on the edge of an ancient Saxon burial ground, now a Christian church with a crumbling churchyard, in the picturesque Sussex village of Hellingly, near Hailsham, on an October night in 1944.

The house, believed to have been inhabited by monks in Jacobean times, had a cloistral atmosphere, making stories of haunting by some past holy order easy to believe. And the present occupant, with a reputation for soothsaying and clairvoyance, only enhanced the atmosphere of medieval spookiness. That's how it seemed, anyway, to the young Australian.

What, in the middle of a tour of operations with Bomber Command, was he doing here?

Cannon, with two members of his crew, Australians like himself, was coming to the end of a hectic spell of leave in war-torn, buzz-bombed, blacked-out, vastly exciting London. They had stayed at the Waldorf Hotel, eaten at the Trocadero, and met old mates at the Codgers off Fleet Street (Cannon pre-war had been a cub reporter on the Melbourne Argus). Another favourite was the Coal Hole in the Strand. For theatres they went again and again to see the show-girls in non-stop variety at the Windmill, with its proud boast that throughout the Blitz 'We Never Closed'. Most theatres did.

Giving scant thought to tomorrows that might never come, they lived far beyond their means as NCO aircrew, and by the time their leave was half-way through they were running short of money.

Clairvoyant Evadne Price. See appendix Two for biographical notes. (Getty Images)

What could they do to raise some cash? 'I know what we'll do,' said Cannon decisively. 'We'll go down to Sussex and see Evadne.'

'Evadne who?'

'Evadne Price.' Evadne, he knew, was married to an Australian. Asked to pay her a courtesy visit, he had done so, soon after his arrival in England. Surely she would be good for a loan.

Hers was a name to conjure with. He knew what a remarkable woman she was, nearing forty now, perhaps, but ageless. She was as dark-eyed, black-haired, gipsy-looking, and vivacious as ever. Actress, playwright, novelist, columnist, mystic, astrologer, and seer, she had recently had plays running in London. But perhaps she would become best-known for her 'What the Stars Foretell' feature in a national newspaper. She'd be bound to help.

Cannon's contact with her was through his former news editor on the *Melbourne Argus*, Keith Attiwill. Evadne had married Attiwill's brother Kenneth, but Kenneth had been reported missing believed killed in Singapore. Evadne had never believed he was dead. Her clairvoyant vision had been vivid. 'I can see him in a small room on an island,' she had insisted. This had proved to be true. He had indeed been on an island, kept in solitary confinement for two years, before news of his survival and whereabouts were known.

The tile-covered house alongside the churchyard at Hellingly, converted into a modern two-storey residence, was called Prior's Grange, which tallied with its reputation. Cannon from the first had found it creepy in a déjà vu sort of way. The three Australians had pitched up in one of the most primeval Sussex villages of the Old Country. One of the cottages that fringed the churchyard was labelled 'The Priest's House', circa 1373. That was the ambience. Evadne Price, though, loved it.

Jack Cannon. To Evadne Price 'looked like some kind of boy scout.' (Cannon)

When he arrived fresh from the boat he had looked so youthful to Evadne, and his dark blue uniform of the RAAF had looked so pristine, that she had thought he was some kind of boy scout. She at once appointed herself his 'English' aunt.

Now, sated with London, and with their pockets empty, the three improvident Australians – Cannon, Ken Frankish and John Treloar – took the train from Victoria to Hailsham and made their way out to Prior's Grange. It was a sizeable structure, with bedrooms enough for all.

Hellingly was on the route from the German temporary V-Bomber sites in France across the Channel to London, and the villagers were already accustomed to the explosion of flying bombs falling prematurely nearby, or intercepted by fighters en route. But like Londoners in the 1940–41 Blitz, they refused to be cowed into subjection. As a stimulus to morale, Evadne was putting on one of her plays that night locally, and the three Australians were invited along.

The play opened with a bang. The bang was a buzz-bomb, which fell a mile away, fortunately in open country, just after the curtain went up. Evadne, who was playing the housemaid, entered ostensibly to answer the telephone, but the effects man, momentarily shocked as the bomb reverberated, missed his cue. 'Was that the telephone?' asked Evadne, with perfect timing. After that the play never looked back.

A party at Prior's Grange wound up the evening. When the other guests left, Evadne asked Cannon to stay behind in the kitchen and help with the dishes. His fellow Australians were packed off to bed. There followed an awkward, almost eerie silence, broken only by the clatter of crockery. Cannon recognised it as a pregnant pause. Evadne, he guessed, was working up to tell him something. That was very much her style. At length she spoke.

'In a fortnight's time, those two boys upstairs are going to be killed, with the rest of your crew. I can see you coming out of a wood with your face bleeding and with an injured leg, walking with the aid of a stick.'

It sounded so fanciful, with so much gory detail, that he laughed it to scorn. 'That's great. Thanks very much.' He laughed again, but mirthlessly this time. Within a few days, as he knew full well, they'd be back on ops over Germany. They were only half way through their tour. What could he possibly say to the others?

'I'm so sure of it,' went on Evadne, 'that I'll be writing to your adjutant naming myself as your English next of kin.'

In the next moment they were interrupted, and soon they all went to bed. He slept fitfully, disturbed by noises that proved imaginary, and at first he blamed the monks. Then he remembered Evadne's flash of clairvoyance. He hadn't been dreaming at all. What could he do?

He tried to rationalise it. It had been an exciting evening. They had been made a great fuss of, the three Australians, and they had all been a bit high after the show. Tongues had been loosened, hair let down, nonsense talked. Surely Evadne, when he spoke to her in the morning, would tell him to forget about it. But the chance to have a private word with her never came. Soon they were on their way back to London.

Evadne might have been right about her husband, probably was. But credence to these stories was often fed by rumour and gossip. As for professional stargazers, of which Evadne was one, he argued that they were wrong as often as they were right. Two or three days later, after another thrash in town, Cannon had almost forgotten about it. It was nonsense anyway. Soon they were back on their squadron, No.460 (RAAF), at Binbrook in Lincolnshire.

Stuart and Denis Richins aged thirteen and eleven in Australia. (Phyllis Handley)

Cannon's crew had comprised exclusively senior NCOs until a month earlier, when their pilot, Denis Richard Garth Richins, from Tamworth, New South Wales, had been commissioned. They had begun on an RAF squadron, but the CO of 460 Australian Squadron was an old school-mate of Richins, and some time earlier he had promised Richins that he and his crew should fill the next vacancy that came up. Such gaps occurred all too frequently on operational squadrons, and just before they went on leave at the end of September 1944 they were posted to Binbrook.

Binbrook was a long-established peacetime station, where accommodation was of pre-war standard, and Cannon and his NCO colleagues were allotted a married quarter to themselves. Richins, now commissioned, looked in daily to keep an eye on them. Only twenty-two himself, he acted the father figure.

While three of Denis Richins' crew were enjoying the sights of London, Denis himself had been visiting an aunt in Swindon, Wiltshire – his

Wren Stobo.

mother's sister. He had first visited the family some months earlier, with his elder brother Stuart, also a pilot, in his case flying Mosquitoes. In their dark-blue uniforms they had created quite a stir locally, as their twenty-two-year-old cousin Phyllis (now Phyllis Handley) remembers. 'Those two strapping six-footers', she called them.

She was particularly taken with the younger boy, Denis. Stuart seemed more serious-minded. Denis, a bank clerk in peacetime, like Stuart, was always laughing. He loved the quaint ways of the English, especially their place-names, which caused him endless amusement. His favourite was an airfield he had once visited – Little Snoring, in Norfolk. Little Snoring! (He was not to know that his own fate was to be poignantly linked with that airfield.)

This time Denis was paying his visit alone. Six months earlier Stuart had been killed, flying Mosquitoes.

All too soon, leave was over, and on the night of 23 October the main force of Bomber Command was detailed for an attack on the Krupps works at Essen. The target would be marked by the Pathfinders. Among the many hundreds in the main force were 26 Lancasters of 460 Squadron.

Selected crews were briefed to aim at a specific wing of the factory, Richins' crew among them. Their bomb-aimer, Flight-Sergeant Wren Stobo (named Wren, it was said, after Sir Christopher), a married man with a daughter back home, had a reputation for accuracy – in his case of bombing – consistent with his namesake.

Of the seven-man crew, all were Australians except the flight engineer, Sergeant Eric Sunderland. A quiet, diffident lad from Shipley, Yorkshire, just twenty years old, he joined the six Australians at their four-engined bomber conversion unit and was shaken at first by what Cannon called 'their raucous ways'. But he proved expert on the job and soon settled down in the cockpit beside Richins. Ken Frankish, the navigator, and John Treloar, the radio operator, had been Cannon's companions on leave. Both were twenty-one. The massive Frankish, from Western Australia, was a talented cricketer who would certainly play one day for Western Australia – if he survived the war. Treloar, whose father had fought with the Anzacs at Gallipoli, came from the same town as Richins.

Cannon occupied the mid-upper turret. Dick Bergelin was the tail gunner. Cannon was the baby of the crew, Stobo at twenty-six the oldest. Teased as the granddad, he seemed impossibly mature to Cannon.

Stobo was a likeable eccentric, with a fund of superstitions. One of them was that he must always kiss at least one of the WAAFs before take-off. There was no shortage of volunteers: they always lined up to see the crews

Denis Richins. (Phyllis Handley)

off, treating them, in an offhand manner, like heroes. Sometimes, as this evening, they crammed into the aircrew trucks in a flurry of banter and accompanied them out to dispersal, making dates as they went. This didn't inhibit Stobo from performing his second superstitious rite of the day – wetting the Lancaster's tail-wheel. Everyone watched for it and cheered as he did it.

More than one distinguished flying man left something to remember him by with these warm-hearted ladies.

It was a blustery autumn evening, scattering the leaves and bringing with it a thin, driving rain. Darkness would overtake them as they crossed the North Sea, providing cover when they reached enemy territory.

Once clear of the English coast, Cannon and Bergelin tested their guns. On an earlier trip, a daylight raid on Walcheren Island – when

Stuart Richins. (Phyllis Handley)

Stobo had distinguished himself with a direct hit on the target – Cannon had fired at what he was warned was a Focke-Wulf 190, diving in to attack them. His fire seemed accurate and he thought he was going to start his career with a victory. Then he spotted the aircraft's markings. He had nearly shot down a Yankee Thunderbolt.

At night it was even more difficult. Gunners tended to shoot at anything that didn't have four engines. Cannon was always scared of blasting away at a Mosquito in mistake for a Junkers 88.

As Richins' Lancaster, H-for-Harry Two, climbed to its bombing height of 18,000 feet, Cannon switched on his electrically heated clothing. Already the temperature in his turret seemed below freezing and he couldn't get warm. It was easy enough, in these conditions, to lose concentration, but he was forcing himself to keep alert.

Over the French coast they ran into a cold front, giving thick cloud right up to 18,000 feet and beyond. They continued in cloud to the bomb-line. The route had been well chosen to avoid enemy defences, and not until they were approaching Essen after two hours' flying did they meet intense flak.

The Pathfinders were less punctual than usual, it seemed, but they saw the first marker go down, a single red flare, at 19.35. This was followed by a single green flare, but no other markers appeared for seven anxious minutes. Then a red target indicator cascaded down – but was soon lost in cloud. Groups of red and green flares followed, but the greens were too scattered to be of much help. The Pathfinders were having a bad night. Fixing their position as best he could, Frankish gave Richins a change of course and they left the main force and headed for their briefed individual target.

Even now the flak was mostly moderate, and there was no sign of enemy fighters. Searchlights, too, criss-crossing the night sky, were no more than minimal. They were carrying one 4,000-pounder, five 1,000-pounders, and six 500-pounders, plus about a thousand 44lb incendiaries and, entrusted with a special task, they were determined to fulfil it.

Getting what guidance they could from the markers, they began their bombing run. Cannon, from his station on top of the fuselage, peered down and watched the black and red puffs of flak come eddying up towards them in deceptive slow-motion. He could smell the sulphurous stench of the flak-bursts, but there was nothing he could do about it

They had just dropped their bombs when he saw something that looked like a red hot coal climbing into the sky towards them, lazily, inexorably. This one was going to be close. It was said that when you could smell the flak you were for it. He knew now that this one had their name on it. He could still see the fiery, incandescent orb soaring towards them as oblivion came.

How long he had been unconscious he had no idea. It might be twenty minutes, it might be many hours. Rain was falling incessantly through the trees that were surrounding and shrouding him. He was still wearing flying boots, still in flying kit, couched in some sort of open space. The rhythmic lapping of the raindrops had penetrated his brain and woken him up. He wasn't really sure whether he was unconscious or dead. Something had knocked him out over the target and he was slowly coming round. That must be it. But he could remember nothing.

Impenetrable darkness smothered and stifled him. Instinctively his fingers scrabbled for his watch, which he always kept at his bedside. But there was no watch, and no bedside, only the dankness of what seemed to be rain-soaked undergrowth. It was totally mystifying, but at least he knew he wasn't in bed. He was lying in a patch of damp bracken, under a canopy of trees.

He was lapsing again into unconsciousness, almost willing it. He was luxuriating in it. Then the raindrops, accumulating in the foliage above him into larger globules, became so persistent that he stirred again. Where was he? Where was he last night? He certainly had a headache. Was he suffering from a massive hangover? Lingering in his nostrils was a sulphurous stench, something reminiscent of his last moments of consciousness. Where had he smelt it before? Was that the key? Memory, still blank round the edges, was coming to life at the centre.

They had been sent to bomb Essen. The Krupps works at Essen. That much he could remember. Dimly he recalled their bombing run, separate from the main force, then he had seen that lambent ascending flame. It must have destroyed them.

Where, then, was the wreck of the Lancaster? Where were the others? How had he got here?

He must have baled out. But he had no recollection of doing so. He couldn't even remember collecting his parachute from its stowage. He felt for his parachute harness, and was mystified to find it wasn't there. He was sure he'd been wearing it in the plane. He had had it on in the turret.

Without it he couldn't have baled out. Why had he taken it off?

Every question that came to him only intensified his bewilderment. They'd been shot down over the target, that much was certain, and he was lying in a forest somewhere on the edge of the Ruhr. They had been due over Essen at 19.30. They must have crashed soon after that. His watch, which he now realised was still on his wrist, showed after midnight. More than four hours to account for.

The last thing he remembered was the evasive action Richins was taking and the stench of explosive. His subconscious was telling him that he had heard shots since then. And explosions, too. That made sense. The Germans would have seen the Lancaster crash and would be out looking for survivors. Very probably they had captured the crew already. He had to get moving.

Richins had always made them take the escape and evasion talks seriously, and he tried to remember what he'd been told. One phrase stuck out in his mind. *Travel by night. Hide by day.*

Before dawn he had to put some distance between himself and the crashed plane. It couldn't be far away. There was no doubt they must have crashed. That was about the only thing that made sense. But which way should he head? He remembered the scarf in his escape kit, stuffed into a capacious pocket in his flying suit. Printed on that scarf was a map. Whether the noise of shooting and explosions he had heard had been real or imaginary, it had faded, and he could discern no traffic noise. In any case he must get started.

He removed his collar-stud and unscrewed it: the base was a miniature compass. He risked striking a match, shielding it with his scarf. Imagining that he must be still somewhere near Essen, he had two choices: to head west for Holland or south-west for Belgium. But might it not be possible to reach the Allied lines, with the progress that had recently been made?

It was an optimistic plan, rendered still more so by his instant collapse when he tried to stand. His left leg crumpled, oozing blood. He still had to get away from his pursuers, they must be somewhere near, and he began slowly and painfully to crawl like a crab through the forest. He had no clear idea whether he might be scrambling away from them or towards them, but he resolved to keep moving.

The autumn was not yet sufficiently advanced to have denuded the trees, and the branches above him shut out the sky. He was dragging himself around in the darkness, with orientation uncertain. He lit another match and felt he was going round in circles.

Suddenly the tree-trunks ahead acquired definition. Beyond them he fancied he glimpsed an open space, with reflected light seeping through. Keeping within the sanctuary of the forest, he looked for a chance to reconnoitre the route he had chosen.

He could hear the sound of bullets again, sometimes a single shot, sometimes rapid bursts, more like machine-gun fire. There was certainly a search on. Sifting through the crash area, no doubt, looking for him, and he supposed the others. He listened intently, but couldn't be sure where the sound was coming from. He just hoped he was getting farther away.

Reaching the clearing, he was frustrated to find that dawn, which he sensed was breaking, was blanketed by a seasonal ground-mist. There was certainly open ground ahead, but he could discern no detail. Then, rising like wraiths out of the mist, the dome-like turrets of what looked like a castle stood strangely suspended in mid-air. Four turrets, one at each corner. Nothing could have looked more menacingly Teutonic, and he floundered back into the forest. A building like that would be heavily guarded. He began to imagine the barking of dogs.

Exhausted by his efforts, and sick with nausea, he sank back to rest. Only one thing could possibly restore him: a cigarette. He inhaled the smoke avidly, hiding the glow of the cigarette under his jacket. Then he ate a malted milk tablet from his emergency pack and felt better.

The morning fog was really a blessing. Instead of waiting for nightfall, he might get safely clear of the wood in daylight, putting a useful distance between him and the crashed plane.

As first light seeped under the horizon the mists expanded, rolling around him as in some fanciful film. He almost wondered if he were in another world already. But a light drizzle, reassuringly earthy, was still falling. Now was the time to work his way into the open.

Somehow he had to evolve a more practical method of propulsion. Choosing a stout branch from the forest floor, he found that with its support he could hobble along. Thus he emerged from the wood just as Evadne had predicted.

Keeping a hedge at his shoulder for safety, he advanced laboriously across the field. He was about half-way when, not twenty yards distant, he saw something move. He shrank at once into the base of the hedge. He hoped it was some species of animal. But he knew in his heart it was not. It was the figure of a man, crouched over his work, mercifully facing away from him for the moment, apparently hoeing the ground. If he waited for the man to move away, he might wait all day. But his cover was flimsy. When the sun came up and the mist cleared, his hiding-place would be revealed.

He recalled another phrase from the escaper's guide. 'A man alone in a field is the best person to help you.'

Could that be true? So far as he could see the man was unarmed. A sudden confrontation might fluster him. It might be worth a try. What had he got to lose?

His helplessness suddenly seemed doubly agonising. Would it be more sensible to give himself up? Surely that was premature. He pulled out the card in his escape-gear which listed foreign expressions, and looked for 'Where am I?' He would try it in German.

He could still make out the ghostly figure of the farmer – as he supposed him to be. The man, intent on his hoeing, was almost squatting, still presenting his back. No half-measures now. He had the man at a disadvantage. He would rely on that.

Tucked into one of his suede leather flying boots was another item of escape equipment – a long-bladed sheath-knife. He withdrew it, then limped shakily towards the man. He judged that he was in his mid-forties, about his own height. His colouring looked Aryan enough, but he also had the ruddy complexion of the countryman. He might not be unfriendly. He crawled the last few feet to the man and gripped him by the thigh, prodding with the tip of his knife. 'Wo bin ich?' he demanded.

The man looked round in amazement. In doing so he saw an apparition. His attacker seemed a mixture of madman and the macabre. He was supporting himself on an improvised crutch, his face was badly contused, blood was dripping from a wound in his head, and he was muttering unintelligibly.

Rendered momentarily speechless, the farmer was weighing up his assailant, too astonished to be scared of him, sure that if it came to a struggle he could be easily overcome. He was aware of the knife, but resolved to take his time. Meanwhile he made no attempt to answer.

Getting no reaction, Cannon tried him in broken French. 'Comment s'appelle ce place ici?' When this, too, brought no response, Cannon increased the pressure on the knife, and his speech reverted to his native Australian. 'Where the hell am I, mate?'

Slowly, at first incredulously, the man began to smile. His dialect was as foreign to Cannon as any lingo he'd encountered, but the words he enunciated began to make sense.

'Ye be in Norfolk, lad. Over there' (pointing) 'be King's Lynn'.

Dumbfounded, he staggered drunkenly. What did the man mean, Norfolk? How could he be in Norfolk? Then the man took his arm protectively and helped him across what he now saw was a well-kept lawn. He had come down on some sort of estate, and the man, he was to learn, was chief gardener. He had been hoeing an onion-bed.

The castle Cannon had glimpsed was Houghton Hall, ancestral home of the Cholmondeley family, built originally in the Eighteenth Century by Sir Robert Walpole, Britain's first Prime Minister. No wonder it looked forbidding to Cannon. Late the previous day the housekeeper, Daisy Dye, had begun her usual round of blacking-out every window in the house. Every aperture had to be screened and checked, not least the 70-foot-long picture gallery. Hitler's secret weapons, the flying-bomb and the rocket, had been unleashed some months earlier, and there were rumours of launchings from ships off the Norfolk coast.

Later that evening, when she first heard the sound of engines, Daisy Dye had been thankful she had completed the black-out job. If they were hit now they couldn't blame her: that was her instinctive thought. But the roar grew to a crescendo second by second until it became thunderous. She knew now from hard experience what the sound was. It was a doomed plane, engines faltering, returning from a raid over Germany.

In the next moment the plane, already on fire, crunched and tore into a large beech tree with lacerating force and minimum recoil, tearing off the port wing before ploughing on short of a water-tower and an avenue of lime trees, reverberating like an earthquake. It seemed the house itself must disintegrate. As for the occupants of the plane, poor devils. There was no chance for anyone in there.

'There was a terrific explosion,' remembers the housekeeper, 'then a sheet of flame spread across the whole area.

'The flames were so brilliant they lit up the whole picture gallery, so I could see every detail of the paintings and the tapestries.

'Then came a series of smaller explosions and a huge banging as the engines, which had broken away from the plane, speared half a mile across the ground before ploughing into a field.

'My husband Fred, the chief gardener, and young Lord John Cholmondeley, on leave from the army, were the only other people on the property at the time. They raced towards the burning bomber but were driven back by the heat.

'Within minutes dozens of local men were on the scene. They tried to fight the fire and get to the crew. We all knew nobody could have survived that first explosion, but a big search was made in case

'For hours ammunition was bursting and zinging in all directions. And the explosions kept recurring as the fuel tanks blew up.

'By 3 a.m. the last of the rescue party had given up and gone home. We went to bed worrying about the men who had died and thinking of their families. It was a nightmare.'

Next morning Fred Dye was confronted by the apparition of Cannon, and Dye helped him into the Hall. He sat him down before a log fire, then went off to fetch his wife – and call an ambulance. Soon Daisy Dye was cleaning the blood off his face and examining the wound, making him tea and cooking him breakfast. No one mentioned that they had been up half the night, trying to rescue his comrades.

He was taken to hospital at the nearby RAF Station of Bircham Newton, which he guessed Richins had been trying to reach. Cannon

was given sedatives which quietened him for two or three days, but he was not badly hurt. Then he started asking questions.

All he was able to learn was that after he was apparently knocked unconscious over the target his crew had turned for home. Staggering under a weight of ice that accumulated on the airframe, they had been unable to climb above it, but they had sent an SOS to say they had been hit, and had wounded on board, and they kept in touch with base as they fought their way back across Holland and the North Sea,

Wren Stobo's watch, found by Bert Lee.

nursing their crippled plane towards the nearest haven, the RAF airfield at Bircham Newton, Norfolk, crashing almost within sight of their goal.

Of the seven men on board, Jack Cannon, already unconscious, was the one whose chances must have seemed the worst. In the event, he was the only one to survive.

The Squadron Diary recorded the tragedy briefly. 'One aircraft, H-Harry Two, Flying Officer D.R.G.Richins, crashed at 12.56 in a field adjacent to Bircham Newton. Six men were killed and one baled out.'

So he had baled out after all! Yet he had no recollection of doing so. He just could not believe it, could not reconcile himself to a conclusion so at variance with his admittedly tortured memory. But he knew he must put it out of his mind. The shock of losing his mates was enough to be going on with.

It remained a mystery that one day he would hope to solve. Meanwhile he was grateful for the message – when he was ready to leave hospital – that 'he was to report to Mrs K.Attiwill (Evadne Price) at Hellingly in Sussex.' Sitting in the churchyard in the late autumn sunshine with Evadne, he began his rehabilitation.

Thirty-seven years after the bodies of Cannon's crew had been recovered from the wreck at Houghton Hall, one particularly persistent East Anglian archaeological digger, Bert Lee, of Fakenham, Norfolk, with his son Arthur, was successful in unearthing many items of the crews' effects from the crashed plane, now almost entirely hidden – among them a cap badge, belt buckles, glasses, buttons, even watches. One such, a gold wrist-watch, Wren Stobo's, was inscribed: 'To Wren from Flo 7.11.36.'

These and many other artefacts from wartime crashes and wrecks in East Anglia were collected together informally after the war to form a small private museum, sited on an old wartime airfield owned by farmer Tommy Cushing, some 15 miles east of Houghton Hall. (This museum has since been permanently established as the Norfolk and Suffolk Aviation Museum at Flixton, near Bungay, Suffolk.)

'I own the old airfield,' Cushing told me, writing in 1983, 'and I have collected or been given many interesting items over the years. One man has been very helpful and does not seem to be happy unless he is up to his neck in mud digging in the airfield pits.' This was Bert Lee, who has produced photos and diagrams of the crash site. 'One of his digs recently was Jack Cannon's Lancaster,' continued Cushing, and he admitted to being especially curious to know more about the inscription on the watch. 'Flo was presumably a girl friend of Wren. I wonder what happened to her?' Any efforts that may have been made over the years to find her have been unsuccessful, but we know now, through Jack Cannon, that the watch was a gift from Wren's girl-friend Florence Hedley, to mark his birthday, also their engagement. Seven months later, on 24 May 1937, they were married.

There was more, much more. On 8 March 1939 a child Frances was born, at the Royal Hospital for Women, Paddington, New South Wales. They were then living at Bellevue Hill, Sydney. Her father's occupation was given as 'Golf Attendant'. This was well-suited to Wren's congenial temperament.

Sixty years later, on 23 May 2003, after Frances's address had become known to Jack Cannon, she wrote:

> 'I was five years old when the plane crashed and I can still feel the utter despair and devastation of my mother's crying when someone knocked on our door and told her the news. I wouldn't have known anything about death and dying, but I did know the feeling of sadness, of being alone and somehow guilty.'

Frances had been too young to get to know her father: she was still only three when he volunteered for the air force, and he completed his training in Canada. Then it had been on to a squadron in England, with no home leave, followed by eleven sorties over Germany. Finally came the knock on the door.

After that awful period of devastation, Flo made what she could of her life. 'My mother remarried when I was seven years old,' Frances says, 'and she asked me to keep a secret. I was not to talk of my father – I had a new one.

> 'I had a new home, as well as a new Daddy, we moved to a new neighbourhood, and I went to a new school. No one knew us before we moved in. My mother, whose life had been so tragically interrupted – she had been married for seven years – determined to make a fresh start.
> 'It was my mother's way of making my stepfather feel secure as the head of the family. He was always good to me and I always called him Dad.'

Soon the new family was completed when Flo gave birth to a boy. Whether it was the intention or not, young Frances kept the secret through the years that followed, and never told anyone that 'Dad' was not her real Dad. It simply did not arise.

It was not until ten years ago that she even told her own children – there were three of them by then – and it was not until Flo died three

Wren Stobo's daughter Frances (right) and grand-daughter Letitia at the memorial at Canberra, December 2003.

years ago that she brought the subject up with her half-brother John. It transpired that he had always known, but somehow the subject had never come up in the home and wittingly or unwittingly he too had kept the secret.

Frances now resolved to write at last to her closest friends and tell them the 'secret'. 'That,' she says, 'was a tremendous weight lifted off my shoulders.'

Although she had come to understand her mother's reaction, it was a burden she was relieved to shed, and once having rid herself of it she wanted desperately to know more, and to see if the one man who might be able to tell her, the sole survivor of her father's crew, Jack Cannon, of whom she had read in a magazine, was still alive.

Thus she went, as recently as 6 December 2003, to a Bomber Command Commemorative Ceremony at the War Memorial in

Canberra, when a wartime Lancaster, G for George, of none other than 460 Squadron, Royal Australian Air Force (Cannon's own squadron), having been completely restored, was the main exhibit at the opening ceremony. The event was highly publicised, more than 3,000 people attending, and although, as she discovered afterwards, Jack Cannon was there, she still didn't know whether he was alive, and had no luck in finding him that day. But with her youngest daughter Letitia she was able to lay a wreath on the memorial. It had been fashioned by Letitia herself, Wren's granddaughter, with, as Frances says, 'love and feeling'. Daughter and granddaughter cried together.

Two days later, on 8 December, Frances records: 'I went back to the War Memorial to spend some time with my own thoughts, talking to my father. I found that the wreath Letitia had made had been moved – to the centre of the memorial.'

Next Frances went to the Department of Veterans' Affairs, also in Canberra, where she found an address for Jack. Although now seventy-nine he proved to be fit and well, and he was soon talking to Frances. 'She was absolutely overcome when visiting me in Melbourne', says Jack. 'She says it was one of the biggest thrills of her life.'

Meanwhile, she met members of the Squadron Association 'who opened up their arms to me. It was so good for my soul to be able to acknowledge my father in this way, to be proud of him dying for his country and his family. I was finally able to grieve – something I had held back all those years.'

The name of the old airfield owned by Cushing was the one that – as Phyllis Handley remembers – had once given Denis Richins such cause for amusement: Little Snoring! Ironical that he, or some of his personal effects, should end up in Cushing's collection at Little Snoring.

Both these 'strapping six-footers' from Tamworth, New South Wales, who would never be forgotten in Swindon, were gone.

When I first wrote a short account of this story, in 1983, and mentioned the name of Cannon's pilot, Denis Richins, it brought a letter from Swindon, from none other than Phyllis Handley, who told me how she had met the boys. That was my first contact with her. She had never forgotten them. 'I am wondering' she had written, 'if the pilot Denis Richins was my cousin. Both Denis and his brother Stuart visited their aunt (my mother) in Swindon and I was able to meet them.' She was of course correct. She continued: 'My mother and Denis's parents are now deceased but I write to their sister, she is in a Nursing Home in Australia.'

Working on the story again twenty years later, in 2003, I turned up her original letter, and wrote again, somewhat tentatively, in the hope

I might find her. It was a wonderful surprise to find that she was still going strong at eighty-four. The boys' parents were dead, but after 60 years she had kept faith with her two Australian cousins. Her own parents too were dead, as was her husband, and she was living alone in a retirement flat. Was it conceivable, after all this time, and so many changes in her life, that she had access to any photographs of her cousins? They came by return of post.

Tragedy had meanwhile pursued the boys' parents in a particularly poignant way. On their way to England from Tamworth to visit the boys' graves – in Cambridge – they had reached Sydney when their mother had a heart attack and died, and their father too never made it. Even their sister Berice was now dead.

Twenty years passed, from that night in 1944, before Jack Cannon felt able to turn the clock back and try to retrace his steps. Working then as London representative of an Australian newspaper, he decided to go back to Houghton Hall and renew his wartime acquaintance with Fred and Daisy Dye. Over the years, some fresh clues might have emerged which might explain what happened. Instead, what he learned only compounded the riddle.

The two trees which the Lancaster crashed into while attempting to land.
(Bert Lee)

The water tower on the left side of which the Lancaster finally crashed. (Bert Lee)

He learned from eye-witnesses how the Lancaster, ploughing into the wood, had hit a huge beech tree. Fred Dye took him out and showed him the tree. A lower branch still showed the effects of that violent moment of amputation, retaining a lop-sided look that new growth could not conceal. Next Dye took him to a different part of the

The tree that severed the port wing still bears the scar (viewed from the west – see diagram p 176, taken from position one). (Bert Lee)

wood, at least 400 yards short of where the wreck had ploughed in, and pointed to the high branches of another tree. 'That,' he said, 'is where your parachute harness was found.'

Finally he showed him where, in a third direction, his parachute pack, still unopened, had turned up with other items some days later.

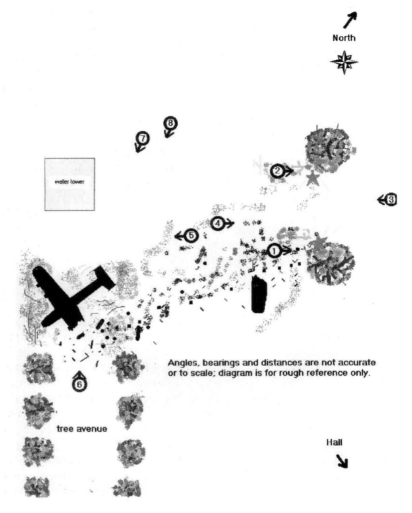

North

Angles, bearings and distances are not accurate
or to scale; diagram is for rough reference only.

water tower

tree avenue

Hall

A reconstruction of the known path of the Lancaster. (Bert Lee)

He had come up to Norfolk in an endeavour to clear up a mystery, and he was now more bewildered than ever. The conclusion he had originally come to, all those years ago, was that, in a semi-conscious state, he must have baled out. But his harness had apparently been torn off, he had had no chance to don his pack, and it must have been thrown out undamaged when the plane hit the ground. Neither, in any case, was anywhere near the spot where Dye estimated Cannon had found himself when he came to.

What about the record in the squadron diary? This could have been no more than an assumption. How else but by parachute, the squadron recorders must have argued, could he have survived?

Cannon was quite sure he had been wearing his parachute harness. He certainly had no recollection of clipping his pack on. But if he hadn't baled out – and it was obvious now he couldn't have done – why wasn't his pack still strapped in its rack at the time of the crash, to be incinerated with the rest of the plane? And what happened to his harness?

One man, aviation archaeologist Bert Lee, has a theory. 'I feel pretty sure that as the aircraft banked steeply between the two large trees, losing chunks off the wings, Cannon's turret was torn off, with him unconscious in it. This would account for his description of regaining consciousness under a tree, with his parachute landing elsewhere.

'As the turret broke away he must have been flung out. Then his harness, snagging on a branch and acting as a brake, suspended him momentarily before disintegrating, releasing him at low speed. In effect he was slowed to a standstill before being laid gently to the ground, a long way short of the crash.

'I know it's just a theory. But all the facts would then fall neatly into place.' They would indeed.

Jack had one more outstanding duty – to find and visit Eric Sunderland's parents at Shipley. They took him to the local church where Eric was buried, then to the Congregational Club, and finally to their home. They had maintained Eric's bedroom as if he had never left it. His uniform was preserved on a hangar, his shirt was ironed and the collar starched, his cap, his shoes and his tie were beside the bed. Most moving of all was that his nearly-new polished black-and-silver motor-cycle was on a framed stand beside the bed. 'It was a very traumatic moment,' remembers Jack.

Even sixty years after the crash Jack protests that he still can't answer the obvious questions – another twenty years after his abortive attempt at elucidation back in 1964. But we now have Bert Lee's theory, surely irresistible.

Cannon's injuries over the target must have been what ultimately saved his life. Unconscious in the mid-upper turret, he had been hurled out violently enough on impact, accounting for his head injuries, but his fall to earth had been retarded and cushioned, as Bert Lee deduced.

Since his visit to Houghton Hall in the autumn of 1964, and again after further conjecture, Jack Cannon has simply had to accept his survival as miraculous. What he can't explain, though, is how the phenomenon of second sight, sixth sense, clairvoyance, paranormal perception, intuition – whatever his 'English Aunt' liked to call it – could have cast its shadows before.

CHAPTER TEN

Jim Hall – Washed-out Jamaican Pilot Saves Bomber Crew, Rhine Crossing, March 1945

'Bomb doors open! Steady up for the bombing run!'

Flight Sergeant Jim Hall, the mid-upper gunner in the centre of a box of six Mitchell Mark II B25 bombers, had a kaleidoscopic view of the action. They were approaching the target in daylight, on a brilliant, sunny morning, not a cloud in the sky. A hint of haze in the atmosphere was reflecting the sunshine. It was the first day of spring, 21 March 1945, and this was his seventy-first operational flight – his seventieth with his present crew.

As No. 4 in the formation, Hall's plane was tucked in directly under the leader. Nos. 2 and 3 were above him left and right of centre, and Nos. 5 and 6 were formating just behind, virtually wing-tip to wing-tip, but all at separate heights, clear of each other's slipstream. They had found that this was the best formation for defence against German fighters, though nowadays they rarely saw them.

Varying his gaze second by second, the twenty-year-old Hall squinted apprehensively at the proximity of the other five Mitchells before focusing on the target 12,000 feet below.

'Left, left.. ...steady…..steady…..'

Six Allied armies were massing for the crossing of the Rhine, the final step towards victory in Europe. But first they were relying on the men of the air forces to smash the enemy supply routes and make their crossing feasible. Maximum effort had been ordered.

The twin-engined Mitchells, of No.180 Squadron of the Second Tactical Air Force, RAF, had taken off from their base at Melsbroek,

Brussels at 09.13 and set course north-east for Bocholt, 120 miles distant, 12 miles across the Rhine into Germany. It wasn't long before the railway marshalling yards they had been briefed to attack were in sight.

A few moments earlier they had been dodging and weaving in perfect unison to confuse the flak predictors. Now, with the German gunners putting up a tremendous box barrage straight ahead, which they would have to fly through, their progress became frustratingly smooth, rhythmic and undeviating. It was a paradox that provoked a wry grin from Jim Hall.

'Left.....left.....steady.....'

All life seemed to be concentrated into a narrow span of time that might last less than half a minute. But as the flak bursts crept closer, and the curtain of fire seemed impenetrable, time was atrophied.

'Steady.....steady.....'

Soon the whole box, carrying 24,000lbs of bombs between them, would drop at a signal from the leader. Why didn't he drop the damn things now? They must be right in the middle of the barrage, bang over the target.

'Bombing.....bombing.....Go!'

At last! Hall had already swung his turret to starboard, but he glimpsed the leader's bombs, falling lazily away. His attention, however, was caught by something else – the No.2, Roy Clipsham, whose crew, like his own, were on their second tour. He knew them all. The formation had opened up a little for the bombing run, and Hall was staring straight up into Clipsham's bomb-doors. The bombs were releasing erratically. Something was wrong.

Without consciously counting, he knew that only seven bombs had gone. The eighth must have hung up.

For a split second he had a clear view of the bomb, jammed in the bomb-bay. Then came a cataclysmic explosion which reduced the flak-bursts to pinpricks and blew in the roof of his own turret. For a moment he lost consciousness. When he came to, his own plane was descending in a steep spiral, out of control.

Bits of Roy Clipsham's aircraft were cartwheeling around them. There had been five men in that Mitchell, including a photographer, and it was curtains for them all. The plane had broken up. The refractory bomb must have collected a direct hit.

To the left he could see the No.3, Bobbie Kennard, an Australian, also on his second tour, going down in flames. A single parachute, stark as a question mark, hung apparently motionless in the sky.

Choked by the smoke that filled his turret and nauseated by the stench of cordite, Hall pressed the release catch on his seat and tumbled with

some difficulty out of his turret. As he did so he heard the other two regular crew-members, Pilot Officer R.J. Roberton, navigator, and Flying Officer R.W.Butler, air gunner – both Australians – calling to the pilot, Dick Perkins, 'Dick! Are you all right, Dick?' They were crawling towards the cockpit from their stations, one in the nose, the other in the tail, to find out why the plane was diving out of control.

Dick Perkins, the pilot, had had a premonition that morning that something was wrong. He couldn't put his finger on it, but he had done all his cockpit checks twice over. Squadron superstitions didn't usually bother him. One was the notion that it was fatal to get commissioned on the squadron – and he had recently been commissioned. Often, as it seemed, disaster followed. The other was that it was fatal to take an extra 'bod', a supernumerary crew-man. That too was reckoned to bring bad luck, but that one didn't bother him either.

In fact, the extra man was not some gash volunteer but a fully trained waist gunner, listed on the Battle Order, Warrant Officer Donald Freeman. Not all the Mitchells carried the extra gun position, but this one did. Freeman was more apprehensive at the thought of flying with a strange crew than Perkins was of taking him. And with waist guns available on each side of the fuselage and downward firing guns in the tail, it was more than likely that he might make himself useful.

Dick Perkins. (Angela Perkins)

Perkins, coming from a distinguished military background, had surprised family and friends by preferring the RAF for his wartime service. And amongst his companions during training he had found most in common with men from the Dominions, and he had chosen two Australians and a Jamaican to make up his crew. Either that or they had chosen him. The Jamaican was Jim Hall.

Despite having led a sheltered life in Jamaica as the son of the Assistant Director of Medical Services (Dr.J.M.Hall, MBE), Jim spoke and acted with the uncomplicated directness of the colonial. Although lightly built and far from robust, he had a reassuring 'presence', suggesting an innate maturity. This maturity had enabled him to suffer setbacks without resentment.

Chief among these setbacks had been his rejection as pilot. He had expected to pass, and others had expected it of him. But one mistake had been enough. Coming in to land one day under instruction, in a Canadian-built Finch II biplane – he hadn't yet got as far as going solo – he had missed a warning red Very light fired from the control tower, and soon afterwards they had washed him out. It seemed a trivial error, and he always told himself they must have been looking for an excuse to fail him. Which he realised later they probably were: 75 per cent of his course were washed out. There were too many pilots under training,

Perkins taking off in his B-25 from Melsbroek, Brussels. (Angela Perkins)

Perkins in his cockpit of a B-25, showing his number of 'strikes'. (Angela Perkins)

and not enough navigators, wireless operators and gunners. But whether he was making excuses for himself he was never quite sure.

Offered the chance of a transfer to air gunner, he had accepted. If that was what they needed, so be it.

All that had been back in Canada eighteen months previously. After crew training on Venturas, conversion to Mitchells and a tour and a half with 180 Squadron – the tour had been gradually extended from 30 trips to 50, and then beyond, after a short break – his brief spell as a trainee pilot seemed a lifetime ago.

Dick Perkins had felt the slight lift as the bombs were released, then a sledge-hammer blow had knocked his right leg off the rudder-bar. He let out a yell, not so much from pain as from shock, although the pain, too, soon became excruciating. Before he realised what was happening, he was staring at the ground 12,000 feet below as the Mitchell plunged almost vertically downhill.

Christ, he thought! It's happened at last! He fought to pull the stick back and drag the nose up, but the controls, heavy at the best of times in a Mitchell, were solid. To get some leverage he tried pressing down on the rudder-bar with both feet, but all he succeeded in doing was putting on sharp left rudder, which sent the plane into a steep spiral. Unknown to him as yet, his right leg was useless.

A jagged hole in the starboard wall of the cockpit revealed where the flak – Perkins thought it was flak, but Hall thought it was flying debris – had crashed into him. It had smashed through his right thigh. Some of it had penetrated his left leg too and come out the other side.

It was impossible to move the control column. The air-flow over the elevators was too strong. The only hope was to wind her out on the elevator trimmer. His fingers felt for the knurled wheel, and there was a response. The relief was intense, yet he operated the trimmer cautiously. They were going down so fast that if he wound her out too quickly she might break up.

Members of the crew were struggling forward to reach Perkins. The extra man, Donald Freeman, at the waist gun, watched in astonishment as the white-faced tail gunner, Dickie Butler, crawled past him over the bomb-bay and hauled himself through to the front. As it happened, Butler was a small man. But Hall got there first, where he found Perkins still fighting the controls. Unable to apply right rudder to counteract the spiral, he threw the port throttle wide open and half-closed the other. Slowly the Mitchell straightened out. But he still couldn't synchronise the engines.

Appalled at first by the scene of devastation in the cockpit, Hall found that fragments of instruments and instrument panel had been scattered everywhere. The stench of scorched clothing and burnt skin choked his throat, and swirling smoke stung his eyes. Worst of all, blood was spattered all round the cockpit.

'Are you all right, Dick?'

'Yes, I'm all right. Been hit in the leg.'

Hall looked down and saw that blood was pumping out of the skipper's right leg at an alarming rate. He would not last long like this. There was dual control in the Mitchell, and someone would have to take over. Hall was already climbing into the right-hand seat. If he could hold the plane briefly while the others attended to Dick, they might have a chance.

By this time 'Robbie' Roberton had managed to crawl back from the nose section, while Butler, after his scramble forward, had joined them in the cockpit. First on the scene, but the most junior, Hall was tacitly accepted as co-pilot. As Perkins finally got the engines synchronised

Jim Hall. (Alan Cooper)

and trimmed the Mitchell out into level flight, he motioned to Hall to take over. He looked as good as done for. Although they had lost at least 5,000 feet, everyone was icy calm.

Apart from the few minutes dual that Perkins had given him during their conversion course on to Mitchells, Hall had not flown for eighteen months, and then it had been in a light aircraft, a single-engined biplane, elementary, obsolescent and primitive. He had not even been judged capable of flying that. Now, in a cockpit that on his side was little more than a shell, he was being asked to take over a crippled but massive and totally modern, highly sophisticated war machine in which, so far as he could see, most of the instruments he would need had been knocked out.

Even as he grabbed hold of the control column he realised it was useless. All the leads on this side had been severed. If he was going to fly the aircraft, they would have to get Dick out of his seat.

Although still fully conscious, Perkins was weakening perceptibly. He had fought and won a life-or-death struggle to bring the Mitchell under control, and the struggle had prostrated him. If they didn't stop the bleeding he would die. He indicated to Hall that they must swap over, and between them the other two lifted him out of his seat.

Meanwhile another Australian pilot, Tom Crawley, No.6 in the shattered formation, had been watching Perkins' Mitchell falling out of the sky. He himself had had the nose section of his aircraft smashed in the explosion. But he had retained full control. Joined in the cockpit by his pale and shocked navigator, they watched what looked like the end of Perkins. Just when they had written him off they saw the plane miraculously recover. Then the stricken Mitchell seemed to wallow and bucket like a waterlogged boat: they could not know it, but Perkins and Hall were changing places. They breathed again as Hall, safely established in the left-hand seat, held the plane steady.

'What's it feel like, Jimmy?'

The switch to the more friendly 'Jimmy' was meant to be encouraging. Meanwhile Hall, overwhelmed by the size of the wings and the engine nacelles on either side, so vast and unfamiliar to him, was content to say nothing and to make as few adjustments as possible. Perkins had set the plane up. His first touch on the stick alarmed him by its weight, something for which even the practice flight with Perkins all those months ago had left him unprepared. But the whole commotion of changing seats had given him no time to think about it. Eventually he felt he had to say something. 'She feels all right,' he told Perkins, and added: 'Bit heavy, though.' For the rookie Hall it was a masterpiece of understatement.

The realisation was dawning on them all that the change-over was more than a temporary expedient. It was as well it came slowly. Staying temporarily airborne was all that mattered for the moment. What lay ahead of them was beyond contemplation.

In civilian life Dickie Butler had had some training as a vet, and he set about applying a tourniquet to Perkins' leg below the hip, and gave him morphine. The impossibility of his regaining the left-hand seat was becoming apparent. It would be up to Hall. And with dual control destroyed already, Hall's mistakes, if he made any, could not be corrected – except by him. In a badly crippled bomber that might or might not stay up, he was going solo for the first time.

Had he been kidding himself all this time about the reason why they had washed him out, months ago in Canada? Had they decided he wasn't up to it? He would soon know.

There could be no question of abandoning the aircraft. They would never get Dick out. None of them would countenance leaving him. Perkins did not even broach the idea. He knew what their answer would be. As for the spare man, he didn't come into their thoughts. In any case, unknown to them all, some of the parachute packs had been damaged.

If there was one word that Perkins would have used about Hall it was 'unflappable'. That mysterious quality of 'presence' was anathema to any form of panic. Perkins felt confirmed in his character assessment: he looked unflappable now. In fact, the Jamaican's feelings belied his looks. He was facing something altogether outside his experience, and his mind was spinning with a kind of centrifugal force which on every revolution seemed to throw out the question: 'How am I going to get the damn thing down?'

With the link to one control column severed, there was no saying what damage the other link might have sustained, or how long the plane might stay up. Already the port engine was running roughly, and they were losing height. But straight ahead he could see the broad expanse of the Rhine. Once across that they would be over friendly territory, where they must put down on the first runway they saw. Quite apart from the damage to the plane, expert medical treatment was urgently needed for Perkins.

Hall remembered for the first time that back towards the tail was an extra man who must be wondering what the hell was going on up front. Sensibly enough, Freeman had kept out of the way, fearing to aggravate what must be a chaotic cockpit scene. Hall tried to reach him on the inter-com, but it was dead. Then he thought of the radio – the VHF voice radio, which had superseded the old wireless. The set was to his left, and he switched it on.

'Mayday! Mayday! Mayday! This is Oxo Brown 4. Do you read? Over.'

'Oxo Brown Four from Base. Change to Emergency Channel B and call Eindhoven. Call-sign Gigantic.'

Even Eindhoven was 40 miles away, which meant 15 minutes' flying. It was 15 minutes too long. But he called them and told them what had happened. They came back with a course to steer of 250 degrees, and he glanced ruefully at the shattered compass. Then even the voice radio went dead. From the position of the sun he guessed he was heading south-west, and when this was confirmed by Roberton, he held his course.

'There's an airfield! Straight ahead!'

The shout came from Butler, who was standing behind him. It was an airfield all right, but a tiny one, designated B90. There was a makeshift runway of PSP – pierced steel planking – but it looked frighteningly short. It would have to do.

'It isn't German, is it?'

'No. It's British all right. I can see Spitfires.'

They had spotted a front-line landing strip occupied by Johnnie Johnson's fighter wing. The runway was long enough for Spitfires, but desperately short for a Mitchell.

Half-insensate from the morphine and stupefied by the loss of blood, Perkins was still able to reason. He roused himself sufficiently to attempt the role of instructor, mostly at little more then a whisper, to pass on to Hall, making an effort to talk him down. Hall, isolated as though in a vacuum, was nevertheless reacting correctly if subconsciously. There was not much else Perkins could do.

With no indicated air speed, no boost gauges, and no rev counters, Hall's only judgement of speed came from the throttle settings. With no certainty that either engine was developing full power, Hall was keeping both throttles wide open, at the same time easing the Mitchell into a shallow dive. What he feared above all else was to lose flying speed.

The crux would come when he began the landing attempt. He reckoned he was doing over 200 miles an hour, dramatically fast for a safe touch-down. Sooner or later he would have to reduce speed, yet to stall on the final approach was a recurring nightmare. Better to fly the plane into that steel planking and trust it would absorb the shock.

There were other factors complicating the landing. The hydraulics had been damaged, the bomb-doors, having been opened, wouldn't close, and that meant that undercarriage and flaps were suspect. Any attempt to lower the undercarriage might result in one wheel locking down and the other staying up, fatal for the landing attempt. The same was true of the flaps. Essential though they were for reducing speed, they might flip the plane over on its back if they failed on one side. There was no doubt in Hall's mind – and Perkins assented, by a nod of the head – that a wheels-up landing at above normal speed must be the choice.

They were over the landing strip now, height about 2,000 feet. As Hall began a left-hand circuit, Roberton fired two red distress flares to warn airfield control.

'The runway's on your side, Jimmy,' Perkins confirmed, again trying to imply reassurance by his extended use of the name. 'Can you see it?'

'I've got it.'

Before moving back to brace themselves in their own crash positions, the two Australians between them fitted flak helmets on Perkins and Hall and checked their straps.

Steering a course parallel with the runway, keeping it in sight and absorbing the topography, Hall was letting down steadily. A mile or so past the runway he turned left prior to lining up for his final approach. It wasn't until the PSP lay straight ahead that they saw the wind-sock. Perkins saw it first. They were coming in down-wind.

'We're up-wind, Jimmy! You'll have to go round!' Somehow Perkins kept the urgency out of his voice, as though it were a routine approach, and Hall reacted coolly. Any attempt to land down-wind on such a desperately short runway, even wheels up, was rejected. Turning away to starboard, Hall flew at right angles to the runway for a half-minute or so, then turned left to complete the down-wind leg. With the runway now behind him, he turned until he was at right angles to it and watched it in his port window until it swam into line. Then he turned in on his second attempt at a final approach.

All this manoeuvring had cost him precious height. He was down to 500 feet.

There was an avenue of poplars not far short of the runway coming from this direction. For a normal, flap-assisted approach they presented no problem: pilots simply floated their aircraft in over the top. But for the long, low, flat approach to which Hall was committed, they offered an obstruction.

He would have to turn in over the tops of the trees before immediately cutting the throttles, to guard against overshooting. There was rough ground beyond, but he thought he was going to make it. He was settling down nicely on an imaginary line that would just clear the tree-tops when the penultimate shock came. The control caravan fired him a red.

For a moment he was flying that ancient Fleet trainer again, reliving the whole confidence-sapping experience. He had missed the signal then, they had washed him out, and it had changed his life. It was as vivid as any flash-back. But now he thought, to hell with that! Another circuit, and a climb away to execute it, was not to be thought of. He could see no other aircraft anywhere near the approach. Perhaps they thought he was too low, crediting him with an expertise he didn't have. He didn't care if they washed him out for ever now. The test he was trying to pass did not depend on obeying instructions from the ground.

He was flying a badly damaged aircraft that might at any time become uncontrollable or break up. Perkins had lost too much blood to be kept waiting any longer. Whatever their priorities were on the ground, they could scarcely be more urgent than his. He could still see nothing else in the circuit, and he maintained his course.

The ground controller was trying to warn him to land on the grass beside the runway, keeping the runway clear of obstruction. This was normal procedure for a crash landing. The controller had realised by now that he was dealing with an emergency. Perkins guessed at once what they were after, but he made an instant decision not to interfere. Hall was committed, and to divert him now was to court disaster. The runway was something clearly defined: it had lateral limits, a beginning, a middle, and an end. It gave Hall something to aim at, and to Perkins that was decisive.

To Hall the runway seemed very like, in his imagination, the deck of an aircraft carrier. The whole picture was clearly etched on his mind, the distances judged and estimates made. Come what may, he was going through with it.

He was coming in too high and too fast. He knew that already, and as the pierced steel planking rushed into focus, it became frighteningly clear. He was reaching for the throttle levers when he heard Perkins shout: 'Throttle back!'

As soon as he did so the aircraft sank. For a moment he thought he had judged it right. Then they were almost into the trees.

'More throttle.....more throttle.....'

He rammed the throttles open and roared in over the trees, brushing the tops. The impression of speed was terrific, but he eased the stick forward. A moment ago the ground had been racing past him. Now it was soaring up at him. He could see individual holes in the PSP as he levelled out.

'Right – chop!'

Hall cut the throttles but this time nothing happened. They were careering along fifty feet above the runway as smoothly as in a fly-past. Then his stomach rocketed into his throat as the plane dropped. It struck the runway a shattering blow, metal on metal, tearing off the bomb-doors, sending debris in all directions, then bouncing skywards twenty, thirty, even forty feet from the deck.

'Hold it, Jimmy! For Christ's sake, hold it!'

If Hall panicked now, the crash might be fatal. But he sat there mesmerised, keeping the stick absolutely central, while the Mitchell regained its equilibrium unaided. Then it plunged into the runway in straight and level flight, spreading the impact.

'SWITCHES!'

He had forgotten the switches. Prompted by Perkins, he switched them off almost as they hit. This, almost certainly, saved them from fire. Meanwhile Hall's abiding memory was of the individual blades of the propellers bending back like an umbrella as each one hit the ground.

Crash tender and ambulances screamed into action and Perkins was soon lifted out. No one had been hurt in the actual crash. Ambulance men carried Perkins off on a stretcher, for surgery that would save his life – and eventually, after two years in hospital, restore him to a measure of health, though he would always limp. Hall's impression of what had caused their misfortune was confirmed by the bits they took

Dick Perkins after he had recovered, in 1948, with his parents at Buckingham Palace. (Angela Perkins)

out of Perkins, which showed, after analysis, that he hadn't been hit by flak, as he'd thought, but by jagged fragments of a British bomb.

Donald Freeman, the extra man, pale and shaken but otherwise unharmed, had emerged meanwhile from the rear of the plane. Feeling a 'spare bod' as never before, he had been aware, when Butler, the tail gunner, crawled past him and over the bomb-bay, after the plane's sudden dramatic dive, that there had been carnage up front. All he could do to help was keep out of the way, and he composed himself as best he could. The bonding that the crew shared, after 70 raids together, had united them in their peril, but this solace was denied Freeman, and there was nothing he could do about it. Hall had tried to call him, but the inter-com was dead, and Freeman, as Perkins was the first to admit afterwards, was forgotten.

When the plane skidded along the runway Freeman jettisoned the rear hatches before stepping out of the plane. He was so quick to do so that the ambulance and fire tender crews tracking the wreck (before it came to a stop) thought the uninjured Freeman was an idle spectator, not realising he was a member of the crew. He had survived it all, and his experience, because of his isolation, must surely have been doubly terrifying.

As they reached the ambulance, Freeman saw – and recognised – the man on the stretcher, and asked, bewildered, 'What happened to *him*?'

He turned even paler when he learned the truth.

They gave Jim Hall the CGM (Conspicuous Gallantry Medal) and Dick Perkins the DSO (Distinguished Service Order). Two days later the Rhine Crossing was made.

When I visited Jim Hall in Ipswich in 1978 he had recently recovered from a heart attack. He had further attacks after that, and as my original story did not appear until 1983, he did not live to see it. But he had seen and corrected the draft copy.

So too had Dick Perkins. It took him two years to fight back from his injuries, but he then trained as an architect, practising for many years as 'Richard Perkins and Partners' in Reading, Berks. I recently heard from his wife Angela, to tell me of his passing, and she writes: 'Things finally caught up with Dick and he died in March 2001 after a longish stay in hospital, fifty-six years and one day after his little 'incident'. We had three children, he always encouraged them to be totally independent, and they always said 'he was their rock'. We never met anyone who didn't like him. His last few years had not been easy, but he kept battling and was courageous to the last.' He had reached his eightieth year.

I also heard from the 'extra man', Donald Freeman – by then residing in Spain – to correct me on errors made in my original story.

APPENDIX ONE

The Edrich Citation

'On the morning of 12th August 1941, Blenheim bombers carried out simultaneous attacks on the great power-stations near Cologne. A strong force attacked the power station at Knapsack, while a smaller force attacked two power stations at Quadrath. These missions involved a flight of some 250 miles over enemy territory which was carried out at an altitude of 100 feet. At Knapsack the target was accurately bombed and machine-gunned from between 200 and 800 feet. At Quadrath both power stations were hit from the height of the chimneys; the turbine house at one of the two stations was left a mass of flames and smoke. The success of this combined daylight attack and the co-ordination of the many formations of aircraft depended largely on accurate timing throughout the flight. That complete success was achieved, despite powerful opposition from enemy ground and air defences, is a high tribute to the calm courage and resolute determination displayed by the following officers and airmen, who participated in various capacities as leaders and members of the aircraft crews.'

The list of awards included DSOs, DFCs, and DFMs. Edrich was one of those awarded the DFC, and the recommendation for his citation read, in part: 'This officer had the difficult task of bringing his formation in to attack the main power station immediately after the leading box had attacked. This needed fine judgement as it was imperative that the target should be bombed from as low an altitude as possible. He had to delay his attack in order to avoid his formation being destroyed by explosions from the delay action bombs of the previous boxes. This required coolness and courage .....

'Squadron-Leader Edrich led his formation in at exactly the right height and time, all aircraft dropping the bombs in the centre of the target area. By carrying out his orders with the greatest exactitude and determination, he must be given credit for a large part of the success of the attack.'

Evadne Price –
A Brief Biography

An intriguing mix of mystery and mistaken identity blur the beginnings of Evadne's childhood. She is said to have been born at sea, in the Indian Ocean, the daughter of a sea captain and an artist, in 1896 – somewhat prematurely, as we now believe – and educated at schools in Australia, Belgium and England. Yet in an interview for a Self Portrait, published by the National Library of Australia in 1977, she denies ever having been to Australia until much later in life. She was, it seems, born in 1905. We also know that she packed into her long life a colourful image of herself as writer, playwright, journalist, actress, war correspondent, and astrologist, comparable with almost any popular figure of her time.

By her own account, she was born in Sussex, one of five children, of Bohemian parents. When her father died, her mother, a talented and ambitious but struggling artist, farmed the children out elsewhere, in Evadne's case to a sister – another ambitious but less impecunious artist. The aunt lived in Chelsea. Nothing more is heard of the siblings.

Whatever stage Evadne's education may have reached, her aunt was too busy with her canvases to give it much thought. Evadne was simply told to make herself scarce from nine in the morning until five in the evening, and given a shilling to buy herself lunch. This, in the back streets of Chelsea, where Evadne wandered for most of the day, was passable pocket money.

That she should get into picaresque company was perhaps inevitable, and Evadne, already stage-struck, landed a part in a small repertory company. She was now fifteen. Here she learned of the Theatre Girls' Club, with accommodation in Soho. It was cheap, the aunt approved, and thus she embarked on a stage career.

After understudying for a role in a West End show, she took over the star part when the principal fell ill. She then played a Chinese maid

(Aldwych, 1920), and landed a star part in 'The Rose and the Ring' (Wyndhams, 1923). She was playing juvenile or *ingénue* roles.

Disillusioned with the glamour of acting, or finding it too demanding, she began writing, turning out a string of popular novels for children, and graduating to the field of adult romances and magazine serials, under the pseudonym Helen Zenna Smith. But the theatre remained her first love, and she excelled at writing plays. These were to become her *raison d'être*.

Some time in the 1920s she married, but her first husband died. Combining journalism with play-writing, she worked for the old *Daily Sketch*, where she met and married Australian writer Kenneth Attiwill. It was to prove a prolific collaboration, yielding London productions for one or the other or both. The research for one of her plays involved learning to fly, 'to get the right atmosphere. I thought I should never like anything better than driving my own car, but that was before I tried aeroplaning.' She quoted a popular song of the time: 'That's my weakness now.'

Asked by a publisher to write a parody on Eric Maria Remarque's best-selling *All Quiet on the Western Front*, she rejected the notion as tasteless, and – seeking help from a gossipy female ambulance driver – wrote a novel instead about women's involvement in the war. *Not So Quiet* had a great success in Europe and America, earning special distinction in France as 'the novel most calculated to promote international peace'.

When war began her husband joined the HAC as a gunner, promising to do 'nothing heroic'. Captured in Singapore, he spent three and a half years as a prisoner, and was eventually awarded the Military Cross. He kept notes throughout his imprisonment, and wrote a best seller about it afterwards.

During her years in Hellingly, when she had those striking visions, about her husband, and then about Jack Cannon, Evadne was working as a war correspondent for *The People*: she was the first woman reporter to visit Belsen Concentration Camp after its liberation. In peacetime she continued to collaborate with her ex-POW husband in further West End plays and films, and they also collaborated in television scripts, notably eighteen months writing for the TV soap *Cross-roads*. But it was in the field of astrological prediction that she achieved personality status, first in her own spot on TV, and then as the regular astrological correspondent for *She* magazine. A colleague, fellow-researcher and author Jeff Watson, writes:

'When I was a journalist for ATV, in the late Sixties and early Seventies, she had a spot on television as an astrologer. I recall Evadne Price dressed as a gipsy, looking into a crystal ball. A rather eccentric lady. It was one of those five-minute spots before the news but it was very popular, and she had a huge following because of her syndicated column in *She* magazine.'

Eventually retiring with her husband to Australia, her reputation caught up with her and for many years the Australian *Vogue* syndicated her star-gazer column. 'She can't stay idle for long' said her husband. She died in 1985, age recorded as eighty.

Index

Page numbers in *italics* refer to illustrations.

Aachen raid 37–38
Abyssinia 24
Alberta Pathfinder 154
Amsterdam power station raid 109–110,
    113–115
Anglo-Persian Oil Company 30
Armstrong Whitworth Whitley 4, *6*, 7, *9*,
    16, 59
Armstrong Whitworth Whitley Mark III
    1–2, 3–4, 7, 8, 9–10, 11–14
Ascroft, Major Peter, RAMC (later
    Professor) 94–95, 105, 106, 107, *107*,
    108
Attew, Ken 72
Attiwill, Keith 156
Attiwill, Kenneth 156–157
Austria 25
Avro Lancaster 124, 125, 126–131, 138,
    143, 146–148, 162, 169, 172, 174
Axford, Sergeant Jack *33*, 34, 42–43, 44

B90 airfield 186, 187, 188–189, 191
Babington, Air Vice-Marshal Philip 89
Baldwin, Air Vice-Marshal Jack 89
Balfour, Arthur 38
Bandon, Paddy, Earl of 55–56
Barber, 'Ali' 2, 12, 13, *18*
Bazalgette, C. Ian 136, 137, 151–153
Bazalgette, Ethel 137, 140, 142–143, 150,
    153
Bazalgette, Ian Willoughby 'Baz/Will',
    VC DFC 92, 136, 137–143, *138*, 144,
    144, 151–152, 154
    Trossy St Maximin V1 Storage Site raid
    145, 146, 147, 148, 149–150, 152–155
Bazalgette, Sir Joseph 142
Bazalgette VC 154
BBC 150–151
Bennebroek 116–117
Bennebroek, Willink van 117
Bennett, Don 141, 142
Bergelin, Dick 161
Beveridge, Flight Lieutenant R.W. 145,
    146, 149–150
Beveridge, Sir William 44, 45
Beveridge Plan 44
Blatchford, Wing Commander H.P.
    'Cowboy' 118

Blomberg, General 22–23
Bocholt railway yards raid 178–180,
    182–185, 186–190
Bodie, Bob 122, 128, 129, *131*, 132, 133,
    135
Boeing Flying Fortress 69
Booth, Wing Commander A.F. 66
Bowles, Sergeant T.W. 'Johnnie' 2, 8, 9,
    10, 11, 12–13, 15, 17, *18*, 19
Box, Allan 81, 82–83, 84, 87, 89, *90*
Bradford, Squadron Leader 35
Branston, Ken 122–123
Bremen raids 57, 59–60, 64–65, 66
Bristol Blenheim 37, 39, 40, 47
    No. 21 Squadron 65, 68, 69, 72,
        73, 74–76, 77
    No. 107 Squadron 48, 56, 57, 59,
        61, 62, 64
Bristol Blenheim Mark IV 46, 51–54, 64
British Expeditionary Force 20, 39
Brooklands Flying School 111
Brophy, Pat 121, 122–123, *123*, 124–126,
    131, 133, 135
    Cambrai raid 126, 127, 128, 129,
        130, 131–132, 133, 134
Brown, Sergeant James Francis
    'Jim/Bomber' 32, 33–34, *33*, 35, 42, 43,
    45
Budden, Flying Officer (later Wing
    Commander, DSO DFC) Harry 16–17,
    19
Butcher, Ted 'Butch' 31–32
Butler, Flying Officer R.W. 'Dickie' 180,
    183, 185, 187, 190

Cabinet 6 *see also* War Cabinet
Cairo, 15th Scottish General Hospital 94,
    95, 105–106
Cambrai raid 125, 126–132
Cameron, Douglas 'Jock' 136, 140–141,
    144, 147–149, 154
Canberra, Department of Veterans'
    Affairs 107
Canberra, War Memorial 171–172
Cannon, Jack 155–156, 157, *157*, 158–159,
    170, 171, 172, 173–177
    Essen, Krupps works, raid 161–162,
        163–164, 168–169

in Norfolk after crash 164–167, 168, 174–175, 177
Carver, Lieutenant Robin 30
Chamberlain, Neville 4, 6, 21, 25–26, 27–28, *32*, 35, 38, 39
Cherbourg raid 65–66
Cholmondeley, John, Lord 167–168
Churchill, Winston 7, 25, 37, 45, 50–51, 54, 56, 57
'Circus' operations 56, 57, 59, 66–67, 69, 73
Clipsham, Roy 179
Cologne power station *70, 71*
Compton, Denis 68
Cope, Major Robert (later Professor) 94–95, 106, 107, 108
Corfield, Pilot Officer Jim 69, 72, *73*
Coshall, Stan 109, 110, 111, *112*, 113, 114, 115
Cotton, Sergeant E. 16, 17
Coty family 2
Cousens, Wing Commander A.S.G. 141–142, 143
Crawley, Tom 184–185
Cresson, Pierre 132, 134
Croll, Lea 99, 101, 102, 103–104
Cushing, Tommy 169, 172
Czechoslovakia 25

Daily Express 44–45
Daily Telegraph 111, 120
de Breyne, Flying Officer Art 121–122, 123, 124, 125, *131, 132*, 134, 135
　Cambrai raid 126, 127, 128, 129, 131, 133
De Spiegel 119, 120
Douglas Boston 110, 118
Duffill, Flight Lieutenant Arthur 110, 118
Dunglass, Lord 38
Dunkirk 39–40, 45
Dye, Daisy 167, 168, 173
Dye, Fred 166–168, 173, 174–175, 176

Edrich, Pilot Officer (later Squadron Leader, DFC) W.J. 'Bill' 46–48, *49, 50*, 66, 67
　Bremen raid 57, 59–60
　with No. 21 Squadron 65–66, 67–70, 72, 73–75, 76–77
　with No. 107 Squadron 48–49, 50, 51–57, 64–65, 66–67
　playing cricket 46, 47, 49–50, 54, 55, 67, 68, 77
　Sylt raid 61–63
Edwards, Hughie, VC 57, *58*, 59, 60, 64, 65, 66

El Alamein 107, 108
Emery, Bill 2, 9, 10, 11, 12, 13, *18*
Eringham 43, 45
Essen, Krupps works raid 160–161, 162–164, 168–169
Evans, Titch 'Taffy' 81, 88–89

Fakenham, Crown Hotel 55
Fleet Finch II 181, 188
Focke-Wulf FW 190: 113
Frankfurt leaflet raid 10, 15–16
Frankish, Ken 157, 158, 161
Freeman, Warrant Officer Donald 180, 183, 186, 190, 191
Friday, Jack 122, 126, 127, 128, *131*, 132

Galland, Adolph 72
Gaudiempre 132, 134, 135
George VI, King *18*, 19
German Public Works student 23–24
Gianacles, Egypt 95, 104, 107
Giddy, Jack 96
Goddard, Geoff 140–141, *144*, 146, 147, 148, 149, 150, 154
Godfrey, Charles 'Chuck' 140–141, *144*, 146, 147–148, 149, 150, 154
Gordon, Gerry 35
Gover, Alf 68
Graham-Hogg, Flight-Lieutenant (later Squadron Leader) Denis 65, 66, 67
Gray (née Lewis), Annie Margaret 'Nan' 31, 36, 41, 43, 44
Gray, Eileen Margaret 31, 36, 43, 44
Gray, Ian William 31, 36, 43
Gray, Flight Sergeant (later Pilot Officer) William Alfred 'Bill/Dolly' 29–32, *31, 33*, 34, 35, 36, 37, 38, 44
　father 41
　shot down and captured 40, 41–42, 43
Griffin, Sergeant Alfred 14–15, 17, 18–19, *18*
　leaflet dropping 1–2, 8, 9, 10, 11, 12, 13

Hall, Flight Sergeant Jim, CGM 181–182, *184*, 185–186, 191
　Bocholt raid 178–180, 183, 184, 185, 186–190
Hamburg raid 91
Handley, Phyllis 160, 172–173
Handley Page Halifax 61
Handley Page Hampden 69
Harte, Bunny 67
Heller, 'Tick' 16
Hellingly 155, 157–158, 169
Hess, Rudolf 22

Hibbert, Ivan 'Van' 140–141, *144*, 146, 149, 154
Hide, Sergeant E. 15–16
Hitler, Adolf 4, 21, 22, 23, 25–26, 27, 56, 119, 143
Hope, Ernie 48, 49, *50*, 51, 53–54, 59, 63, 64, 65
Hopkins, Colonel G.F. 'Hoppy' 73, 74
Houghton Hall 167, 168, 169, 173–175, *173*, *174*, *175*, *176*, 177
House of Commons 21, 24, 25, 35
Howard, Reg 94, 95–97, 99–101
   injuries, operation and recovery 95, 102–107, *105*
Huize Bennebroek 116, 117, 119, 120
Hurnall, Bob 143, 144, *144*

Ijmuiden, Royal Dutch Steel Works 110, 118
Illustrated London News 91
Iraq 25, 26–27, 29, 30
Ironside, General 26

Jackson, Aircraftman 1st Class (later Wing Commander) Roy, DFM MBE 2, 3, 10, 11, 12, 13, 14, *18*, 19
Jeffrey, James 150
Junkers Ju 88: 99, 127

Kay, Wing Commander Cyril 'Cyrus' 80, 81
Kelly, Jim 122, 123, 127, 128, 129, *131*, 132, 133, 135
Kennard, Bobbie 179
Kercher, Wing Commander Bill 67, 69, 72, 76
Khorramshahr 30
Knapsack power station raid 69–70, *70*, *71*, 72–73

Labour Government 44
Langston, Sergeant Jim 69, 72
Late Victorian, the life of Sir Arnold Talbot Wilson 44
Lawton, Joe, AFC 79, 81, 82, 84–85, 86, 87, 89, *90*, 92
Le Havre raid 56
leaflet dropping 3–4, *4*, *5*, 6–7, *6*, 10–11, 15, 18, 32, 125
Lee, Bert *168*, 169, 177
Leeder, Vernon Victor Russell 144–145, *145*, 146, 147, 149, 154
Letgoquart, Raymond 133, 135
Leven, Sergeant, DFM 64
Levy, Professor Herman 44
Lockheed Ventura 109–110, 111, *112*, 113–117, 118

London 24, 79–80, 122, 142, 143, 146, 155
   Chandos Dive Bar 122, 133
   Windmill Theatre 155
London Gazette 30
Longuenese airfield raid 73–75

Mackie, John 150
Mahaddie, Wing Commander (later Group Captain) T.G. 'Hamish' 136, 138–139, 140, *140*, 141
Martin Maryland 96, 97
Martineau's Guide to the English Lake District 31
Mason, Bill 81, 83, 84, 88
Meakin, Squadron Leader 69, 72
Melsbroek, Brussels 178–179, *181*
Merten, Walter 'Willie' (later Air Chief Marshal) 32, 33, 37, 40
Messerschmitt Bf 109: 62–63, 72, 113
Methwold 36, 41
Middleton, Ron, VC 92, 136, 137, 138, 150–151, *151*, 152
Montgomery, Field Marshal Bernard 108
Munich leaflet raid 1–2, 3–4, 7–15, 16–17
Munster raid 81–86
Murray, 'Zeke' 61, 62, 63
Mussolini, Benito 24
Myers, 'Pop', Mrs and daughters 55
Mynarski, Andy, VC 123–126, *124*, *131*, 132, 134, 135
   Cambrai raid 126, 128, 129, 130, 132, 133, 134, 135
Mynarski, Anna 134

Namur raid 37
New Malden, Sycamore Avenue 137–138, 139, 142
Nieuport raids 40
North, Rupert 111, *112*, 113–114, 115, 117–118
North American B25 Mitchell Mark II 178–180, *181*, 182–185, *182*, 187, 189
Norway 35

Operation 'Channel Stop' 66
Orland, LAC Rex *33*, 34, *34*, 42, 43, 44
Orme, Frankie 76

Passavant-en-Argonne 15
Pearse, Harry 48–49, 65
Pennant (née Carver), Ann 30, 44
Perkins, Angela 191
Perkins, Dick, DSO 180–181, *180*, *181*, 182–184, *182*, 185–190, *190*, 191
Petley, Wing Commander Lawrence 'Petters' 48, 49, *49*, 56, 57, 59, 60–61, 64

Phipps, Vic 48, 49, *50*, 51, 52, 53, 64, 72, 75
Portal, Sir Charles 32–33, 50, 89–91
Price, Evadne 155, 156–158, *156*, 165,
    169, 177

Quadrath power stations raid 69–70,
    72–73

RAF Short History 39
Red Cross 41
Resistance 132–133, 148, 149
Ribbentrop, Herr von 22, 23
Richardson, Tony 48, *49*, 60
Richins, Denis Richard Garth 159–160,
    159, 161, *161*, 164, 168, 169, 172, 173
Richins, Stuart *159*, 160, *162*, 172, 173
Richins family 173
Roberton, Pilot Officer R.J. 180, 183, 186,
    187
Rommel, General Erwin 95, 107, 108
Rotterdam harbour raid 65, 76–77
Royal Air Force
    Awards Committee 89, 134
    Bomber Command 36, 37, 43, 81, 160
    Central Gunnery School, Warmwell 28
    Cranwell 47
    No 1 Air Armaments School, Manby 28
    No. 2 Group 48, 56, 61, 65, 66, 67, 68,
        73, 110
    No. 3 Group 80, 138, 139
    No. 11 Group 75
Royal Air Force squadrons
    No. 21: 65, 66, 67–70, 72–77
    No. 37: 30–32, 33–38, *33*, 39, 40–43
    No. 38: 92, 95–97, 99–105, *100*, *105*,
        107–108
    No. 51: 2–4, 7, 8–19
    No. 61: 66–67
    No. 75 (New Zealand) 79, 80–89, *90*,
        91–92
    No. 82: 69, 76
    No. 105: 57, 59, 66
    No. 107: 48–49, *49*, 51–57, 59–65, 66–67
    No. 115: 138–139
    No. 149: 136–137
    No. 180: 178–181, 182–191
    No. 419 (Moose) 125–132
    No. 457 (New Zealand) 109–110, 111,
        112, 113–117, 118
    No. 460 (RAAF) 158–159, 160–164,
        168–169, 172
    No. 635: 141–142, 143–144, 145–148,
        153, 154
Royal Air Force stations *see also* B90
    airfield; Gianacles, Egypt; Melsbroek,
    Brussels; Villeneuve airfield
    Binbrook 158, 159

Bircham Newton 168, 169
Dishforth 122
Downham Market 141, 143, 145
Driffield 61, 63–64
Feltwell 30, 33–35, 37, 39, 40, 41, 44,
    80, 81–82, 89
Heliopolis 105
Linton-on-Ouse 2, *18*, 19
Little Massingham 48–49, *49*, 54, 60,
    64, 65
Little Snoring 160, 172
Lossiemouth 79, 140, 141
Manston 66, 67
Marham 92
Methwold 110, 111, 118
Middleton St George 124, 126
Mildenhall 150–151
Swanton Morley 57, 59
Upwood 47–48, 65, 67, 111
Uxbridge 47
Watton 65, 67, 68, 77
West Raynham 50, 55–56, 65, 66
Russia 57, 69

Safian, Victoria 123
St Neots power station 68, 70
Senantes 148, 149, 150, 153
Senlis-le-Sec 133
Serant, Jeanne 133, 135
shipping strikes 51–54, 66, 75–76
    with torpedoes 95, 97, *98*, 99, 100–104,
        100, *105*, 107–108
Short Stirling 137
Shuttleworth, Dick 67–68, 75, 76–77
    parents and wife 77
Silvester, Wing Commander James 6–7,
    8, 16–18
Simmons, Squadron Leader Peter, DFC*
    46–47, 48, *49*, 51–52, 53, 54
Sinclair, Sir Archibald 28, 39
Sinclair, Group Captain Laurie, GC 68,
    73, *74*, 76–77
Soignies raid 39
*South West Persia: A Political Officer's
    Diary* 44
Sparkes, George 109, 111, 113, 115
Stalag Luft III 118
Stancomb, Flying Officer John 108
Stannard, Bill 110–111, *112*, 113, 115, 118,
    119–120
    and fire aboard aircraft 109–110, 113,
        114–117, 119
    mother 116
Stevenson, AOC 60, 61
Stobo (née Hedley), Flo 169, 170–171
Stobo, Frances 160, 170–171, *171*
    daughter Letitia *171*, 172

Stobo, Flight Sergeant Wren 160, *160*, 161–162, *168*, 169, 170
Straight, Whitney 66–67
Sudetenland 25
Sunderland, Sergeant Eric 160–161, 177
 parents 177
Supermarine Spitfire 66, 69, 72
Supermarine Spitfire V 113, 118
Sylt raid 61–64

Tait, 'Willie' 19
Tedder, Air Marshal 108
Thickens, Sammy 99–100, 101, 102, 104
Times, The 28
Tobruk raids 97, 108
torpedo dropping 95, 97, *98*, 99, *100*, 101–102, *105*, 107–108
Treloar, John 157, 158, 161
Trent, Squadron Leader (NZ) Leonard, VC 110, 113, 118–119
Trossy St Maximin V1 Storage Site raid 143, 145–150
Turin raid 137
Turner, George *144*, 146–148, *149*, 150

V1 flying bomb 142, 143, 146, 150, 157, 158, 167
Vandermeer, Mr 119
Varennes 132
Vermeulen, A.H. 119–120
Versailles, Treaty of 22, 23
Vickers Wellington 20, 37, 39, 41, 42, 43, 59, 80–81, 138
 torpedo dropping *98*, 99, 100, *100*, 101–102, *105*, 107–108
Vickers Wellington IC 34, 35, 41, 81, 82–89, *88*, *91*
Vigars, Roy 121–122, 124, 125, 127, 128, 129, *131*, 132, 133, 134
Villeneuve airfield 2–3, *3*, 7, 16

Waalhaven airfield raid 35–36
Wagstaff, Ralph, DFC 99, 100, 102, 103, 104, 107, 108

Wallis, Barnes 81
War Cabinet 36 *see also* Cabinet
Ward, James Allen 'Jimmy', VC 78–83, *90*, *92*
 and fire in Wellington 83–91, *91*
 shot down and killed 91–93
Watton, Crown Hotel 77
Webster, Wing Commander P.F. 'Tom' 65, 67, 76
Westerland airfield raid 61–64
Westmere 20, 36, 38
Widdowson, Squadron Leader Reuben P. 'Ben' 80–81, 82, 83–84, 85, 88, 89, *90*, *92*
Wiggins, Flying Officer Lloyd, DSO 95, 97, *97*, 99, 100, 101–102, 103, 104–105, 107, 108
Wilson, Pilot Officer Sir Arnold, MP 20–21, 24, *32*, *45*
 desire to join RAF 21–22, 26, 27–28
 Germany, visits to 22–23, 24, 25, 26
 in Iraq 25, 26–27, 29, 30
 joins RAF and training 28–29
 meeting with Hitler 21, 23
 as Member of Parliament 21, 22–23, 24–26, 28, 35, 44–45
 shot down and killed 42–43, 45
 as tail gunner 22, 30–31, *31*, 32–33, *33*, *34*, 35–39, 43, 45
Wilson, Hugh 20, 26, 29, 30, 31, 33, 34–35, 37, 38, 43
Wilson (née Carver), Lady Rose 30, 36, 43, 44
Wilson, Sarah 20, 30, 36, 37, 38, 43
Winnipeg, Pat Mynarski commemorated in 134
Workmen's Compensation: the Need for Social Reform, Volume II 44
Wright, Doug 68
Wynton, Flight Sergeant John W.P. 10, 15–16, 17, 19